U0406537

高等学校教材

无机非金属材料专业英语

大学英语专业阅读教材编委会组织编写

杜永娟 主编

郑昌琼 主审

化学工业出版社

教材出版中心

·北 京·

《无机非金属材料专业英语》是根据大学英语教学大纲（理工科本科用）的专业阅读部分的要求编写的。

全书共分7个部分，33个单元。每个单元包括精读课文，词汇表（附音标），课文注释，练习，阅读材料。内容涉及无机材料物理化学、陶瓷、玻璃、水泥与混凝土、耐火材料，宝石学和无机材料工程。

本教材供已通过大学英语四级的无机材料专业及相关专业学生，同等英语水平的科技人员使用。

图书在版编目（CIP）数据

无机非金属材料专业英语/杜永娟主编. —北京：化学工业出版社，2001.12（2024.11重印）
高等学校教材
ISBN 978-7-5025-3355-7

Ⅰ. 无… Ⅱ. 杜… Ⅲ. 无机材料：非金属材料-英语-高等学校-教材 Ⅳ. H31

中国版本图书馆CIP数据核字（2001）第092180号

责任编辑：杨　菁　徐世峰
责任校对：郑　捷　　装帧设计：于　兵

出版发行：化学工业出版社（北京市东城区青年湖南街13号　邮政编码100011）
印　　装：北京盛通数码印刷有限公司
787mm×1092mm　1/16　印张14¾　字数362千字　2024年11月北京第1版第16次印刷

购书咨询：010-64518888　售后服务：010-64518899
网　　址：http://www.cip.com.cn
凡购买本书，如有缺损质量问题，本社销售中心负责调换。

定　　价：32.00元

前　言

组织编审出版系列的专业英语教材，是许多院校多年来共同的愿望。在高等教育面向21世纪的改革中，学生基本素质和实际工作能力的培养受到了空前的重视。对非英语专业的学生而言，英语水平和能力的培养不仅是文化素质的重要部分，在很大程度上也是能力的补充和延伸。在此背景下，教育部（原国家教委）几次组织会议研究加强外语教学问题，制订有关规范，使外语教学更加受到重视。教材是教学的基本因素之一，与基础英语相比，专业英语的教材问题显得更为突出。

国家的主管部门和广大院校的呼吁引起了化学工业出版社的关注。他们及时的与原化工部教育主管部门和全国化工类专业教学指导委员会请示协商后，根据学校需求，编委会优先从各院校教学（交流）讲义中确定选题，同时组织力量进行编审工作。本套教材涉及的专业主要包括化学工程与工艺、石油化工、机械工程、信息工程、生产工程自动化、应用化学和精细化工、生化工程、环境工程、制药工程、材料科学与工程和化工商贸等。

根据“全国部分高校化工类及相关专业大学英语专业阅读教材编委会”的要求和安排编写的《无机材料非金属材料专业英语》教材，可供材料类及相关专业本科使用，也可作为同等程度（通过大学英语四级）的专业技术人员的自学教材。

本书分为7个部分，33个单元，每个单元包括精读课文，词汇表（附音标），课文注释，练习，阅读材料等。各篇课文之间，课文与阅读材料既有一定联系，又可独立成章，教学时可以根据不同学时灵活选用。课文与阅读材料均来自英文原版教科书、专著、国际著名学术期刊和国际学术会议，绝大部分为20世纪80年代末和90年代以来的出版物。

本教材的内容涉及无机材料物理化学（Part1 ），陶瓷（Part2），玻璃（Part3），水泥与混凝土（Part4），耐火材料（Part5），宝石学（Part6）和无机材料工程（Part7）。基本覆盖了无机非金属材料专业的重要内容，从无机材料科学到工程，从主要无机材料的结构、组成、性质、应用到制备工艺；从传统的无机非金属工程材料，天然无机非金属材料到新型无机材料；材料的加工从高温到新技术。内容具有广泛性、基础性和新颖性。

本书由华东理工大学杜永娟主编，本书第一部分、第四部分与总词汇表由杜永娟编写，第二部分由陈奇编写，第三部分由王中俭编写，第五部分由陈国荣编写，第六部分由刘学良与郭守国编写，第七部分由郑金标编写。全书由杜永娟统稿，郑昌琼（四川大学）主审。华东理工大学博士研究生汪山、硕士研究生刘春玲、王萍、王海鹏，本科生郑爱萍等参加了部分文摘整理和文字处理工作。

本书在编写过程中得到化学工业出版社、全国部分高校化工类及相关专业大学英语专业阅读材料编委会、华东理工大学教务处和四川大学教务处的大力支持；博士生导师郑昌琼教授认真审阅了全书，提出宝贵意见，在此一并表示衷心感谢。

由于时间仓促和编者的水平有限，不足之处在所难免，希望广大读者提出宝贵意见。

编　者

2001年9月

Contents

PART Ⅰ PHYSICAL CHEMISTRY OF INORGANIC MATERIALS

Unit 1 Types of Bonds in Crystals

Ionic Bonds

In some crystals, the atoms are present in a state where their electron system is similar to that of a rare gas, so that their outer shell has either lost excess electrons or has been filled with a total of eight electrons, i. e. , completed. Since the electric neutrality must be conserved, the crystal always simultaneously contains atoms that donate electrons and atoms that accept electrons. The former form positively charged cations, while the latter form negatively charged anions, and the electric charges of ions are integral multiples of the electron charges.

The cohesive forces in these crystals are electrostatic forces acting between the ions. This type of bond is called an ionic bond and the crystals are called ionic crystals. As the electric field of ions is spherically symmetrical, the ionic bonding is isotropic, i. e. , the bonds do not have directional character and every ion attempts to be surrounded by the maximum possible number of ions of the opposite charge, so that the bonds are not saturated. Halide salts of alkali metals represent typical ionic crystals; this is so because alkali metals have only one electron in the outer shell, while halides lack exactly one electron for completion of their outer shell to eight electrons.

This idea is identical with the concept of valency except that the crystal is not considered as a compound of molecules, but rather as a unified structure for which the chemical formula has the meaning of the ratio of the elements and the geometric arrangement is an indispensable part of the description of the substance①. The chemical formula, e. g. , NaCl, does not denote a molecular structural unit here, because every ion in the crystal interacts with several closest neighbours with the opposite sign, so that, for example, each Na^+ ion in NaCl is surrounded by six equivalent nearest Cl^- ions, and vice versa.

Covalent Bonds

An exact quantum mechanical calculation for the hydrogen molecule model, carried out by Heitler and London (1927), revealed that there exist two possible lowest energy states of the hydrogen molecule, composed of the original single-atomic states, and that the lower energy corresponds to a singlet state in which orientations of the spins of electrons are antiparallel②. The energy difference between the two states and the consequent forces, called exchange forces, depend on the overlap of the wave functions of the electrons, which become common for both atoms. Such a bonding is called homeopolar or atomic.

The pairing of electrons in states in which the electrons, according to Pauli principle, differ only in spin orientation is also characteristic for covalent bonds between atoms with more complex electron structures. The bond is again created by the overlap of the single-electron wave functions of atomic orbitals, which combine into the wave function of the common state. The main characteristics of covalent bonds are their saturation and mutual orientation of the bonds when there are several on the given atom; this is always the case except for atomic pairs. Saturation is a consequence of the Pauli principle; every bond contains exactly two electrons. Formally, the bond is similar to an ionic bond with the difference that the electrons are not transferred between atoms but become common property. For electrons in the p- and d- states, the degree of overlap, and thus also the covalent bond, depends not only on the interatomic distances but also on the mutual orientation of the directions of lines connecting the various atoms.

Bond hybridization. A future important property of covalent bonds is hybridization of the atomic orbitals, leading to variation of the valency of a given element in various compounds. The best example of this phenomenon is carbon, the ground state of which has the electron configuration $1s^2 2s^2 2p^2$ with only two p-electrons unpaired, which results in valency of two as, for example, in CO. However, it is known that carbon is usually present in compounds as a tetravalent element. Pauling (1931) explained this phenomenon through orbital hybridization, where carbon is present in the compound in the excited state $1s^2 2s^1 2p^3$, so that it has one unpaired s-electron and three unpaired p-electrons, i. e. , a total of four electrons that can enter into covalent bonds③. From a quantum mechanical point of view, these electrons cannot be considered separately but must be considered as equivalent particles in a single common state. From this also follows that the four bonds, available on carbon in this state, are completely equivalent. As a consequence, the atoms bonded to tetravalent carbon form a configuration of a regular tetrahedron. According to Kimball, the spatial orientations of the covalent bonds have the following shapes for various combinations of atomic orbitals:

atomic orbitals	shape of the hybrid orbitals	coordination number K	atomic orbitals	shape of the hybrid orbitals	coordination number K
a) sp, dp	linear	2	f) dsp^3, d^3sp	trigonal bipyramidal	5
b) sp^2, dp^2, d^2s	planar trigonal	3	g) d^4s	tetragonal pyramidal	5
c) d^2p	trigonal pyramidal	3	h) d^2sp^3	octahedral	6
d) sp^3, d^3s	tetrahedral	4	i) d^4sp	trigonal prismatic	6
e) dsp^2	planar tetragonal	4			

Metallic bonds

In metallic crystals, many of the valence electrons are present in states where they are not localized close to the atoms but can move freely over the crystal, which is reflected in a high conductivity④. The structure of metals can thus be conceived of as being composed of positively charged ions immersed in an electron gas. The term "gas" is not used accidentally here, as the free electrons actually behave statistically like a gas. The bonding between the positive ions occurs through these free electrons. Thus, an ionic bond can be described as containing an electron localized close to an acceptor atom, while the electron in a covalent bond is located between two atoms, and in a metallic bond the free electrons are completely delocalized. Metallic bonding, similarly to ionic, is characterized by isotropy and the consequent large coordination numbers. The ions in a metal tend to be surrounded by the maximum possible number of neighbours. In contrast to ionic bonds, metallic bonds do not require a balance of the electric charge between the elements; the electrostatic equilibrium is between metal ions and electron gas. This is why different metal elements can mix in crystals in practically arbitrary ratios to form alloys.

Van der Waals bonds

Van der Waals bonds are familiar from the kinetic theory of gases as the forces responsible for the deviation of the behaviour of a gas from that of an ideal gas. These are attractive forces between molecules with saturated bonds. Of all the forces in crystals, they are the weakest and mostly responsible for the formation of layered structures with weak cohesion between the layers. Van der Waals forces are present in molecular crystals, in which the molecules constitute the basic structural units. The forces which make the molecules stable are either of ionic or of covalent character while the molecules themselves are bound into crystal by van der Waals forces.

Selected from "Structure and Properties of Ceramics", A. Koller, Elsevier Publ., 1994

Words and Expressions

1. cation [ˈkætaiən] *n.* 阳离子
2. anion [ˈænaiən] *n.* 阴离子
3. cohesive [ˈkəuhiːsiv] *a.* 内聚（力）的；聚合在一起的
4. spherically [ˈsfərikəli] *ad.* 球的；球形的
5. isotropic [aisəˈtrɔpik] *a.* 均质的；各向同性的
6. halide [ˈhælaid] *a.n.* 卤化物（的）；卤族的
7. indispensable [ˌindisˈpensəbl] *a.* 必不可少的
8. vice versa [ˈvaisiˈvəːsə] 反之亦然
9. singlet [ˈsiŋglit] *n.* 零自旋能级
10. antiparallel [ˌæntiˈpærəlet] *a.* 逆平行的；反（向）平的
11. overlap [ˌəuvəˈlæp] *vt.* 与……重叠；与……部分一致
12. wave function 波函数
13. homeopolar [həumiəpɔlə] *a.* 相似极化
14. mutual orientation 相互取向
15. hybridization [ˌhaibridaiˈzeiʃən] *n.* 杂化
16. configuration [kənˌfigjuːˈreiʃən] *n.* 构形；（电子）排布

17. tetravalent [ˌtetrəˈveilənt] *a*. 四价的
18. orbital hybridation 轨道杂化
19. tetrahedron [ˌtetrəˈhiːdrən] *n*. 四面体
20. spatial orientation 空间取向
21. trigonal [ˈtraigənəl] *a*. 三方的
22. pyramidal [piˈræmidəl] *a*. 四方锥的
23. tetragonal [teˈtrægənəl] *a*. 正方晶的
24. bipyramidal [baiˈpirəmidəl] *a*. 四方双锥的
25. octahedral [ˈɔktəˈhedrəl] *a*. 八面体的
26. prismatic [prizˈmætik] *a*. 斜方晶系的
27. Van der Waals fores 范德华力
28. coordination number [kəuˈɔdineiʃən] 配位数

Notes

① 本句的主语部分为 This idea is identical with the concept of valency，其余部分为 except 引导的介词宾语。介词宾语中又包括一个由 for which 引导的定语从句，修饰 unified structure。该定语从句包含两个由 and 连接的并列句。参考译文：这种观念与化合价概念完全相同，只是没有把晶体视为分子化合物，而把它看作一种均一的结构，对它而言，化学式只表示元素之间的比值，而元素的几何排布是描述该物质的必不可少的部分。

② 本句的主要结构为带有两个用 that 引导的宾语从句的主从复合句，主语为 quantum mechanical calculation，它有一个过去分词短语作定语。第一个宾语从句中也有一个过去分词结构 composed of 修饰 energy states，第二个宾语从句中有一个用 in which 引导的定语从句修饰 singlet state。参考译文：亥特勒和伦敦在 1927 年用量子力学精确地计算了氢分子模型，得出氢分子存在由原先的单原子状态构成的两种可能的最低能量状态，其中能量更低的这种对应于电子自旋反平行取向的单一态，又称为零自旋能级。

③ 该句为带有定语从句的主从复合句，where 引导的定语从句说明 orbital hybridation，定语从句中又有一个用 so that 引导的结果状语从句，状语从句中又有一个 that 引导的定语从句，修饰 electrons。参考译文：鲍林（1931）用轨道杂化解释此现象，在此化合物中碳以 $1s^2 2s^1 2p^3$ 的激发态存在，于是它有一个未成对的 s 电子与三个未成对的 p 电子，也就是说，总共有四个电子能形成共价键。

④ 本句以 where 作为引导词引出定语从句，说明 states，在这个定语从句中，又有一个 which 引导的非限制性定语从句，它不是修饰某一个先行词，而是补充说明。参考译文：在金属晶体中许多价电子处于与原子非紧密结合且可以在整个晶体中自由移动的状态，这反映在金属的高电导。

Exercises

1. Translate the following expressions into Chinese or English.
   cohesive force，isotropic，vice versa，quantum mechanics，hybridization of the atomic orbitals，layed structure
   阳离子，阴离子，离子键，共价键，碱金属卤化物，波函数，电子排布（构型），成对电

子，电导，配位数

2. Translate the following sentences into Chinese.

① The simple valence theory is based on the idea that atoms with a small number of electron in their last shell readily lose these electrons to atoms whose last shell is almost complete .

② The classification of bonds into types is not absolute and, in readily, bonds with mixed character occur, such as ionic-covalent, ionic-metallic and covalent-metallic bonds (in semicoductors).

3. Fill in the blanks with suitable words.

① Atoms that give electrons form______, while atoms that accept electrons form_____.

② Carbon atom has_______s-electron and three_______, owing to orbital hybridization these electrons are considered as______in a single common state. As a consequence, the atom bonded to tetravalent carbon form______.

4. Answer following questions.

① Why is the ionic bond isotropic and unsaturated?

② What are the main characteristics of covalent bonds? Why have they such characteristics?

Reading Material 1

Grouping of Ions and Pauling's Rules

In crystals having a large measure of ionic bond character (halides, oxides, and silicates generally) the structure is in large part determined on the basis of how positive and negative ions can be packed to maximize electrostatic attractive forces and minimize electrostatic repulsion. The stable array of ions in a crystal structure is the one if lowest energy, but the difference in energy among alternative arrays is often very slight. Certain generalizations have been made, however, which successfully interpret the majority of ionic crystal structures, which are known. These generalizations have been compactly expressed in a set of five statements known as Pauling's rules.

Pauling's first rule states that a coordination polyhedron of anions is formed about each cation in the structure. The cation-anion distance is determined by the sum of their radii. The coordination number (i. e. , the number of anions surrounding the cation), is determined by the ratio of the radii of the two ions. the notion that a "radius" may be ascribed to an ion, regardless of the nature if the other ion to which it is bonded, is strictly empirical. Its justification is the fact that self-consistent sets of radii may be devised which successfully predict the interionic separations in crystals to within a few percent. The reason why the radius ratio of two species of ions influences the coordination number is apparent from Figl. 1. A central cation of given size cannot remain in contact with all surrounding anions if the radius of the anion is larger than a certain critical value. A given coordination number is thus

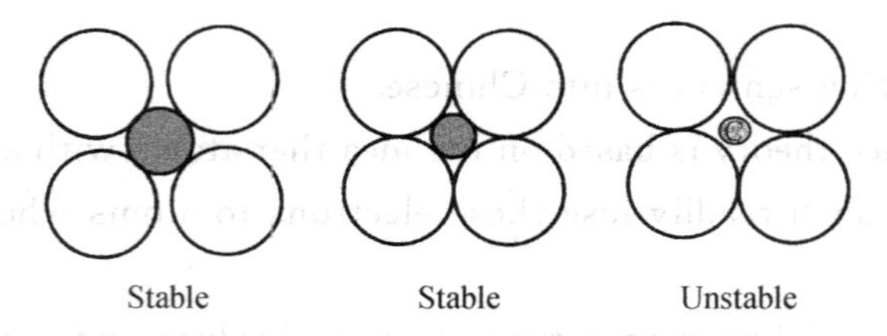

Fig. 1. 1 Stable and unstable coordination configurations

stable only when the ratio of cation to anion radius is greater than some critical value. In a crystal structure the anion is also surrounded by a coordination polyhedron of cations. Critical radius ratios also govern the coordination of cations about anions. Since anions are generally larger than cations, the critical radius ratio for a structure is almost always determined by the coordination of anions about the cations. This is why Pauling's first rule emphasizes the cation coordination polyhedron. For a given pair of ions, the radius ratio places an upper limit on the coordination number of the cation. In general, geometry would permit the structure to form with any one of a number of smaller coordination numbers. The stablest structure, however, always has the maximum permissible coordination number, since the electrostatic energy of an array is obviously decreased as progressively larger numbers of oppositely charged ions are brought into contact. The critical ratios are useful but are not always followed. The reason for this is that the packing considerations have considered the ions to be rigid spheres. A coordination number larger than that permitted by the radius ratio would be assumed if the electrostatic energy gained by increasing the coordination number exceeded any energy expended in deforming the surrounding ions. This consideration becomes especially important when the central cation has high charge or when the surrounding anions have a high atomic number and are large and easily deformed. Similarly, contributions of directional covalent bonding have an effect. Some experimentally observed coordination numbers are compared with predicted values in Table 1. 1.

Table 1. 1 Coordination Number and Bond Strength of Various Captions with Oxygen

Ion	Radius(CN=6)	Predicted Coordination Number	Observed Coordination Number	Strength of Electrostatic Bond
B^{3+}	0. 16	3	3,4	1or3/4
Be^{2+}	0. 25	4	4	1/2
Li^{+}	0. 53	6	4	1/4
Si^{4+}	0. 29	4	4,6	1
Al^{3+}	0. 38	4	4,5,6	3/4or1/2
Ge^{4+}	0. 39	4	4,6	1or2/3
Mg^{2+}	0. 51	6	6	1/3
Na^{+}	0. 73	6	4,6,8	1/6
Ti^{4+}	0. 44	6	6	2/3
Sc^{3+}	0. 52	6	6	1/2
Ar^{4+}	0. 51	6	6,8	2/3or1/2
Ca^{2+}	0. 71	6,8	6,7,8,9	1/4
Ce^{4+}	0. 57	6	8	1/2
K^{+}	0. 99	8,12	6,7,8,9,10,12	1/9
Cs^{+}	1. 21	12	12	1/12

The first rule focuses attention on the cation coordination polyhedron as the basic building block of an ionic structure. In a stable structure such units are arranged in a three-dimensional array to optimize second-nearest-neighbour interactions.

A stable structure must be electrically neutral not only on a microscopic scale but also at the atomic level. Pauling's second rule describes a basis for evaluating local electrical neutrality. We define the strength of an anion as the formal charge on the cation divided by its coordination number. For example, silicon, with valence 4 and tetrahedral coordination, has bond strength 4/4=1; Al^{3+} with octahedral coordination has bond strength 3/6=1/2. (The same considerations are applied regardless of whether all coordinating anions are the same chemical species; the bond strength of Al^{3+} is 1/2 in both the structure of Al_2O_3, where the six anion neighbors are O^{2-}, and that of kaolinite, where the anions surrounding Al^{3+} are $4OH^-$ and $2O^{2-}$. The second rule states that in a stable structure the total strength of the bonds reaching an anion from all surrounding cations should be equal to the charge of the anion. For example, in the Si_2O_7 unit, two bonds of strength 1 reach the shared oxygen ion from the surrounding silicon ions; the sum of the bonds is thus 2, the valence of the oxygen ion. (Note that this implies that, in a silicate based on Si_2O_7 units, no additional cation may be bonded to this shared oxygen.) Similarly in the structure of spinal $MgAl_2O_4$, each O^{2-} is surrounded by one Mg^{2+} which donates a bond of strength 2/4 and three Al^{3+} which donate three bonds of strength 3/6.

Pauling's third rule further concerns the linkage of the cation coordination polyhedra. In a stable structure the corners, rather than the edges and especially the faces, of the coordination polyhedra tend to be shared. If an edge is shared, it tends to be shortened. The basis of this rule is again geometrical. The separation of the cations within the polyhedron decreases as the polyhedra successively share corners, edges, and faces and the repulsive interaction between cations accordingly increases. Pauling's fourth rule states that polyhedra formed about cations of low coordination number and high charge tend especially to be linked by corner sharing. That this is true may be appreciated by recognizing that the repulsive interaction between a pair of cations increases as the square of their charge and that the separation of cations within a coordination polyhedron decreases as the coordination number becomes smaller. A fifth rule state that the number of different constituents in a structure tends to be small. This follows from the difficulty encountered in efficiently packing into a single structure ions and coordination polyhedra of different sizes.

Selected from "Introduction to Ceramics" 2nd Edition, W. D. Kingery, John Wiley & Sons, 1976

Words and Expressions

1. coordination polyhedron 配位多面体
2. empirical [em'pirikəl] *a*. 经验的
3. critical value 临界值
4. permissible [pə'misəbl] *a*. 容许的；许可的

5. deform [di'fɔːm] *vt*. 使变形；破坏……的外形
6. basic building block　基本组成部分
7. bond strength　键强
8. second-nearest-neighbour　次近邻
9. spinel [spi'nel] *n*. 尖晶石
10. linkage ['liŋkidʒ] *n*. 键合；联结

Unit 2 Silicate Structures

Atomic arrangement in hundreds of silicates having complex chemical compositions have in their basic structures a beautiful simplicity and order. At the same time the details of many of the silicate structures are complex and difficult to illustrate without three-dimensional models, and we will not attempt to give precise structure information.

The radius ratio for Si—O is 0.29, corresponding to tetrahedral coordination, and four oxygen ions are almost invariably arrayed around a central silicon. With a bond strength of 1, oxygen ions may be coordinated with only two silicon atoms in silica; this low coordination number makes close-packed structures impossible for SiO_2, and in general silicates have more open structures than those discussed previously. The SiO_4 tetrahedra can be linked in compounds such that corners are shared in several ways. There are four general types. In orthosilicates, SiO_4^{4-}, tetrahedra are independent of one another; in pyrosilicates, $Si_2O_7^{6-}$, ions are composed of two tetrahedra with one corner shared; in metasilicates, SiO_3^{2-} $(SiO_3)_n^{2n-}$, two corners are shared to form a variety of ring or chain structures; in layer structures, $(Si_2O_5)_n^{2n-}$, layers are made up of tetrahedra with three shared corners; in the various forms of silica, SiO_2, four corners are shared.

Silica. Crystalline silica, SiO_2, exists in several different polymorphic forms corresponding to different ways of combining tetrahedral groups with all corners shared①. Three basic structures—quartz、tridymite、cristobalite—each exists in two or three modifications. The most stable forms are low quartz, below 573℃; high quartz, 573 to 867℃; high tridymite, 867 to 1470℃; high cristobalite, 1470 to 1710℃; and liquid, above 1710℃; and liquid, above 1710℃. The low temperature modifications are distorted *derivative* structures of the basic high-temperature forms. (A derivative structure in the sense is one that can be derived from a basic structure of greater symmetry by distorting the structure in space rather than substituting different chemical species②) We confine our attention to the basic high-temperature forms.

High quartz has a structure which can be viewed as composed of connected chains of silica tetrahedra. Compared to the close packed structures discussed in the last section, this is a relatively open structure; for example, the density of quartz is 2.65g/cm^3, compared with 3.59 for MgO and 3.96 for Al_2O_3. However, quartz has a greater density and closer packing than either of the high-temperature forms, tridymite (ρ=2.26) and cristobalite (ρ=2.32).

Orthosilicates. This group includes the olivine minerals (forsterite, Mg_2SiO_4, and solid solutions with Fe_2SiO_4), the garnets, zircon, and the aluminosilicates-kyanite, silimanite, andalusite, and mullite. The structure of forsterite, Mg_2SiO_4, is similar to that found for chrysoberyl, Al_2BeO_4. The oxygen ions are nearly in a hexagonal close-packed structure with Mg^{2+} in octahedral and Si^{4+} in tetrahedral sites. (From a coordination point of view this assembly can also be considered an array of SiO_4 tetrahedra with Mg^{2+} ions in the octahedral holes). Each oxygen ion is coordinated with one Si^{4+} and three Mg^{2+} or with two Si^{4+}.

The structure of kyanite, Al_2SiO_5, consists of nearly cubic close-packed oxygen ions with Si^{4+} in tetrahedral and Al^{3+} in octahedral sites. However, in the polymorphic forms andalusite and sillimanite have much more open structures, with SiO_4 tetrahedra coordinated with AlO_6 octahedra. Mullite, $Al_6Si_2O_{13}$, a common constituent of fired clay products, has a structure similar to that of sillimanite (compare $Al_{16}Si_8O_{40}$ and $Al_{18}Si_6O_{39}$).

Pyrosilicates. Crystalline silicates containing $Si_2O_7^{6-}$ ions are rare.

Metasilicates. Silicates containing $(SiO_3)_n^{2n-}$ ions are of two types-cyclic or chain arrangements of the silica tetrahedra. Some of the discrete cyclic ions observed are the $Si_3O_9^{6-}$ (such as in wollastonite, $CaSiO_3$) and $Si_6O_{18}^{12-}$ (in beryl, $Be_3Al_2Si_6O_{18}$) ions. Minerals with chain structures comprise a large group. Those with compositions corresponding to single chain, $(SiO_3)_n^{2n-}$, are the pyroxenes, and those with double chains, $(Si_4O_{11})_n^{6n-}$, the amphiboles. The pyroxenes include enstatite, $MgSiO_3$; diopside, $MgCa(SiO_3)_2$; spodumene, $LiAl(SiO_3)_2$; and jadeite. The amphiboles include tremolite, $(OH)_2Ca_2Mg_5(Si_4O_{11})_2$, in which isomorphic substitution is widespread. The asbestos minerals are amphiboles.

Framework Structures. Many important silicate structures are based on an infinite three-dimensional silica framework. Among these are the feldspars and the zeolites. The feldspars are characterized by a framework formed with Al^{3+} replacing some of the Si^{4+} to make a framework with a net negative charge that is balanced by large ions in interstitial positions, that is, albite, $NaAlSi_3O_8$; anorthite, $CaAl_2Si_2O_8$; orthoclase, $KAlSi_3O_8$; celsian, $BaAl_2Si_2O_8$; and the like③. The network structures are similar in nature to the cristobalite structure, with the alkali or alkaline earth ions fitting into interstices. Only the large positive ions are from feldspars; smaller ones that enjoy octahedral coordination are from chains or layer silicates.

Much more open alumina-silica frameworks occur in the zeolites and ultramarines. In these compounds the framework is sufficiently open for there to be relatively large channels in the structure④. The alkali and alkaline earth ions present can be exchanged in aqueous solutions, leading to there use as water softeners. In addition, these channels can be used as molecular sieves for filtering mixtures on the basis of molecular size. The size of the channels in the network depends on the composition.

Selected from "Introduction to Ceramics" 2nd. Edition, W. D. Kingery, John. Wiley&Sons, 1976

Words and Expressions

1. close-packed structure 紧密堆积结构
2. orthosilicate [ˌɔːθəˈsilikeit] *n.* 正（原）硅酸盐
3. pyrosilicate [ˌpairəuˈslikeit] *n.* 焦硅酸盐

4. metasilicate [ˌmætəˈsilikeit] *n*. 偏硅酸盐
5. polymorphic [ˌpɔliˈmɔːfik] *a*. 多晶的
6. tridymite [ˈtridimait] *n*. 鳞石英
7. cristobalite [krisˈtəubəlait] *n*. 方石英
8. derivative [dəˈrivətivl] *a*. 被诱导的；衍生的
9. modification [ˌmɔdifiˈkeiʃən] *n*. 改变，修改；变体
10. olivine [ˌɔliˈviːn] *n*. 橄榄石
11. forsterite [ˈfɔːstərait] *n*. 镁橄榄石
12. garnet [ˈgɑːnit] *n*. 石榴石；石榴红色
13. zircon [ˈzəːkɔn] *n*. 锆石
14. kyanite [ˈkaiənait] *n*. 蓝晶石
15. sillimanite [ˈsilimənait] *n*. 硅线石
16. andalusite [ˌændəˈluːsait] *n*. 红柱石
17. mullite [ˈmʌlait] *n*. 高铝红柱石，莫来石
18. chrysoberyl [ˈkrisəˌberil] *n*. 金绿宝石
19. hexagonal [hekˈsægənəl] *a*. 六方晶系的
20. wollastonite [ˈwuləstənait] *n*. 硅灰石
21. beryl [ˈberil] *n*. 绿柱石
22. pyroxene [ˈpaiərɔksiːn] *n*. 辉石
23. amphibole [ˈæmfibəul] *n*. 闪石
24. enstatite [ˈenstətait] *n*. 顽火辉石
25. diopside [daiˈɔpsaid] *n*. 透辉石
26. spondumene [ˈspɔdjumiːn] *n*. 锂辉石
27. jadeite [ˈdʒeidait] *n*. 硬玉
28. tremolite [ˈtreməlait] *n*. 透闪石
29. isomorphic [aisəˈmɔːfik] *a*. 同晶型的
30. asbestos [æzˈbestɔs] *n*. 石棉
31. feldspar [ˈfeldspɑː] *n*. 长石
32. zeolite [ˈziːəlait] *n*. 沸石
33. interstitial [intəˈstiʃəl] *a*. 间隙的
34. ultramarine [ˌʌltrəməˈriːn] *n*. 群青；深蓝色 *a*. 群青的，深蓝色的

Notes

① corresponding to 引导一个现在分词短语，修饰 polymorphic forms，可按中文的习惯，分开译：结晶态的二氧化硅有几种不同的晶型，它们对应于所有角共享的四面体群的不同组合方式。

② That 引导同位语从句，它的先行词为 one，从句中 distorting 开始的结构为现在分词短语作介词 by 的宾语，说明 derived 的总体过程。参考译文：此处衍变结构是指这个结构可以从对称性较高的基本结构经空间畸变得到，而不是经不同类型化学物质置换所得。

③ 从 formed 开始到 interstitial 为一过去分词短语，作后置定语修饰 framework，此短语中

with 后为介词短语，说明形成的过程。其中 replacing 为现在分词，它的动作执行者为 Al^{3+}，to make 为一不定式短语，表示引起的结果。that 开始到 positions 为定语从句，修饰 negative charge，后面部分为长石族的各种矿物。参考译文：长石的特点是由 Al^{3+} 取代骨架中的某些 Si^{4+} 形成铝硅酸盐骨架。取代产生的负电荷由处于间隙的大离子平衡，例如钠长石 $NaAlSi_3O_8$，钙斜长石 $CaAl_2Si_2O_8$，正长石 $KalSi_3O_8$，钡长石 $BaAl_2Si_2O_8$。

④ 此句中 for 后面为不定式 to be 的短语，说明前面形容词的目的。参考译文：这些化合物中骨架足够开放使得结构中有较大的通道。

Exercises

1. Translate the following expressions into Chinese or English.
   three-dimensional models，low temperature modifications，solid solution，hexagonal closed-packed structure，olivine minerals，octahedral hole，tetrahedral site，fireclay products，isotrophic substitution，alumina-silica，framework，tetrahedral coordinations
   紧密堆积结构，衍生结构，铝硅酸盐，锆英石，莫来石，链状排列，长石，角联结的硅氧四体，近似立方紧密堆积的，氧离子，水软化剂，被铝取代的氧
2. Translate the following sentences into Chinese.
   ① The basic building block of silicates，beginning with silicon dioxide，whose modifications were described among AX_2 structure ，is the silicate ion $(SiO_4)^{4-}$，which has tetrahedral shape with the silicon atom in the centre and the oxygen atoms at the vertices.
   ② Silicates often contain the following elements：Li，Na，K，Mg，Ca，Ti，Zr，Mn，Fe，Zn，B，Al，H，F and the hydroxyl group，Al，B，or Be，can replace silicon，as they also form tetrahedra with oxygen. The compounds are then accordingly called aluminosilicate，borosilicate or beryllosilicates.
3. Fill in the blanks with suitable words.
   Because____governs the coordination of anions about cations，in silicate structure____is always surrounded by four oxygen ions；one oxygen ion may be linked with____silicon atoms. It is____that results in the more open structure for SiO_2 and silicate. The general structure types for silicates are____ ____ ____ ____.

Reading Material 2

Structure of Carbides，Nitrides and Borides

The binary compounds of boron，nitrogen and carbon，especially those with the transition metals，form a wide range of structures with a similarly wide range of useful technical properties for industrial applications. They include very hard materials，comparable with corundum and diamond，those with high chemical resistance to corrosive media，with high melting points (up to about 4000℃，the temperature of vaporization of graphite；the highest known melting point 3983℃ is that of tantalum carbide TaC), and with special electrical properties (including semiconductors, metallic phases and superconductors).

In addition to classical applications in turning and machining technology as grinding and cutting materials, these compounds are now used in electronics in the manufacture of integrated circuits and also in space technology or as construction ceramics designed for use at high temperatures in corrosive chemical media.

The Hägg Rules

Empirical rules for the structures of carbides, nitrides, borides and also hydrides were formulated by Hagg in 1931 and are still used, although a number of exceptions have been found. In these rules, the structural criterion is the ratio of the radius of the metal atoms Me in the compound to the radii of light element atoms **X=H, B, N, C**. It states that, for ratio **$r=r(X)/r(Me)<0.59$**, simple structures of types A1, A2 and A3 or a simple hexagonal structure is formed and that the light elements are located in the largest cavities of the elemental metal structure. When $r>0.59$, more complex structures are formed.

Compounds of carbon, nitrogen and boron will be of the greatest interest here, usually with the transition metals, which are known as carbides, nitrides and borides.

Carbides and Nitrides

Of the compounds formed by transition metals with light elements (H, B, C, N, O), only carbides and nitrides have similar structural and bonding types as well as electrical and magnetic properties. This similarity is a consequence of the similarities in the electron structures, dimensions and electronegativities of these atoms. As nitrogen has one electron more than carbon, these two elements behave somewhat differently as do their compounds, where the properties may be shifted; metal carbides of the sixth group behave similarly and form similar structures to the nitrides of metals of the fifth group. Carbides and nitrides of metals of the iron group (Mn, Fe, Co, Ni) are important components of high-grade steels, constituting an independent chapter on these compounds. In general, the formation of carbides and nitrides is characteristic for transition metals. Except for nitrides of metals of the sixth group, carbides and nitrides have high melting points (2000～4000℃). Carbides are components of contemporary solid alloys, used in machining technology; as a consequence of their resistance to high temperatures and corrosive media, they are also employed as high-temperature construction materials. Nitrides of the IV-VI groups are also very hard materials; in addition, their specific electrical properties make them interesting in electronics as a basis for the manufacture of integrated circuits. Some of them are also superconductors.

It can be seen from Table 6. 4 that all the transition metals with the exception of the palladium and platinum groups form carbides and nitrides; in addition, osmium carbide OsC is also formed.

Carbides and nitrides form both crystal structures and intermetallic phases. Their description will be based on their substructures, formed by the metal atoms in the carbides and nitrides of transition metals. In structures, which satisfy the Hagg conditions (Hagg phases) there occur metallic substructures of both types A1 and A3 of close packing, structure A2 and a simple hexagonal lattice, which are close to dense packing arrangements. In the first three substructures, carbon and nitrogen occupy octahedral positions; in structures A1 and A3, these are the familiar regular octahedral, while in structure A2 the octahedron is deformed in the direction of one of the axes. In the simple hexagonal structure, the internodal positions, which have the form of trigonal prisms, are occupied.

The metal substructure in carbides and nitrides (except for cobalt) is not identical with the structure of the metal alone. Andrews and Hughes (1959) empirically determined a correlation between primary metal structures and final structures if carbides or nitrides: Elements originally with structure A3 do not form carbides and nitrides with hexagonal substructure; elements originally with structure A1 do not form carbides, and nitrides with cubic metallic substructure and elements with primary structure A2, as long as they do not have an allotropic modification with close packing, form both carbides and nitrides with cubic and hexagonal metallic substructures.

The physical principles for the formation of one or another structure of carbides and nitrides can be described to a first approximation as a consequence of the atomic dimensions compared with the size of internodal positions in which the C and N atoms are located. However, this is insufficient; for example, the A2 structure contains both deformed octahedral as well as large tetrahedral cavities; the C and N atoms prefer smaller octahedral cavities. As these cavities are often too small, the original structure becomes deformed. This also explains the limited solubilities of elements C and N in a great many metals of groups IV-VI. Well founded explanations of structures usually need a detailed knowledge of the electron structure of the resulting substances.

Selected from "Structure and Properties of ceramics" A. Koller, Elsevier Publ, 1994

Words and Expressions

1. carbide [ˈkɑːbaid] *n.* 碳化物
2. nitride [ˈnaitraid] *n.* 氮化物
3. boride [ˈbɔːraid] *n.* 硼化物
4. corundum [kəˈrʌndəm] *n.* 刚玉
5. tantalum [ˈtæntələm] *n.* 钽
6. superconductor [ˌjupəkənˈdʌktə] *n.* 超导体
7. construction ceramics 结构陶瓷
8. cavity [ˈkæviti] *n.* 孔穴；*a.* 有空腔的
9. electronegativity [iˌlektrəuˈnegətiviti] *n.* 电负性
10. palladium [pəˈleidiəm] *n.* 钯

11. platinum [ˈplætinəm] *n*. 铂
12. osmium [ˈɔzmiəm] *n*. 锇
13. substructure [ˈsʌbstrʌktʃə] *n*. 亚结构
14. internodal [ˈintəˌnəudl] *a*. 节间的
15. cobalt [ˈkəbɔːlt] *n*. 钴
16. allotropic [ˌæləˈtrɔpic] *a*. 同素异型的

Unit 3　Defect Crystal Chemistry

It has already been remarked that point defect populations affect both the physical and chemical properties of materials profoundly. In order to describe these consequences we need a notation for defects that is simple and self-consistent. The most widely employed system is the Kroger-Vink notation which was designed to account for point defect populations in crystals.

When we add or subtract elements from the crystal，we do so by adding or subtracting electrically neutral atoms and thus avoid making judgements and decisions about chemical bond types. When ionic crystals are involved this requires that we separately add or subtract electrons. To illustrate the implications of this idea we will use the notation to describe some defects in a compound of formula MX，where M is a metal and X an anion. It is simplest to do this by discussing the various types of defect that can occur in such a material，and to commence with uncharged atomic defects[1].

Atomic Defects

Vacancies. When empty lattice sites occur，they are indicated by the symbols V_M and V_X for the metal (M) and non-metal (X) sites respectively. In the notation the subscript M indicates a missing metal atom and X a non-metal. If we suppose that the oxide NiO is ionic，V_{Ni} would imply the removal of a Ni^{2+} ion together with two electrons，that is，a neutral Ni atom. Similarly，V_O would indicate a vacancy in the oxygen sub-lattice and implies removal of an O^{2-} ion from the crystal and the subsequent addition of two electrons to the crystal.

Interstitial atoms. When atoms occupy interstitial positions，they are denoted by M_i and X_i for metals and anions respectively. Hence K_I represents an interstitial potassium atom in a crystal .

Impurity atoms. Many materials contain impurity atoms，introduced either on purpose，or as a result of inadequate purification procedures，and it is important to be able to specify the nature of the impurities and where in the crystal they are to be found[2]. This is particularly true for impurities that are deliberately added to control electronic or other properties. In this case the impurity is given its normal chemical symbol and the site occupied is written as a subscript. Thus an Mg atom on a Ni site in NiO would be written as Mg_{Ni}. The same nomenclature is used if an atom in a crystal occupies the wrong site. Thus it is possible for M atoms to be on X sites，written as M_X，or X atoms to be on M sites，written as X_M. A potassium atom on a bromine site in KBr would be written as K_{Br}，for example.

Associated defects. As we will see in following sections，it is also possible for one or more lattice defects to associate with one another，that is，to cluster together. These are indicated by enclosing the components of such a cluster in parenthesis. As an example，

$(V_M V_X)$ would represent a Schottky defect in which the two vacancies were associated as a vacancy pair.

It is seen that the normal symbol for a chemical element represents the species involved, and the subscript represents the position of the atom in the structure③.

Charges on Defects

Electrons and electron holes. The charged defects that most readily come to mind are electrons. Some fractions of the electrons will be free to move through the crystal. These are denoted by the symbol e'. The superscript$'$ represents the negative charge on the electron. Although electrons are the only charged subatomic particles to exist in the structure it often simplifies matters to think about the sites where electrons are missing. This is analogous to thinking about vacacies instead of atoms. In the case of these 'electron vacancies' we use the symbol $h^{\bullet}$ to denote the defect, which is called an electron hole, or, more commonly, simply a 'hole'. Each hole will bear a positive charge of $+1$, which is represented by the superscript.

Charges on Defects. Besides the electrons and holes just mentioned, the atomic defects that we have described above can also carry a charge. In ionic crystals, in fact, this may be considered to be the normal state of affairs. The Kroger-Vink notation bypasses the problem of deciding on the real charges on defects by considering only effective charges on defects. The *effective charge* is the charge that the defect has with respect to the normal crystal lattice. To illustrate this concept, let us consider the situation in an atomic material such as NaCl, which we will suppose to be made up of the charged ions Na^+ and Cl^-.

If we then have a vacancy in the NaCl structure at a sodium position V_{Na}, what will the effective charge on this defect be? To understand this, you must imagine yourself as 'diffusing' through the NaCl structure. Each time a Na^+ ion is encountered, a region of positive charge will be experienced. If, then, we meet a vacancy instead of a normal ion, this will seem not to be positive at all. Relative to the situation normally met with at the site we will encounter a region which has an effective negative charge, that is, a charge relative to that normally encountered at that position equivalent to -1. In order to distinguish effective charges from real charges, the superscript$'$ is used for each unit of negative charge and the superscript$^{\bullet}$ is used for each unit of positive charge. Hence a 'normal' vacancy at a sodium site in NaCl would be written as V'_{Na}, which corresponds to a missing Na^+ ion. Similarly, a 'normal' vacancy at a chlorine site would seem to be positively charged relative to the normal situation in the crystal. Hence the vacancy has an effective charge of $+1$, which would be written $V^{\bullet}_{Cl}$.

With each of the other defect symbols V_M, V_X, M_i, M_X and associated defects such as $(V_M V_X)$ an effective charge relative to the host lattice is also possible. Thus $Zn_i^{\bullet\bullet}$ would indicate a Zn^{2+} at an intersticial site which is normally unoccupied and hence without any pre-existing charge. In such a case, all the charge on the Zn^{2+} ion is experienced as we move through the lattice, and hence the presence of two units of effective charge is recorded in the symbol, viz. 2. Similarly, substitution of a divalent ion such as Ca^{2+} for monovalent Na on a sodium site gives a local electronic charge augmented by one extra positive charge which is then represented as $Ca_{Na}^{\bullet}$.

Suppose now a sodium ion in NaCl, represented by Na_{Na}, is substituted by a potasium ion, represented by K_{Na}. Clearly the defect will have no effective charge, as, to anyone moving through the crystal, the charge felt on encountering the K ion is the same as that experienced on encountering a normal Na ion. This defect is therefore neutral in terms of effective charge. This is written as K_{Na}^{x} when the effective charge situation needs to be specified, the superscript X representing an effectively neutral charge.

It is therefore seen that the idea of the charge on the defect is separated from the chemical entity which makes up the defect. Real charges are represented by n^{+} and n^{-}, while effective charges are represented by n' and n • or x. It is for this reason that the charges on electrons and electron holes mentioned above were written as ' and •, as these charges are also of importance only relative to the surrounding crystal lattice④.

Selected from "Defect Crystal Chemistry and Its Application" K. J. D. Tilley, Blakie&son ltd, 1987

Words and Expressions

1. defect crystal chemistry 缺陷晶体化学
2. notation [nəu'teiʃən] *n*. 表示法
3. self-consistent ['selfkən'sistent] *a*. 首尾一致的；一贯的
4. vacancy ['veikənsi] *n*. 晶格空位
5. subscript ['sʌbskript] *n*. 下标
6. sub-lattice ['sʌbˌlætis] *n*. 亚晶格
7. deliberately [di'libərətli] *ad*. 故意地；审慎地
8. nomenclature [nəu'menklətʃə] *n*. 术语；命名法
9. cluster ['klʌstə] *n*. 凝块
10. Schottky defect 肖脱基缺陷
11. subatomic [ˌsʌbə'tɔmik] *a*. 亚原子的
12. electron hole 电子空穴
13. bypass ['baipɑːs] *v*. 越过；避开
14. divalent [dai'veilənt] *a*. 二价的
15. entity ['entəti] *n*. 实体；统一体

Notes

① It 是 to do this 与 to commence 两个不定式短语的形式主语，不定式短语中有一 that 引导的宾语从句修饰 defect。科技文章中经常使用这样的形式。参考译文：最简单的是讨论这种物质中可能出现的各种类型的缺陷，并从不带电的原子缺陷开始。

② 此句基本结构为并列句，前半句中 introduced 至 purification procedures 是省略了 being 的独立分词，说明杂质的来源；后半句中 it 为形式主语，从 to be able 至句末为不定式短

语作真正的主语，此短语中还有一个 cohere 引导的宾语从句，与 the nature of the imparities 并列作为 specify 的宾语。参考译文：许多物质中含有杂质原子，它们或者是有目的的引入，或者因净化工艺不适当的缘故，重要的是确定这些杂质的本质和在晶体的何处可寻得。

③ It 是形式主语，这次它的实际主语是 that 引导的主语从句，主语从句为一用 and 连接的并列句。参考译文：可见常用的化学元素表示所涉及的物质，下标则表示该元素在此结构中的位置。

④ It 作为形式主语代表 that 引导的主语从句，主语从句中还含有一个 as 引导的原因状语从句。参考译文：正因为这个原因，上述的电子和电子空穴带有的电荷各用′与˙表示，因为这些电荷只有相对于周围的晶格才显得重要。

Exercises

1. Translate the following expression into Chinese or English.

point defects, chemical formulate, commence with, charged interstitial site, host lattice, non-metal, effectively neutral charge, vacancy pair

缺陷化学，化学方程式，净化工艺，缔合缺陷，电子空穴，亚原子粒子，有效电荷，一价阴离子，二价阳离子

2. Translate the following paragraphs into Chinese.

① One departure from ideality involves the motion of an atom from a normal site to an interstitial position. This type of disorder, which results in equal concentrations of vacant lattice sites and interstitial atoms, is called Frenkel disorder.

② In FeO, for example, it is possible to have Fe^{3+} ions in addition to the normal Fe^{2+} ions. In this case, the Fe^{3+} ions are indicated as $Fe_{Fe}^{\cdot}$.

3. Fill in the blanks with suitable words.

① The notation V_M and V_X are used to represent____for M and X atoms in a binary compound MX, while____and____indicate respectively interstitial site occupied by M and X atoms.

② The superscripts + and − are used to indicate____ions, whereas the superscript · and ′ indicate____and____with respect to the host lattice.

Reading Material 3

Solid Solution

Solid solutions are very common in crystalline materials. A solid solution is basically a crystalline phase that can have variable composition. Often, certain properties of materials, e. g. conductivity, ferromagnetism, are modified by changing the composition in such a way that a solid solution forms and great use may be made of this in designing new materials that have specific properties.

Simple solid solution series are one of two types: in substitutional solid solutions, the atom or ion that is being introduced directly replaces an atom or ion of the same charge in the parent structure; in interstitial solid solutions, the introduced species occupies a site that is normally empty in the crystal structure and no ions or atoms are left out. Starting with these two basic types, a considerable variety of more complex solid solution mechanisms may be derived by having both substitution and interstitial formation occurring together and/or by introducing ions of different charge to those in the host structure.

Substitutional Solid Solutions

An example of a substitutional solid solution is the series of oxides formed on reacting together Al_2O_3 and Cr_2O_3 at high temperatures. Both of these end member phases have the corundum crystal structure (approximately hexagonal close packed oxide ions with Al^{3+}, Cr^{3+} ions occupying two-thirds of the available octahedral sites) and the solid solution may be formulated as $(Al_{2-x}Cr_x)O_3$; $0 \leqslant x \leqslant 2$. At intermediate values of x. Al^{3+} and Cr^{3+} ions are distributed at random over those octahedral sites that are normally occupied in Al_2O_3. Thus, while any particular site must contain either a Cr^{3+} or an Al^{3+} ion, the probability that it is one or the other is related to the composition x. When the structure is considered as a whole and the occupancy of all the sites is averaged out, it is useful to think of each site as being occupied by an 'average cation' whose properties, atomic number, size, etc, are intermediate between those of Al^{3+} and Cr^{3+}.

If a range of simple substitutional solid solutions is to form, there are certain minimum requirements that must be met. The ions that are replacing each other must have the same charge (otherwise vacancies or interstitials would also be created) and be fairly similar in size. From a review of the experimental results on alloy formation, it has been suggested that a difference of 15 percent in the radii of the metal atoms that are replacing each other is the most that can be tolerated if a substantial range of solid solutions is to form. For solid solutions in non-metallic systems, the limiting difference in size that is acceptable appears to be rather larger than 15 per cent, although it is difficult to quantify this. To a large extent this is because it is difficult to quantify the sizes of the ions themselves. Let us use the Pauling crystal radii (in angstroms) for the alkali cations as an example, i. e. Li^+ 0. 60, Na^+ 0. 95, K^+ 1. 33, Rb^+ 1. 48, Cs^+ 1. 69. The radii of K^+, Rb^+ and Rb^+, Cs^+ pairs are both within 15 per cent of each other and it is common to get solid solutions between, say, corresponding Rb^+ and Cs^+ salts. However, Na^+ and K^+ salts also commonly form solid solutions with each other (e. g. KCl and NaCl at high temperatures) and the K^+ ion is ~40 per cent larger than the Na^+ ion. Sometimes, Li^+ and Na^+ replace each other over limited ranges of compositions and Na^+ is ~60 per cent larger than Li^+. The difference in size of Li^+ and K^+ appears to be too large for any significant ranges of solid solution to form, however. If instead, one uses the Shannon and Prewitt radii based on $r_{O2-} = 1.26$A, similar effects are seen regarding the differences in size of the alkali cations.

In systems that exhibit complete ranges of solid solution, it is essential that the two end-member phases be isostructural. The reverse is not necessarily true, however, and just because two phases are isostructural it does not follow that they form solid solutions with each other; e. g. LiF and CaO both have the rock salt structure but they are not miscible with each other (i. e. they do not react together to form solid solutions) in the crystalline state. While complete ranges of solid solution form in favourable cases, as for example, with Al_2O_3-Cr_2O_3 at high temperatures, it is far more common to have only partial of limited ranges of solid solution. In such cases, the restriction that the end-member phases be isostructural no longer holds. For example, the minerals forsterite, Mg_2SiO_4 (an olivine), and willemite, Zn_2SiO_4, are partially soluble in each other, as shown by their phase diagram. The crystal structures of olivine and willemite are quite different; olivine contains approximately hexagonal close packed oxide layers but close packed oxide layers are not present in willemite. Both contain SiO_4 tetrahedra but magnesium is coordinated octahedrally in olivine and zinc is coordinated tetrahedrally in willemite. Both magnesium and zinc are flexible ions in their coordination requirements, however, and are happy in either tetrahedral or octahedral coordination. Thus, in the forsterite solid solutions, $(Mg_{2-x}Zn_x)SiO_4$, zinc replaces magnesium in octahedral sites whereas in the willemite solid solutions, $(Mg_{2-x}Zn_x)SiO_4$, magnesium replaced zinc in the tetrahedral sites. Mg^{2+} is a slightly larger cation than Zn^{2+} and this is reflected in the observation that, in oxide structures, magnesium shows a slight preference for octahedral coordination whereas zinc appears to prefer tetrahedral coordination.

Aluminium is also capable of being four or six coordinate to oxygen and this is shown in the system $LiAlO_2$-$LiCrO_2$, in which $LiCrO_2$ forms an extensive range of solid solutions, $Li(Cr_{2-x}Al_x)O: 0<x<0.6$; in these, Cr^{3+} and Al^{3+} are in octahedral sites. $LiAlO_2$ contains tetrahedrally coordinate Al^{3+}, however, and the dislike of Cr^{3+} for tetrahedral coordination is shown by the complete absence of solid solutions of $LiCrO_2$ in $LiAlO_2$.

In systems where the two ions that are replacing each other are of considerably different size, it is usually found that a larger ion may be partially replaced by a smaller one, but it is much more difficult to do the reverse and replace a small ion by a larger one. For example, in the alkali metasilicates, rather more than half the Na ions in Na_2SiO_3 may be replaced by Li^+ at high temperatures (~800℃) to give solid solutions $(Na_{2-x}Li_x)SiO_3$, but only ~10 per cent of Li^+ in Li_2SiO_3 may be replaced by Na^+.

Many types of atom or ion may replace each other to form substitutional solid solutions. Silicates and germanites are often isostructural and form solid solutions with each other by $Si^{4+}=Ge^{4+}$ replacement. The lanthanide elements, because of their similarity in size, are notoriously good at forming solid solutions with each other in, say, their oxides. Indeed, one cause of the great diffculty experienced by the early chemists in trying to separate the lanthanides was this very easy solid solution formation. Anions may also replace each other in substitutional solid solutions, e. g. AgCl-AgBr solid solutions, but these are not nearly as common as the solid solutions formed by cation substitution, probably because there are not many pairs of anions that have similar size and coordination/bonding requirements. Many alloys are nothing more than substitutional solid solutions, e. g. in brass, copper and zinc atoms replace each other over a wide range of compositions.

Interstitial Solid Solutions

Many metals form interstitial solid solutions in which small atoms, e. g. hydrogen, carbon, boron, nitrogen, etc., can enter into empty is well known for its ability to 'occlude' enormous volumes of hydrogen gas and the product hydride is an interstitial solid solution of formula PdH_x: $0<x<0.7$, in which hydrogen atoms occupy interstitial sites within the face centred cubic palladium metal structure. There is still uncertainty as to whether hydrogen is in octahedral or tetrahedral holes and it appears that the sites occupied may depend on the composition x.

Selected from "Solid State Chemistry and Its Application" A. R. West, John Wiley & sons ltd. 1984

Words and Expressions

1. ferromagnetism [ˌferəuˈmægnitizəm] *n*. 铁磁性
2. substitutional [ˌsʌbstiˈtjuːʃənəl] *a*. 取代的
3. occupancy [ˈɔkjupənsi] *n*. 占据
4. Pauling crysta radii 鲍林晶体半径
5. isostructural [ˌaisəˈstrʌktʃərəl] *a*. 同种结构的
6. miscible [ˈmisibl] *a*. 可溶混的
7. magnesium [mægˈniːzjəm] *n*. 镁
8. zinc [ziŋk] *n*. 锌
9. germanite [ˈdʒəːmənait] *n*. 赭石；亚锗酸盐
10. lanthanide [ˈlænθənaid] *n*. 镧系元素；镧（系卤）化物
11. notoriously [nəuˈtɔːriəsli] *ad*. 臭名昭著地，声名狼藉地
12. brass [brɑːs] *n*. 黄铜
13. occlude [ɔˈkluːd] *v*. 夹杂；挡住
14. uncertainty [ˌʌnˈsəːtənti] *n*. 不确定性

Unit 4 Surfaces and colloids

In 1915 Wolfgang Ostwald described the subject matter of colloid and surface science as a "world of neglected dimensions." The reason for such a description stemmed from the unique nature of interfaces and colloidal phenomena -they could not be readily interpreted based on "classical" atomic or solution theories, and the regions of space involved were beyond the reach of existent experimental techniques. Science has since taken a firm theoretical and experimental hold on the nature of matter at its two extremes: at the molecular, atomic, and subatomic levels, and in the area of bulk materials, including their physical strengths and weaknesses and their chemical and electrical properties. Legions of chemists, physicists, materials scientists, engineers, and others are continuously striving to improve on that knowledge in academic and industrial laboratories around the world. Between those two extremes still lies the world referred to by Ostwald, and even with the latest advanced techniques for studying the region between phases, a great many mysteries remain to be solved. For that reason, I like to refer to the study of interfaces and colloids as entering the "twilight zone." That "region" of the physical world represents a bridge not only between chemical and physical phases, but also plays a vital but often unrecognized role in other areas of chemistry, physics, biology, medicine, engineering, and other disciplines[①].

Our understanding of the nature of the interfacial region and the changes and transformations that occur in going from one chemical (or physical) phase to another has historically lagged behind that in many other scientific areas in terms of the development and implementation of both theoretical and practical concepts[②]. That is not to say, however, that we are particularly ignorant when it comes to interfacial and colloidal phenomena. Great strides were made in the theoretical understanding of interactions at interfaces in the late nineteenth and early twentieth centuries. Modern computational and analytical techniques made available in the last few years have led to significant advances toward a more complete understanding of the unique nature of interfaces and the interactions that result from their unique nature. However, because of the unusual and sometimes complex character of interfaces and associated phenomena, the development of fully satisfying theoretical models has been slow. By "fully satisfying" is meant a theory that produces good agreement between theory and experiment in situations that are less than "ideal" or "model" systems.

The degree of "satisfaction" one obtains from a given theory is quite subjective, of course, so there exists a great deal of controversy in many areas related to colloids and interfaces. For the surface and colloid scientist (as in all science), such controversy is not bad, since it represents the fuel for continued fundamental and practical research. However, for the practitioner who needs to apply the fruits of fundamental research, such uncertainty can sometimes complicate attempts to solve practical interfacial and colloidal problems.

It is likely that for every trained surface and colloid scientist in academic and industry, there are hundreds of scientists, engineers, and technicians whose work directly or indirectly involves some surface and/or colloidal phenomena. And very probably, of those hundreds, a relatively small percentage have been formally introduced to the subject in more than a cursory way during their scientific training. It therefore becomes necessary for them to learn "on the fly" enough of the subject to allow them to attack their problems in a coherent way. This book has been designed in a way and at a level that will (hopefully) provide a useful introduction to surface and colloid science at an undergraduate or graduate level while at the same time serving as an accessible reference for those already trained in other fields of science but needing some initial guidance into the twilight zone.

It would be practically impossible to list all of the human activities (both technological and physiological) that involve surface and colloidal phenomena, but a few examples have been listed in Table1. 2. For purposes of illustration, the examples in Table1. 2 have been divided into four main categories, each of which is further divided (somewhat arbitrarily, in some cases) according to whether the main principle involved is "colloidal" or "interfacial."③ More exact definitions of what those two terms imply will be given in the appropriate chapters; however, for present purposes one can think of "colloidal" as being a state of subdivision of matter in which the particle (or molecular) size of the basic unit involved varies from just larger than that of "true" molecular solutions to that of coarse suspensions-that is, between 10 and 10000 nm. "Interfacial" phenomena may be defined in this context as those related

Table1. 2 Some Common Examples of Surface and Colloidal Phenomena in Industry and Nature

Surface Phenomena	Colloidal Phenomena
Products Manufactured as Colloids or Surface Active Materials	
Soaps and detergents(surfactants)	Latex paints
Emulsifiers and pesticides	Aerosols
(nonsurfactant)	Foods(ice cream, butter, mayonnaise, etc.)
Herbicides and pesticides	Pharmaceuticals
	Lacquers, oil-based pants
	Oil and gas additives
Direct Application of Surface and Colloidal Phenomena	
Lubrication	Control of theological properties
Adhesion	Emulsions
Foms	Emulsion and dispersion polymerization
Wetting and waterproofing	Drilling muds
	Electrophoretic deposition
Use for the Purification and/or Improvement of Natural or Synthetic Materials	
Tertiary oil recovery	Mineral ore separation by flotation
Sugar refining	Grinding and communition
Sintering	Sewage and wastewater treatment
Physiological Applications	
Respiration	Blood transport
Joint lubrication	Emulsification of nutrients
Capillary phenomena in liquid	Enzymes
Arteriosclerosis	Cell membranes

to the interaction of at least one bulk phase (solid or liquid) with another phase (solid, liquid, or gas) or a vacuum in the narrow region in which the transition from one phase to the other occurs④. As will quickly become apparent, the two classes of phenomena are intimately related and often cannot be distinguished. For present purposes (and according to this author's preference) the examples have been divided according to those definitions based on the principle phenomenon involved.

By examining each subdivision in Table1. 2, one can quickly see that interfacial and colloidal phenomena are ubiquitous. We and our world simply would not function or even exist as we know it in their absence.

Selected from "Surface, Interface and Colloids" 2nd edition, D. Meyer, Wiley Vch Inc. 1999

Words and Expressions

1. improve on 提高，改善
2. twilight [ˈtwailait] *n*. 微光，曙光；*a*. 微明的
3. implementation [ˌimplimenˈteiʃən] *n*. 实现
4. suspension [səsˈpenʃən] *n*. 悬浮液
5. surfactant [səːˈfæktənt] *n*. 表面活化剂
6. emulsifier [iˈmʌlsifaiə] *n*. 乳化剂
7. stabilizer [ˈsteibilaizə] *n*. 稳定剂
8. aerosol [ˈɛərəsɔl] *n*. 气溶胶
9. herbicide [ˈhəːbisaid] *n*. 除草剂
10. pesticide [ˈpestisaid] *n*. 杀虫剂，农药
11. pharmaceutical [fɑːməˈsjuːtikəl] *a*. 制药的，医药的；*n*. 成药，药品
12. lacquer [ˈlækə] *n*. 漆，漆器
13. rheological [riːˈɔlədʒikəl] *a*. 流变学的
14. emulsion [iˈmʌlʃən] *n*. 乳浊液，乳液
15. drilling mud 钻井泥浆
16. electrophoretic [iˈlektrəufəretic] *a*. 电泳的
17. sewage [ˈsjuːidʒ] *n*. 污水，污物
18. respiration [rəspəˈreiʃən] *n*. 呼吸作用
19. lubrication [ljuːbriˈkeiʃən] *n*. 润滑（作用）
20. capillary [kəˈpiləri] *a*. *n*. 毛细管（的）；毛细作用（的）
21. arteriosclerosis [ɑːˈtiəriəuskliəˈrəusis] *n*. 动脉硬化
22. emulsification of nutrient 营养乳化作用
23. enzyme [ˈenzaim] *n*. 酶
24. ubiquitous [juˈbikwitəs] *a*. 普遍的，无处不在的
25. cell membrane 细胞膜

Notes

① 此句是用 not only……but also 连接的并列复合句。参考译文：物理世界的这个范畴不仅是化学相与物理相之间的桥梁，而且在化学、物理、生物、医药工程和其他学科的领域中起到非常重要但往往尚未被认识到的作用。

② 本句是一个用 that 引导的定语从句的主从复合句，句中出现的第二个 that 是 behind 的介词宾语，它后面省略了 understanding。主句的主要骨架为 our understanding has lagged behind that。参考译文：就理论和实践的开发和利用而言，我们对于界面区域本质的了解以及从一个化学（或物理）的相到另一个相的改变或转变的理解，历史上就落后于对其他科学领域的理解。

③ 此句为带有一个用 of which 引导的定语从句的主从复合句，定语从句中又带有一个 whether 引导的介词宾语从句。参考译文：为了说明，表 1.2 中的例子划分为四个部分，其中的每一个又根据涉及的主要原理是“胶体”还是“界面”再作进一步的分类，（在有些情况下，略带有人为的因素）。

④ 此句为一用 however 作为连词的并列复合句，尽管原文中 10000nm 后面用了一个句号，但从上下文关系与意义的完整来说，整个句子应延续到 occurs. 句子的第一部分有一个 what 引导的定语从句，第二部分说明 colloidal 的定义，其中有一个用 in which 引导的定语从句，修饰 a state of subdivision，第三部分说明 interfacial 的定义，也含有一个用 in which 引导的定语从句，修饰 the narrow region。

Exercises

1. Translate the following expressions into Chinese or English.
   world of neglected dimension ，take hold on，improve on
   experimental and analytical technique，agreement between theory and experiment
   accessible reference，physiological activity，lubrication
   rheological property，polymerization，mineral ore separation by flotation
   胶体，界面，表面，超出现有实验技术可达，物理强度，学科，落后于，独特的性质，许多争论，区分，根据，真溶液，悬浮液，乳浊液，表面活性剂，稳定剂，电泳沉积，细胞膜，污水处理。

2. Translate the following paragraphs into Chinese.
   ① It is desirable to understand the structure，composition，and properties of the boundaries of a solid and the interface between phases，for they have a strong influence on many mechanical properties，chemical phenomena，and electrical properties.
   ② The composition and structures of surfaces depend a great deal on the condition of formation and subsequently treatment. For example，it is found that freshly fractured oxide surfaces have high chemical reactivity compared with the same surfaces after they are allowed to stand in the air or are heated at high temperatures.

3. Fill in the blanks with suitable words.
   Between the two extremes of the nature matter：____and____there are regions called as ____and____. Interface refers to the region between two phases，which can be solid-solid，

____, ____, ____, and____, while colloid is a state of subdivision of matter whose basic unit is larger than that of____, but smaller than that of____.

Reading Material 4

Surfaces and Interfaces

Surface science in general and surface chemistry in particular have a long and distinguished history. The spontaneous spreading of oil on water was described in ancient times and was studied by Benjamin Franklin. The application of catalysis started in the early 1800s, with the discovery of the platinum-surface-catalyzed reaction of H_2 and O_2 in 1823 by Dobereiner. He used this reaction in his "lighter" (i. e., a portable flame source), of which he sold a large number. By 1835 the discovery of heterogeneous catalysis was complete thanks to the studies of Kirchhoff, Davy, Henry, Philips, Faraday, and Berzelius. It was at about this time that the Daguerre process was introduced for photography. The study of tribology, or friction, also started around this time, coinciding with the industrial revolution, although some level of understanding of friction appears in the work of Leonardo da Vinci. Surface-catalyzed-chemistry-based technologies first appeared in the period of 1860 to 1912, starting with the Deacon process ($2HCl+1/2O_2 \longrightarrow H_2O+Cl_2$), SO_2 oxidation to SO_3 (Messel, 1875), the reaction of methane with steam to produce CO and H_2 (Mond, 1888), ammonia oxidation (Ostwald, 1901), ethylene hydrogenation (Sabatier, 1902), and ammonia synthesis (Haber, Mittasch, 1905～1912). Surface tension measurements and recognition of equilibrium constraints on surface chemical processes led to the development of the thermodynamics of surface phases by Gibbs (1877). The existence of polyatomic or polymolecular aggregates that lack crystallinity and diffuse slowly (gelatine and albumin, for example) was described in 1861 by Graham, who called these systems "colloids." Polymolecular aggregates that exhibit internal structure were called "micelles" by Nageli, and stable metal colloids were prepared by Faraday. However, the colloid subfield of surface chemistry gained prominence in the beginning of the 20th century with the rise of the paint industry and the preparation of artificial rubbers. Studies of light bulb filament lifetimes, high-surface-area gas absorbers in the gas mask, and gas separation technologies in other forms led to investigations of atomic and molecular adsorption (Langmuir, 1915). The properties of chemisorbed and physisorbed monolayers, adsorption isotherms, dissociative adsorption, energy exchange, and sticking upon gas-surface colloids were studied. Studies of electrode surfaces in electrochemistry led to the detection of the surface space charge (for a review of electrochemistry in the 19th, see reference). The surface diffraction of electrons was discovered by Davisson and Germer (1927). Major academic and industrial laboratories focusing on surface studies have been formed in Germany (Haber, Polanyi, Farkas, Bonhoefer), the United Kingdom (Rideal, Roberts, Bowden), the United States (Langmuir,

Emmett, Harkins, Taylor, Ipatief, Adams), and many other countries . They have helped to bring surface chemistry into the center of development of chemistry-both because of the intellectual challenge to understand the rich diversity of surface phenomena and because of its importance in chemical and energy conversion technologies.

In the early 1950s, focus on chemistry research shifted to studies of gas-phase molecular processes as many new techniques were developed to study gas-phase species on the molecular level. This was not the case in surface and interface chemistry, although the newly developed field-ion and electron microscopies did provide atomic level information on surface structure. The development of surface-chemistry-based technologies continued at a very high rate, however, especially in areas of petroleum refining and the production of commodity chemicals. Then in the late 1950s, the rise of the solid-state-device-based electronics industry and the availability of economical ultrahigh vacuum systems-developed by research in space sciences-provided surface chemistry with new challenges and opportunities, resulting in an explosive growth of the discipline. Clean surfaces of single crystals could be studied for the first time, and the preparation of surfaces and interfaces with known atomic structure and controlled composition was driving the development of microelectronics and computer technologies, New surface instrumentation and techniques have been developed that permit the study of surface.

As a result of this sudden availability of surface characterization techniques, microscopic surface phenomena (adsorption, bonding, catalysis, oxidation and other surface reactions, diffusion, desorption, melting and other phase transformation, growth, nucleation, charge transport, atom, ion and electron scattering, friction, hardness, lubrication) are being reexamined on the molecular scale. This has led to a remarkable growth of surface chemistry that has continued uninterrupted up to the present. The discipline has again become one of the frontier areas of chemistry. The newly gained knowledge of the molecular ingredients of surface phenomena has given birth to a steady stream of high technology products, including: new hard coatings that passivate surfaces; chemically treated glass, semiconductor, metal, and polymer surfaces where the treatment imparts unique surface properties; newly designed catalysis, chemical sensors, and carbon fiber composites; surface-space-charge-based copying; and new methods of electrical, magnetic, and optical signal processing and storage. Molecular surface chemistry is being utilized increasingly in biological sciences.

Condensed phases—solids and liquids—must have surfaces or interfaces. The suit of an astronaut maneuvering in outer space represents a solid-vacuum interface; a basketball player jumping to score is a moving solid-gas interface; a sailboat moving over the waves is a solid liquid interface; a tire slides at the solid-solid interface. The surface of a lake is a liquid-gas interface. Olive oil poured on top of an open bottle of wine to prevent air oxidation forms a liquid-liquid interface. These interfaces exhibit remarkable physical and chemical properties. The chemical behavior of surfaces is responsible for heterogeneous catalysis (ammonia synthesis, for example) and gas separations (as in the extraction of oxygen and nitrogen from air) by selective adsorption. Mechanical surface properties give rise to adhesion, friction, or slide. Magnetic surfaces are used for information storage (e. g., magnetic tape or computer disk drive). Optical surface phenomena are responsible for color and texture perception, total internal reflection needed for transmission through glass fibers, and the generation of second and higher harmonic frequencies in nonlinear laser optics. The electrical behavior of surfaces often gives rise to surface charge build-up, which is used for image transfer in xerography and for electron transport in integrated circuitry.

Surfaces and interfaces are the favorite media of evolution. Both photosynthetic and biological systems-the brain and the leaf-evolve and improve by ever increasing their interface area or their interface-to-volume ratio. The spine of the sea urchin has remarkable strength that is achieved by the layered structure of an inorganic-organic composite, namely, single-crystalline calcium carbonate that grows on ordered layers of acidic macromolecules deposited on layers of protein.

Selected from "Introduction to Surface Chemistry and Catalysis". G. A. Somorjai, John Wiley&Sons Ltd. 1994

Words and Expressions

1. catalysis [kə'tælisis] *n.* 催化
2. heterogeneous ['hetərəu'dʒiːnjəs] *a.* 异种的、非均质的，多相的
3. tribology [ˌtraib'ɔləkʒi] *n.* 摩擦学
4. Surface-catalycal-chemistry-based technology 表面催化化学技术
5. methane ['miːθein] *n.* 甲烷，沼气
6. ethylene ['eθilin] *n.* 乙烯
7. constraint [kən'strein] *n.* 限制，约束，强制
8. crystallinity [kristə'liniti] *n.* 结晶度，(结) 晶性
9. gelatine ['dʒelətin] *n.* 明胶，动物胶
10. albumin ['ælbjumin] *n.* 清蛋白
11. micelle [mi'selə] *n.* 胶束，胶态分子团
12. absorption [əb'sɔːpʃən] *n.* 吸收
13. isotherm ['aisəuθəːm] *n.* 等温线
14. collision [kə'liʒən] *n.* 碰撞
15. diffraction [di'frækʃən] *n.* 衍射
16. solid-state-device-based 固态器件
17. frontier ['frʌntiə] *n.* 新领域，前沿
18. sensor ['sensə] *n.* 传感器
19. surface-space-charge-based copying 表面空间电荷复印
20. texture perception 构造感觉
21. xerography [zi'rɔgrəfi] *n.* 静电印刷术、干印术、静电复印术

22. photosynthetic [ˌfəutəusinˈθetik] *a*. 光合的
23. spine [spain] *n*. 脊柱
24. urchin [ˈəːtʃin] *n*. 海胆
25. composite [ˈkɔmpəzit] *a*. 混合的，复合的；混合体，合成物
26. protein [ˈprəutiːn] *n*. 蛋白质；*a*. 蛋白质的

Unit 5 Diffusion

The oscillations of atoms are characterized by small average amplitudes up to temperatures near the melting point of the crystal. Nevertheless, some atoms may occasionally attain, even at temperatures below the melting point, a considerable energy that exceeds the mean for the whole crystal. Energy fluctuations of this kind may occur, for example, when all the atoms that are located on one side of the atom of interest simultaneously move towards this atom, thereby imparting to it a considerable momentum. If, moreover, all the atoms on the other side move away from the atom at the same instant, then it can be displaced from its normal position to another site in the structure. These thermally activated jumps of atoms or of other elements of the structure (e. g. a vacancy) from one position of the structure to another constitute the fundamental mechanism of the migration of individual atoms in a crystal, known as *diffusion*. Here a distinction can be made between the diffusion of native atoms of the structure of a given crystal, known as *self-diffusion*, and the diffusion of atoms that are extraneous to the crystal structure.

The simplest mechanism of diffusion in the bulk of a crystal consists in a migration of the atom (ion) from a lattice point to its adjacent vacancy. This is referred to as the *vacancy mechanism*, since, in view of the very low vacancy concentration in a crystal and the indistinguishability of individual atoms (or ions) of one kind, it is advisable to consider this mechanism in terms of the movements of vacancies rather than atoms. In ionic crystals it is also reasonable to make a distinction between the vacancy mechanism in the cationic sub-lattice and that in the anionic sub-lattice, since the cationic vacancies travel more easily in the cationic sub-lattice, and similarly for the anionic vacancies①.

This is because in this situation the repulsion due to charges of the same sign is a minimum. Vacancies exhibit a measurable mobility at temperature equal to one fourth of the melting point of the substance, in Kelvins.

Another point defect capable of relatively easy migration in the structure is an interstitial ion (or atom). The measurable mobility of interstitials is observed just above a temperature of 273K. A typical *mechanism* of interstitial diffusion consists in jumps of interstitial atoms from one interstitial position to another. The jumps may also be effected in such a way that an interstitial ion knocks on an adjacent ion (atom) at a lattice point, which then jumps to an interstitial position and occupies its site. The latter mode is referred to as the *interstitial mechanism with displacement*.

The direct interchange of positions between neighboring ions (or atoms) with no participation of point defects is an alternative mechanism, whose variant is the *ring mechanism*. This interchange is accomplished here by a concerted motion of the ions of one kind along a ring-shaped circumference. A number of other variants and modifications of the mechanisms of diffusion in crystals may be conceived; however, due to lack of space, these will not be presented here. The interested reader is referred to the pertinent references listed at the end of this section.

In some crystals such as the tungsten bronzes and polyaluminates of the β-Al_2O_3 type, voids are present in the perfect structure, and in concentrations that considerably exceed the equilibrium concentration of vacancies. In the zones containing voids diffusive jumps may occur with a greater facility than in the close-packed zones. Compared with crystals, glass also has a loose structure. Although the previous discussion was concerned primarily with diffusion in the crystal bulk it should also be borne in mind that in many cases, it is the *high-diffusivity paths* that are of paramount importance②. In addition to structural voids, the high-diffusivity paths also comprise grain surfaces and boundaries, which are of significance for diffusion in polycrystals. For the above reasons the discussion of the diffusion in the bulk of crystals has been supplemented, wherever possible and practicable, by the data on diffusion in the high-diffusivity paths.

Since atom jumps during diffusion require the surrounding structure to be strained, it is therefore intuitively evident that, for close-packed crystals, the energetically most preferred are the vacancy mechanism and the interstitial mechanisms.

Figurel. 2 illustrates the jump of an atom from the interstitial position A to the adjacent position C, an element of the interstitial mechanism of diffusion. The atom here has to pass through an intermediate position B, which it can attain only if its energy is sufficient to overcome the repulsive forces exerted by the atoms surrounding this position③. The changes in energy corresponding to the consecutive positions of the ion (or atom) are schematically shown in Figurel. 2. Therefore, for an atom to jump from one position to another the energy barrier has to be overcome, whose value is determined by the difference in the energy of the atom in point B and point A or C (energy minimum). Accordingly, for an atomic jump a definite activation energy, E^*, is required.

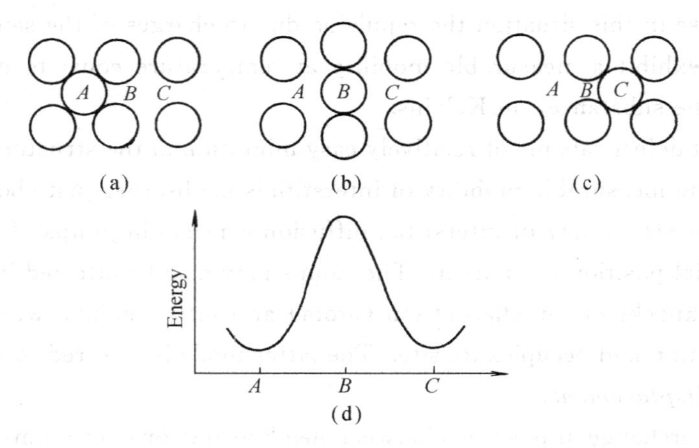

Fig. 1. 2 Successive stages of the jump of an interstitial atom to an adjacent interstitial position (a-c); changes in energy of an atom during such (d)
(after P. D shewan Diffision in Solids, McGraw-Hill, New york, 1963)

Each oscillation of an atom at an equilibrium position can actually be regarded as an attempted jump to an adjacent position. In the majority of cases, however, these attempts are unsuccessful to the energy barrier; yet once in a while a thermal fluctuation arises at a given crystal site which enables the atom to overcome this barrier. Therefore, the frequency with which atoms jump among interstitial positions is, to a first approximation, proportional to the product of the frequency of oscillation of an atom and the probability of occurrence of a fluctuation large enough for an atom (ion) to acquire an energy equal to at least E^*④. If $\Gamma_{at,i}$ denotes the frequency of atomic jumps by the interstitial mechanism, v the frequency of oscillation of atoms (ions), and P_l the probability that a thermal fluctuation will occur that is high enough to impart to one interstitial atom an energy equal to E^*, the frequency of the jumps is given by $\Gamma_{at,i}=vP_l$.

$$P_l=\exp\left(\frac{-E^*}{kT}\right) \qquad \Gamma_{at,i}=v\exp\left(\frac{-E^*}{kT}\right) \tag{1. 1}$$

Where k is Boltzmann's constant and T is the absolute temperature. The jump frequency tells us how often an atom abandons its normal position, but says nothing about the direction the atom will choose during its jump. As expected, the choice of direction of successive jumps of interstitial ions is random. At a temperature of 1300K, the frequency of oscillations, v, is of the order of $10^{13}s^{-1}$, and the value of Γ_i, found from equation (1. 1) for typical E^* values, amounts to $10^7-10^8 s^{-1}$. In other words, an atom (or ion) remains in the interstitial position for a long time between successive jumps. During that time an equilibrium condition is established between the atom of interest and the crystalline environment; from 10 to 50 vibrations are sufficient to effect this. As a result, the momentum of the atom in a specific direction, imparted to that atom during the jump, has been lost before a subsequent jump occurs. Additionally, the atom in an interstitial position has identical surroundings; at a moderate concentration of point defects, an atom is surrounded, for example, in a cubic structure, by six equivalent interstitial positions, and the choice of any one of these is entirely haphazard.

Selected from "Constitution and Properties of Ceramic Materials".
R. Pampuch, Elservier Publ. 1991

Words and Expressions

1. diffusion [di'fju:ʒən] n. 扩散
2. oscillation [ɔsi'leiʃən] n. 振动，振荡
3. fluctuation [flʌktju'eiʃən] n. 波动，起伏
4. momentum [məu'mentəm] n. 动量
5. vacancy mechanism 空位机理
6. indistinguishability [indis'tiŋgwiʃəˌbiliti] n. 难辨性
7. interstitial mechanism 填隙机理
8. ring mechanism 环形机理
9. displacement [dis'pleismənt] n. 移动，取代，位移

10. circumference [sə'kʌmfərəns] *n.* 圆周
11. tungstun bronze 钨青铜
12. polyaluminate [pɔliə'ljuːmineit] *n.* 多聚铝酸盐
13. void [vɔid] *n.* 空位；*a.* 空的
14. consecutive [kənsekjutiv] 连续的
15. activation energy 活化能
16. haphazard [hæp'hæzəd] *n.* 偶然性

Notes

① 带 since 引导的原因从句的主从复合句，主句中 it 为不定式 to make 的形式主语，that 后面省略了 vacancy mechanism，从句中 similarly for the atomic vacancy 也是一省略形式。参考译文：在离子晶体中，较合理的是区分阳离子亚晶格和阴离子亚晶格中的空位机理，因为阳离子空位更易于在它的主晶格中移动，阴离子空位亦然。

② 带 although 引导的让步从句的主从复合句，主句中的 it 为 that 引导的主语从句的形式主语，主语从句中有一 it is that 的强调形式。参考译文：尽管以前的讨论主要涉及在晶体整体中的扩散，但应该牢记的是，在许多情况下，正是高扩散率通道最为重要。

③ Which 引导的定语从句为非限制性定语从句，它修饰的不是某个词，而是前面做过的动作，定语从句中还有一个 if 引导的条件从句。参考译文：这里，这个原子必须通过一个中间位置 B，只有当它的能量足以克服周围原子施加的斥力，它才能做到这一点。

④ With which 引导一个定语从句，修饰 frequency，谓语为 is proportional to the product of. 参考译文：因此，作为一极近似，原子在相邻间隙位间跃迁的频率正比于原子振动频率与原子（离子）出现热起伏并获得大于或等于 E^* 的能量的几率的乘积。

Exercises

1. Translate the following expressions into Chinese or English.

   average amplitude，momentum，thermal activated jump，lattice point，anionic vacancy，ring mechanism，interstitial mechanism with displacement，high diffusivity path，repulsive force，energy barrier，equilibrium position.

   熔点，能量起伏，自扩散，空位机理，阳离子亚晶格，熔点的一半，间隙扩散，活化能，一极近似，正比于，绝对温度，平衡条件，相邻间隙位。

2. Translate the following paragraphs into Chinese.

   When an atom moves from one lattice site to another by a diffusion jump，there is an intermediate position of high energy. Only a certain fraction of the atoms present in the lattice have sufficient energy to overcome this energy barrier to moving from one site to another.

   As the temperature is increased，the fraction of atoms present which have sufficient energy to surmount this barrier increases exponentially，so that the temperature dependence of diffusion can be represented as $D=D_0\exp(-G^*/RT)$

3. Answer the questions.

   ① What is the definition of diffusion? self diffusion?

② why can only a few atoms or ions diffuse through lattices?

③ On which factors does the frequency of atomic jumps depend in the interstitial mechanism?

Reading Material 5

Phase Transitions

Phase transitions are important in most areas of solid state science. They are interesting academically, e. g. a considerable slice of current research in solid state physics concerns soft mode theory, which is one aspect of phase transitions, and they are important technologically, e. g. in the synthesis of diamond from graphite, the processes for strengthening of steel and the properties of ferroelectricity and ferromagnetism. This chapter discusses structural, thermodynamic and kinetic aspects of phase transitions and their classification. A few of the more important phase transitions are described; others are mentioned elsewhere in this book.

What Is a Phase Transition?

If a crystalline material is capable of existing in two or more polymorphic forms (e. g. diamond and graphite), the process of transformation from one polymorph to another is a phase transition. The terms *transition* and *transformation* are both used to describe this and are interchangeable. In the narrowest sense, phase transitions are restricted to changes in structure only, without any changes in composition, i. e. to changes in elements or single-phase materials. A much wider definition that is sometimes used includes the possibility of compositional changes, in which case more than one phase may be present before and/or after the transition. However, one then has to try and draw a dividing line between polymorphic transitions, on the one hand, and chemical reactions, on the other. The easiest solution is probably to try and avoid giving a precise definition of phase transitions.

Phase transitions are affected by both thermodynamic and kinetic factors. Thermodynamics gives the behavior that should be observed under equilibrium conditions and, for a particular material or system, this information is represented by the phase diagram. Phase transitions occur as a response to a change in conditions, usually temperature or pressure but sometimes composition. The rates at which transitions occur i. e. kinetics, are governed by various factors. Transitions that proceed by a nucleation and growth mechanism are often slow because the rate controlling step, which is usually nucleation, is difficult. In martensitic and displacive phase transitions, nucleation is easy, occurs spontaneously and the rates of transition are usually fast.

Buerger's Classification: Reconstructive and Displacive Transitions

We can begin with the classification scheme of Buerger (1961) which initially divides phase transitions into two groups: reconstructive and displacive transitions. Reconstructive transitions involve a major reorganization of the crystal structure, in which many bonds have to be broken and new bonds formed. The transition, graphite • diamond, is reconstructive and involves a complete change in crystal structure, from the hexagonal sheets of three-coordinated carbon atoms in graphite to the infinite framework of four-coordinated carbon atoms in diamond, and vice versa. The quatz = cristobalite transition in SiO_2 is also reconstructive because although there is no difference in coordination between the two polymorghs-both structures are built of SiO_4 tetrahedra linked at their corners to form a three-dimensional framework-the polymorphs have different types of framework structure and many Si—O bonds must break and reform in order that the transition may take place. Because many bonds must break, reconstructive transitions usually have high activation energies and, therefore, take place only slowly.

Often, reconstructive transitions may be prevented from occurring, in which case the untransformed phase is kinetically stable although thermodynamically it is metastable. A classic example is the occurrence of diamond at normal temperatures and pressures. At 25℃ and 1 atmosphere, graphite is the stable polymorph of carbon, but for kinetic reasons the transition diamond→graphite does not occur at detectable rates under ambient conditions.

Since there is often no structural relationship between two polymorphs separated by a reconstructive phase transition, there may also be no relation between the symmetry and space groups of the two polymorphs.

Displacive phase transitions involve the distortion of bonds rather than their breaking and the structural changes that occur are usually small. For this reason, displacive transitions take place readily, with zero or small activation energies, and cannot usually be prevented from occurring. As well as a structural similarity, a symmetry relationship exists between the two polymorphs such that the symmetry of the low temperature polymorph is lower than, and belongs to a subgroup of, that of the high temperature polymorph. Example are provided by the three main polymorphs of silica: quartz, tridymite and cristobalite, all of which undergo displacive, low-high transitions. These transitions involve small distortions or rotations of the SiO_4 tetrahedra, without breaking any primary Si—O bonds.

The distinction between reconstructive and displacive phase transitions is shown schematically in Fig. 1. 3. In order to convert structure A into any of the other structures, B, C and D, bond breaking is necessary and the transition is reconstructive. On the other hand, interconversions between structures B, C and D do not involve bond breaking but only small rotational movements. These transitions are therefore displacive.

A more detailed and specific classification scheme, also due to Buerger, is given in Table1. 3. First coordination refers to bonds between nearest neighbor atoms (e. g. Si and O in SiO_4 tetrahedra), i. e. to the first coordination sphere of a particular atom. Second coordination refers to interactions between next nearest neighbor atoms (it is probably not true to regard these interactions as bonds), e. g. between adjacent silicon atoms in a chain of corner-sharing SiO_4 tetrahedra. Transformations involving first coordination can take place by two

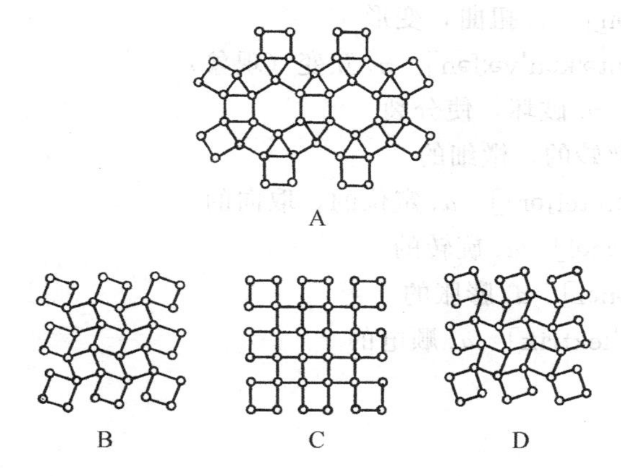

Fig. 1. 3 Transformation from structure A to any other structure requires the breaking of first coordination bonds. Transformations among B, C and D are distortional only. (After Buerger, 1961)

mechanisms: (a) by completely disrupting the crystal structure of the original polymorph, as in graphite=diamond, or (b) by a much more subtle and easier method involving dilation.

Table 1. 3 *Classification of Phase Transitions*

Type of transition	Examples
1. Transition involving first coordination	
(a) Reconstructive (Slow)	Diamond ⇌ graphite
(b) Dilational (Rapid)	Rock salt ⇌ CsCl
2. Transition involving second coordination	
(a) Reconstructive (Slow)	Quartz ⇌ cristobalite
(b) Displacive (Rapid)	Low ⇌ high quartz
3. Transitions involving disorder	
(a) Substitutional (Slow)	Low ⇌ high $LiFeO_2$
(b) Orientational and Rotational (Rapid)	Ferroelectric ⇌ Paraelectric $NH_4H_2PO_4$
4. Transitions of bond type (Slow)	Grey ⇌ white Sn

Selected from "Solid State Chemistry and Its Application", A. R. West, John. Wiley & Sons Ltd. 1984

Words and Expressions

1. phase transition 相变
2. ferroelectricity [ferəuiˌlek'trisiti] *n*. 铁电现象
3. transformation [ˌtrænsfə'meiʃən] *n*. 转变
4. kinetics [kai'netiks] *n*. 动力学
5. nucleation [ˌnjuːkli'eiʃən] *n*. 核化
6. martensitic [mɑːtən'sitik] *a*. 马氏体的
7. displacive [dis'pleisiv] *a*. 位移性的
8. reconstructive [ˌriːkən'strʌktiv] *a*. 重建的
9. ambient ['æmbiənt] *a*. 周围的，外界的

10. distortion [dis'tɔːʃən] *n*. 扭曲，变形
11. interconversion [ˌintəːkən'vəːʃən] *n*. 互变（现象）
12. disrupt [dis'rʌpt] *v*. 破坏，使分裂
13. subtle [sʌtl] *a*. 微妙的，微细的
14. orientational [ˌɔːriən'teiʃənl] *a*. 定位的，取向的
15. rotational [rəu'teiʃənəl] *a*. 旋转的
16. dilational [dai'leiʃənəl] *a*. 膨胀的
17. paraelectric [pærəi'lektrik] *a*. 顺电的

PART Ⅱ CERAMICS

Unit 6 Ceramic Fabrication Process: Conventional Routes to Ceramics

Solid ceramic bodies are generally produced by using the process of powder compaction followed by firing at high temperature. Sintering or densification occurs during this heat treatment and is associated with joining together of particles, volume reduction, decrease in porosity and increase in grain size. The phase distribution or microstructure within the ceramic is developed during sintering and fabrication techniques used for shaping ceramics are described here. The aim of these techniques is to produce microstructures suitable for particular applications.

(a) Precipitation from solution

Alumina occurs as the mineral bauxite and is refined in the Bayer process whereby ore is initially dissolved under pressure in sodium hydroxide so that solid impurities (SiO_2, TiO_2, Fe_2O_3) separate from sodium aluminate solution. This solution is either seeded with gibbsite crystals (α-$Al_2O_3 \cdot 3H_2O$) or undergoes autoprecipitation to bayerite (β-$Al_2O_3 \cdot 3H_2O$) after its neutralisation with CO_2 gas. Temperature, alumina supersaturation and amount of seed affect particle size during crystallisation.

Problems can arise when two or more components are coprecipitated. Thus, different species do not always deposit from solution at the reaction pH, while washing procedures can selectively remove a precipitated component as well as dissolve entrained electrolyte. The difficulty in maintaining chemical homogeneity is serious as inhomogeneities have a deleterious effect on the mechanical and electrical properties of ceramics. Because precipitation results in agglomerated powders, grinding, dry-milling or wet-milling with water or a non-aqueous liquid are used for particle size reduction so that powder compacts will sinter to near theoretical density①.

Precipitation reactions are not restricted to oxides and hydroxides. Hence, for the high-T_c oxide superconductor $La_{1.85}Ba_{0.15}CuO_4$, La, Ba and Cu oxalates were deposited from electrolyte solutions and sintered in air at 1373 K. Because these materials reversibly intercalate O_2, the annealing temperature and rate of cooling, which affect their superconducting properties and the Cu^{3+}/Cu^{2+} ratio must be carefully controlled.

(b) Powder mixing techniques

Multicomponent oxide powders are synthesised from conventional mixing techniques by initially blending together starting materials, usually metal oxides and carbonates, after which the mixtures are ground or milled. Comminuted powders are then calcined, sometimes after compaction, and the firing sequence may be repeated several times with intermediate grinding stages. As for coprecipitation, impurities can be introduced into the ceramic from the grinding operation; grinding also results in angular-shaped powders.

Several problems are associated with mixing powders. High temperatures required for reaction between components can result in loss of volatile oxides, while milling may not comminute powders sufficiently for complete reaction to occur on calcination. It is difficult to obtain reproducible uniform distributions of material in ball-milled powders especially when one fraction is present in small amounts as occurs in electroceramics whose properties are often controlled by grain boundary phases containing minor quantities of additives②. The $YBa_2Cu_3O_{7-\delta}$ superconductor was synthesised by mixing Y_2O_3, $BaCO_3$ and CuO, grinding and heating at 1223K in air. Powder was then pressed into pellets, sintered in flowing O_2, cooled to 473K in O_2 and removed from the furnace.

(c) Uniaxial pressing

In uniaxial pressing a hard steel die is filled with either dry powder, or a powder containing up to several weight percent of H_2O, and a hard metal punch is driven into the die to form a coherent compact. Van der Waals forces cause aggregation of fine powders so that binders such as polyvinyl alcohol and lubricants are incorporated into them by, for example, spray-drying in order to improve their flow properties and homogeneity of the product. It is important that the unfired or green body has adequate strength for handling before the firing operation, during which organic additives are decomposed. Uniaxial pressing can be readily automated and is particularly suited for forming components with a simple shape such as flat discs and rings that can be produced to close dimensional tolerances, thus avoiding post-firing diamond machining operations.

(d) Hot uniaxial pressing

Hot uniaxial pressing or hot-pressing involves simultaneous application of heat and pressure during sintering. A refractory die, usually graphite, is filled with powder, which, after compaction, is heated in an inert atmosphere. Hot-pressing produces higher density and smaller grain sizes at lower temperatures compared with uniaxial pressing and is particularly suited for fabrication of flat plates, blocks and cylinders. Stresses set up by the applied pressure on contacts between particles increase the driving force for sintering and remove the need for very fine particle sizes. Additives such as magnesium oxide and yttrium oxide, which are often used for Si_3N_4, allow achievement of theoretical density at lower temperatures. These sintering aids result in formation of a liquid phase and particle rearrangement because of capillary forces arising from the Laplace equation and by dissolution-recrystallisation processes. However, advantages brought about by additives have to be offset by degradation in mechanical behaviour of sintered components especially at high temperature because glassy and crystalline grain boundary phases derived from them often have inferior properties compared with the matrix③.

(e) Solid-state sintering

The driving force for sintering is reduction in surface free energy associated with a decrease of surface area in powder compacts due to removal of solid-vapour interfaces. Vapour-phase nucleation is described by using the Kelvin equation, which is also applicable to mass-transport process in a consolidated powder. The vapour-pressure difference across a curved interface can enhance evaporation from particle surfaces and condensation at the neck between two particles, particularly for particle diameters of several micrometers or less, such as occur in ceramic fabrication. Although this evaporation-condensation process produces changes in pore shape and joins particles together, the centre-to-centre distance between particles remains constant so that shrinkage and densification do not occur. The driving force for mass transport by solid-state processes for ceramic powders with low vapour pressure is the difference in free energy between the neck region and surface of particles. As for the evaporation-condensation pathway, transport from surface to neck by surface and lattice diffusion does not cause densification. This is produced only by diffusion from the grain boundary between particles and from the bulk lattice. Covalent ceramics such as Si_3N_4 are more difficult to sinter to high density than ionic solids, for example Al_2O_3, because of lower atomic mobilities, although difficulties can be overcome by using very fine powders ca. 0.1μm diameter, high temperature and high pressure.

Impurities such as oxygen and chlorine in Si_3N_4 often migrate during sintering to grain boundaries where they reduce the interfacial surface energy and impair densification, creep behaviour, oxidation resistance and high-temperature strength.

Selected from "Chemical synthesis of advanced ceramic materials", David Segal,
Cambridge University Press, Cambridge, 1989.

Words and Expressions

1. sintering [ˈsintəriŋ] *n.* 烧结
2. porosity [pɔːˈrɔsiti] *n.* 气孔率，多孔性，
3. grain size 粒度，颗粒大小
4. microstructure [ˈmaikrəstrʌktʃə] *n.* 显微结构
5. alumina [əˈljuːminə] *n.* 氧化铝
6. bauxite [ˈbɔːksait] *n.* 铝土矿，(铁) 矾土
7. impurity [imˈpjuəriti] *n.* 杂质，不纯物
8. gibbsite [ˈgibzait] *n.* 三水铝石 (α-$Al_2O_3 \cdot 3H_2O$)
9. bayerite [beiəˈrit] *n.* 三水铝石 (β-$Al_2O_3 \cdot 3H_2O$)
10. neutralisation [njuːtrəlaiˈzeiʃen] *n.* 中和 (作用，法)
11. supersaturation [sjuːpəˈsætʃəreiʃen] *n.* 过饱和
12. crystallisation [ˌkristˈlizeiʃən] *n.* 结晶 (作用)，晶化
13. deposit [diˈpɔzit] *v.* (使) 沉积，涂，覆
14. inhomogeneity [ˈinhɔmoudʒeˈniːti] *n.* 不 (均) 匀性，不同类 (质)，多相 (性)
15. deleterious [deliˈtiəriəs] *a.* 有害 (毒) 的，有害杂质的
16. agglomerate [əˈglɔməreit] *v.* (使) 聚结，结块，成团；*n.* & *a.* 烧结块 (的)，附聚

物（的）

17. grinding [ˈgraindiŋ] *n*. 研磨，磨碎
18. oxalate [ˈɔksəleit] *n*. 草酸盐
19. intercalate [inˈtəːkəleit] *vt*. 添加，插入
20. annealing [əˈniːliŋ] *n*. & *a*. 退火，退火的
21. multicomponent [mʌltikəmˈpəunənt] *a*. 多成分的，多元的
22. calcine [ˈkælsin] *v*. 煅烧，烧成；calcination *n*. 煅烧，焙解
22. grain boundary *n*. 颗粒界面，晶界
23. additive [ˈæditiv] *n*. 添加剂；*a*. 加成的
24. pellet [ˈpelit] *n*. 片，粒化（料），丸
25. binder [ˈbaində] *n*. 粘结剂
26. polyvinyl [pɔliˈvainil] *n*. & *a*. 聚乙烯（的）
27. spray-drying *n*. 喷雾干燥
28. green body *n*. 生坯，未烧坯
29. yttrium [ˈitriəm] *n*. 钇（Y）
30. rearrangement [ˌriəˈreindʒmənt] *n*. 重排
31. matrix [ˈmeitriks] *n*. 基体，基质
32. shrinkage [ˈʃriŋkidʒ] *n*. 收缩（性，量，率）
33. impair [imˈpɛə] *v*. 削弱，损害
34. creep [kriːp] *n*. 蠕变

Notes

① 本句含有 because 引导的原因状语从句和 so that 引导的结果状语从句。参考译文：因为沉淀会产生团聚的粉体，因此研磨、干磨或者使用水或非水性液体的湿磨可用于减小粒径，以便粉末密实体可以烧结至接近理论密度。

② 在 when 引导的时间状语从句中 as occurs in electroceramics 作定语从句；whose 引导的定语从句修饰 electroceramics。参考译文：在球磨制备粉体的情况下，难以得到可重复生产的均匀分布的粉料，尤其当电子陶瓷生产中一部分原料的用量很少时更是如此；电子陶瓷的性质常由含有少量添加剂的晶界相所控制。

③ 主语部分中 brought about by additives 的分词短语作定语修饰 advantages。参考译文：然而，引入添加剂所带来的优点不得不抵消烧结组分的机械性能下降的不足（尤其在高温下），因为由添加剂产生的玻璃和晶界相常具有比基体差的性质。

Exercises

1. Translate first paragraph into Chinese.
2. Translate the following phrases into English or Chinese.

   ① 退火和烧结温度

   ② 颗粒尺寸分布

   ③ 颗粒的重排和团聚

   ④ 喷雾干燥和煅烧

⑤ 共沉淀和过饱和
⑥ shrinkage and densification
⑦ Van der Waals forces and aggregation of fine powders
⑧ glassy and crystalline grain boundary phases
⑨ ball-milled powders and hot uniaxial pressing
⑩ the driving force for mass transport by solid-state processes for ceramic powders

Reading Material 6

Ceramics Fabrication

Slip casting, injection molding, isostatic pressing and reaction-bonding are all conventional technique for synthesis of traditional and advanced ceramics on both the laboratory and industrial scale.

(a) Slip casting

Slips are suspensions of one or more ceramic materials in a liquid, usually water, with a particle size around 1μm and may be considered as colloidal systems. The slip casting technique involves pouring a slip into a porous mold often made from plaster of Paris which absorbs liquid and deposits solid material at the mold walls. Excess slip is drained off after which the cast is removed and then fired. Slip casting is a very versatile technique and has been used for manufacture of tableware, sanitaryware, crucibles, tubes, thermocouple sheaths and gas turbine stators. However, three factors affect the quality of a cast. First, particles must remain in suspension so that deposition occurs evenly on the mold walls. Secondly, high solid contents (ca. 70 wt%) improve the drainage rate and thirdly, low viscosity is required in order to prevent incorporation of air bubbles into the ceramic and to ease filling of the mold.

As for other colloidal dispersions the stability of slips is controlled by interaction forces between particles. Strong ceramics can be obtained in the absence of particle aggregates, which are avoided by using deflocculating agents in the slip. These materials, normally surface-active agents, probably act by adsorption at the solid-liquid interface, for both oxide and non-oxide ceramics, which modifies the interaction energy between particles. However, particle size, pH and ionic strength affect slip stability and rheological properties of these systems, important for controlling liquid drainage from the dispersions.

(b) Injection molding

Injection molding is a plastic forming technique in which ceramic powder is added as a filler to an organic polymer, usually a thermoplastic, to form a plastically deformable mixture that is injected, by using a combination of heat and pressure, by a plunger into the mold. The viscosity before injection is an important parameter for controlling even filling of the mold and avoiding air bubbles in finished components. Large amounts of polymer are used, typically 30 volume %, although solid content in the mixture can be maximised by optimisation of the particle size, but binder removal is a difficult step as it can produce cracking and voids. Injection molding is used extensively in the plastics industry and has the potential for production of components with complex shapes such as turbine blades.

A second plastic-forming technique, extrusion, is related to injection molding although extrusion dies open at one end in contrast with those used in the latter process. Extrusion is particularly useful when articles with long length and uniform cross-section are required. It has been applied to clay-based materials for manufacture of bricks, tiles and pipes, although these systems exhibit the required plastic behaviour without polymer additives. However, other ceramic systems have been extruded, e. g. cordierite, $2MgO \cdot 2Al_2O_3 \cdot 5SiO_2$, as monolithic honeycomb structures used for catalyst supports in the treatment of vehicle exhaust emissions.

(c) Isostatic pressing

Hot-pressing is limited by the strength of graphite dies and fabrication of articles with simple shapes. In isostatic pressing, a mold is filled with powder and then subjected to high pressure transmitted through liquid in a pressure vessel. The mold deforms to compress powder and regains its original shape when the pressure is released. Both cold and hot isostatic pressing are used for fabrication, the latter referred to as HIP, which was used initially in 1955 for cladding nuclear fuel elements but currently finds many applications. Compared with uniaxial pressing techniques, isostatic pressing yields green compacts with higher and more uniform density in a wider variety of geometries although accurate shaping is difficult.

(d) The reaction-bonding technique is associated with Si_3N_4 and SiC ceramics. For the former, silicon articles are fabricated by a variety of processes including uniaxial pressing, injection molding and slip casting. These parts are then reacted with N_2 to form the reaction-bonded silicon nitride (RBSN) components that can be produced in complicated designs with a high degree of dimensional accuracy because no shrinkage occurs during nitridation, although the non-oxide ceramics contain about 15 volume % porosity. Because of its porosity, reaction-bonded materials has inferior strength compared with hot-pressed silicon nitride. However, Mangels & Tennenhouse showed that post-sintered reaction-bonded silicon nitride (PSRBSN) could be obtained with 95% of theoretical density and a strength and microstructure similar to hot-pressed material. In this technique, sintering aid is incorporated into RBSN, either Y_2O_3 to Si powder before nitridation or MgO impregnating RBSN with a magnesium chloride solution after which the reaction-bonded components is heated between 2053 and 2198 K under an N_2 gas pressure of 2. 1 MPa. This post-sintering technique offers near-net shape fabrication of high-density, high-strength components such as turbocharger rotors and keeps machining to a minimum.

Selected from "Chemical synthesis of advanced ceramic materials", David Segal, Cambridge University Press, Cambridge, 1989.

Words and Expressions

1. slip casting *n*. 注浆成型，泥浆浇注
2. injection molding *n*. 喷射模制成型
3. isostatic pressing *n*. 等静压成型
4. sanitaryware [ˌsænitəriˈwɛə] *n*. 卫生洁具
5. crucible [ˈkruːsibl] *n*. 坩埚
6. thermocouple sheath 热电偶套
7. colloidal [kəˈlɔidəl] *a*. 胶体的，胶态的
8. deflocculate [diˈflɔkʌleit] *v*. 反絮凝，解胶
9. plunger [ˈplʌndʒə] *n*. 活塞，圆柱，插棒
10. extrusion [eksˈtruːʒən] *n*. 挤出，挤压
11. cordierite [ˈkɔːdiərait] *n*. 堇青石
12. monolithic [mɔnouˈliθik] *n*. 单片（块），*a*. 整体的，单块的
13. honeycomb [ˈhʌnikɔm] *n*. 蜂窝状物，*a*. 蜂窝状的
14. nitridation [naitraiˈdeiʃən] *n*. 氮化
15. impregnate [ˈimpregneit] *v*. 注入，浸渍（透，润）
16. turbocharger [təːbouˈtʃɑːdʒə] *n*. 蜗轮增压机

Unit 7 Treatment after Firing: Grinding and Glazing

Many ceramic products can be taken directly from the kiln, inspected, and shipped to the customer. Certain other products, however, require additional processing to meet customer specifications. These postfiring processes are grouped under the general category of finishing operations and may include grinding to meet critical size or surface finish requirements and application of adherent coatings for protection, decoration, or other special needs. Technical ceramics are carefully examined for flaws before shipment to the consumer. Cracks and pits can sometimes be detected visually or by dye penetration tests. X-ray and ultrasonic techniques may also be used to detect flaws.

Grinding

Most ceramic products can be fired to meet customer specifications on dimensions without further processing. By calculating the proper oversized dimensions of the formed part from dimensions specified by the customer, and by knowing the shrinkage of the ceramic associated with drying and with firing, a manufacture can usually fire to a given size and shape specification①. Frequently, special firing techniques are required to insure meeting a specification. The ceramic parts may have to be supported by refractory kiln furniture to prevent warping or slumping during firing. Solid refractory setters or setters of the same composition as the parts being fired may be placed under certain parts to help control shrinkage and warpage. A layer of refractory grain such as calcined clay or fused alumina may be required to keep parts from reacting with or sticking to setters or refractories during firing. Tubes and rods are frequently hung by collars into refractory saggers so that gravity tends to keep them straight during firing.

If the manufacture cannot meet the dimensional and surface finish specifications of the customer by special firing techniques, then the ceramics must be ground and (or) polished after firing. Diamond tooling is usually required to grind hard materials such as alumina ceramics, but silicon carbide, alumina, or other abrasives may be used for softer materials. Disks may be lapped to the proper flatness, thickness, and surface finish. Centerless grinders are often used to grind the outer diameters of cylinders and rods. Small parts as well as the diameters of disks or the ends of cylinders may be ground on tool post grinders.

Very close size tolerances are commonly required on technical ceramic parts. The dimensions of these parts are frequently measured under carefully controlled humidity and temperature conditions with specialized measuring devices. Special grinding and polishing techniques are always required under these circumstances.

Glazing

Many ceramics are glazed after firing. A *glaze* is a special glass coating designed to be melted onto the surface of a ceramic body and to adhere to that surface during cooling. Glazes are used primarily to seal the surface of a porous ceramic to prevent absorption of water or other substances. The resulting smooth impermeable surface is also attractive and easy to clean. In high-tension insulators, a glaze ensures maintenance of good electrical properties even in the rain. Special colors and textures can be developed within the glaze to provide decoration and sales appeal.

The major constituent of a glaze is generally finely ground silica, with the addition of constituents rich in alkalies such as sodium and potassium oxides to lower the melting point of the glaze and alkaline earths such as calcium oxide to impart chemical durability. Lead oxide and boric oxide are also frequent glaze constituents. The overall composition is always adjusted in order to control the thermal expansion of the glaze, which must be equal to or slightly less than that of the underlying body. Additives are used to color the glaze or make it opaque.

Most glazes are prepared by wet-grinding together various raw materials along with a specially prepared commercial *frit*. The frit is a glass containing all originally soluble materials, all coloring oxide, and those materials which are toxic in uncombined form. Frits are produced commercially by melting and quenching a glass made up of the required chemical constituents. Quenching may be accomplished by pouring the molten frit directly into water or by roll-quenching in which the frit is quenched between water-cooled steel rolls②. After quenching, the frit is ground, dried, bagged, and shipped to customers for use in formulating glazes or enamels.

To make the glaze, the frit is placed in a ball mill along with clays and other insoluble materials and milled to a definite particle size with the proper amount of water. Binders may be added to aid in application. The milled glaze slip may be applied to the ceramic by spraying or dipping, and patterns can be added by printing. Spraying is used in many automated processes. The powdered glaze dries rapidly on the ceramic surface, and special drying is usually not required before firing.

Glazes can be applied to green ceramics and to completely vitrified ceramics; however, ware is generally *bisque-fired* before glazing③. Bisque firing is a low-temperature firing that removes the volatiles from the ware and accomplishes part or all of the firing shrinkage, thus assuring better success in the glazing operation. The body and glaze are then finish-fired together (*glost-fired*). Electrical ceramic ware is frequently completely matured and then glazed at a lower temperature than the maturing temperature of the body. Low-cost items such as pottery can frequently be sprayed in the green state and the body and glaze can be matured together. (In the *china process* the ceramic body is first fired to maturity; then the glaze is applied and matured by firing at a lower temperature. In the *porcelain process*, the bisque-fired body and glaze are matured together in the final glost-firing operation.) It is usually necessary to warm previously vitrified ware before the glaze slip is applied or it will not adhere properly.

Various glaze defects can occur in the different stages of production. *Crawling* (uneven coverage) occurs when the glaze slip does not satisfactorily wet the body. This can often be corrected by changing or increasing the amount of organic binder in the glaze slip. *Crazing* (fine network of cracks) occurs if a matured glaze has a higher coefficient of thermal expansion than the body. *Shivering* (shearing away of the coating in spots) occurs when the matured glaze has too low a coefficient of thermal expansion compared to the body. Pitting can be traced to volatiles in the glaze or body.

Selected from "Ceramics: industrial processing and testing", J. T. Jones and M. F. Berard, Iowa State University Press, Ames, Iowa, 1993.

Words and Expressions

1. kiln [ˈkiln] *n*. 窑，炉
2. flaw [ˈflɔː] *n*. 裂纹，裂痕，瑕疵
3. frit [ˈfrit] *n*. 熔块，玻璃料
4. quenching [ˈkwentʃiŋ] *n*. 淬火，骤冷
5. collar [ˈkɔlə] *n*. 套管（环），卡圈
6. sagger [ˈsægə] *n*. 匣体
7. abrasive [əˈbreisiv] *n*. 磨料；*a*. 磨蚀的，磨损的
8. glaze [ˈgleiz] *n*. 釉料，上釉；*v*. 施釉
9. impermeable [imˈpəːmiəbl] *a*. 不可渗透的，不透水的
10. alkali [ˈælkəlai] *n*. 碱性，强碱
11. vitrify [ˈvitrifai] *v*.（使）玻璃化
12. bisque firing 素烧（初次焙烧）
13. glost-firing *n*. 釉烧
14. crawling [ˈkrɔːliŋ] *n*. 釉卷缩，缩釉
15. crazing [ˈkreiziŋ] *n*. 细裂，龟裂，碎纹裂
16. shivering [ˈʃivəriŋ] *n*. 瓷釉剥落，脱釉
17. shearing [ˈʃiəriŋ] *n*. 切变，剪切

Notes

① 两个并列的 by 开头的介词短语作状语；associated with 为词组，意思为：伴随……（产生）。本句的参考译文：通过由客户指定的样品的大小来计算出略大的成型部件的尺寸，和通过了解陶瓷样品在干燥和烧成中的收缩率，一个制品常能烧成至设定的尺寸和形状。

② 本句中 in which 引出的是限制性定语从句，roll-quenching 意思为对辊淬冷。参考译文：通过将熔体直接倒入水中或由熔体在水冷却的钢辊间进行对辊淬冷，可以实现淬冷。

③ 本句中 Glazes can be applied to green ceramics 意思为：釉可以施加在陶瓷生坯（未烧陶瓷）上；ware：器皿。

Exercises

1. Translate the last paragraph into Chinese.
2. Translate the following phrases into English or Chinese.

① 切割、研磨、抛光
② 釉的热膨胀系数
③ 熔块和着色氧化物
④ 素烧和釉烧
⑤ 细磨的磨料
⑥ crack, pit and flaw
⑦ grinding, glazing and decoration
⑧ to prevent warping or slumping during firing
⑨ the milled glaze slip be applied to the ceramic by spraying, dipping, and printing
⑩ the maturing temperature of the body

Reading Material 7

Metallizing, Sealing, Sputter Deposition Process and Chemical Vapour Deposition

Metallizing

Ceramic parts sometimes need to be bonded directly to metal parts, a process that is especially common in the electronics industry. The process consists of first metallizing the surface of the ceramic and then soldering or brazing the hardware to the metallized ceramic surface. In one process a mixture of molybdenum and manganese metal powder is ground in organic solvents and binders and painted or sprayed onto the ceramic surface. The coating is then fired onto the ceramic in a furnace containing a cracked ammonia reducing atmosphere (hydrogen plus nitrogen) at a temperature sufficient to form an adherent cermet layer. Metal parts with expansion coefficients near that of the ceramic may then be attached to the metallized (cermet) area using solder or brazing alloys of metals such as lead, copper or silver. The metallized areas are often plated with nickel, silver, or gold before soldering or brazing to improve wetting by the molten solder alloy.

Glass-to-ceramic seals

Many glasses have been developed to solder ceramics to other glasses. Techniques of application of the glass solder to the joint vary with the products being produced. Sometimes solder glass rings can be used to form the joint, and solder glass powders are used in other applications. The thermal expansion coefficient of the solder glass must be compatible with both the ceramic and the glass being bonded. The seal is made by heating the glass and ceramic parts together until they become hot enough to soften the solder glass. Glass-to-ceramic seals are extremely common in a wide range of products from automobile spark plugs to cathode ray tubes.

Sputter deposition process

The basic sputter deposition process involves removal of atoms from the surface of a solid or liquid by energetic ion bombardment and collection of the sputter species on a solid surface. A target, consisting of the material to be deposited, is held at a negative potential ranging from a few hundred volts to a few kilovolts. For a critical value of the chamber pressure (1×10^{-3} Torr to -1 Torr), the application of the voltage strikes a discharge in the vicinity of the target. The target, because of its negative potential, is bombarded by the ions present in the plasma. The discharge is sustained by the stochastic ionization of the gas atoms/molecules by the secondary electrons emanating from the target. In situations when the gas ions are sufficiently heavy, the bombardment of the target leads to sputtering of the target surface by a momentum transfer process. Argon, because of its higher atomic number and non-reactivity, is the commonly used sputtering gas. Since the sputtering rate is directly dependent on the number of ions striking the target, its magnitude can be increased by increasing the ion density in the vicinity of the target. The higher ion densities are realized by application of magnetic fields. This modification of the sputtering process is known as magnetron sputtering. If the target material is electrically conducting, voltage can be used for sputtering.

Chemical vapour deposition

Chemical vapour deposition (CVD) has become one of the basic technologies in semiconductor industry. CVD is the technique to grow solid layers on substrates by decomposition of chemical vapours at elevated temperatures, using high frequency electric fields or other energy sources. The deposition of single crystal layers on substrates of the same crystalline type is called epitaxy. It offers the possibility to adjust the impurity concentration in the deposited film by controlling their concentration in the reactant vapour. In contrast to the diffusion process, where an impurity concentration gradient is inherent, the epitaxial growth is able to make homogeneously doped layers and thus can form abrupt junctions with the underlaying substrate.

The most important parameters for CVD are temperature, pressure, and velocity of the gas flow through the reactor chamber.

Besides the single crystal growth (epitaxy) CVD is widely used for depositing polysilicon, silicon nitride, Si_3N_4, and SiO_2.

The most common deposition chemicals are $SiCl_4$, SiH_4, $SiHCl_3$, SiH_2Cl_2, NH_3 (for Si_3N_4), AsH_3, B_2H_6, PH_3 (impurity doping) and others. Hydrogen is mostly used as the carrier gas.

Selected from "Advanced ceramic processing and technology, vol. 1", J. G. P. Binner, Noyes Publications, Park Ridge, New Jersey, 1990.

Words and Expressions

1. molybdenum [mɔ'libdinəm] *n*. 钼 (Mo)

2. manganese [mæŋgə'niːz] *n.* 锰 (Mn)
3. lead *n.* 铅 (Pb)，铅制品
4. braze [breiz] *vt* & *n.* 钎接，铜（钎，硬）焊
5. wetting [wetiŋ] *n.*（变，润，浸）湿
6. thermal expansion coefficient 热膨胀系数
7. spark plug *n.* 火花塞
8. cathode ray tube 阴极射线管
9. sputter deposition 溅射沉积
10. bombardment [bɔm'bɑːdmənt] *n.* 轰击，碰撞
11. plasma ['plæzmə] *n.* 等离子体，等离子区
12. stochastic [stə'kæstik] *a.* 随机的，机遇的，推测的
13. emanate ['eməneit] *v.* 发出，放射，析出
14. argon ['ɑːgən] *n.* 氩 (Ar)
15. epitaxy ['epitæksi] *n.* 外延，（晶体）取向生长
16. chemical vapour deposition 化学气相沉积
17. doping ['doupiŋ] *n.* 掺杂，加添加剂

Unit 8 Electronic Ceramics: Electrical Insulators and Conductors

There are literally hundreds of applications of advanced ceramics that depend primarily on the reaction of the material to applied electric or magnetic fields. Some of these are enumerated here, along with a brief description of the special characteristics that make these materials useful for particular applications. In many cases, while the electronic properties are paramount, for many of these applications there are also stringent mechanical and thermal property requirements that must be met.

Many ceramic materials are electrical insulators and, consequently ceramics have been used for years for dc and low-frequency ac electrical insulator shapes ranging from large, high-voltage suspension insulators for power transmission lines to simple, low-voltage shapes for lamp and switch bases. These shapes have traditionally been made from clay-based porcelains and are not usually included in the advanced ceramics category. On the other hand, the utilization of advanced ceramic electrical insulator materials suitable for more exotic applications is growing very rapidly. The materials most often used are alumina ceramics, beryllia ceramics, aluminum nitride, and a variety of special glasses, including those that can be converted into crystalline form after shaping (glass-ceramics). The most important electrical properties of such insulation materials are very low electrical conductivity, low dielectric constant (a low tendency to polarize or store charge), a high dielectric strength (resistance to breakdown under large voltage drops), and, for high-frequency applications, low dielectric losses (low propensity to convert energy in the alternating field into heat).

A wide variety of shapes are made from advanced ceramic insulator materials, many of which are so intricate that they must be made by injection molding or isostatic pressing followed by machining and finishing[①]. An especially important ceramic insulation application is as smooth substrates for thick film and thin film deposition of circuitry. Substrates are usually made as thin (a few mm), flat rectangular sheets utilizing tape-casting technology. Most frequently, discrete electronic devices such as silicon chips or discrete capacitors will be attached to the film circuitry on the substrate to form what are known as hybrid circuits. It is not at all unusual for multilayer ceramic substrates to be employed. Multilayer substrates are made by thick-film printing of circuitry onto unfired ceramic tapes using metal inks, then stacking and laminating the green tapes together to form a sandwich structure, and then "cofiring" the ceramic and metal inks to form a single mutilayer substrate. The circuits on different layers of the multilayer structure are connected at appropriate points by metal-filled holes called vias in the intervening ceramic layers. Substrates not only support the circuitry, but they also provide for dissipation of heat generated in the circuitry, either by absorbing it themselves or by conveying it to an attached heat sink. When substrates and their associated circuitry are fitted with external leads and are encapsulated to protect the circuitry from the environment, the entire assembly is usually called an electronic package.

Ceramic insulator materials are also commonly used as capacitor dielectrics-that is, as the material placed between the plates of a capacitor to serve as the charge storage medium. While any insulating material can be used for such an application, it is usually desirable to use materials that will allow the maximum amount of charge storage (capacitance) in the smallest possible device. This consideration means that materials with very high dielectric constants should be used. In addition to high dielectric constant, a capacitor dielectric should have high dielectric strength and low dielectric losses and should exhibit minimal variations in these properties with temperature or voltage changes. The most important group of advanced ceramic capacitor dielectric materials consists of combinations of barium titanate ($BaTiO_3$) with a variety of other oxides used to modify its fundamental properties. There are hundreds of titanate-based materials in use. Ceramic capacitor dielectric are often made in the form of small, thin discs or thin-walled hollow tubes, with the plates being deposited on each side by thick film techniques.

A very important and rapidly growing form of high-rating ceramic capacitor, called a ceramic chip capacitor, is made by a process similar to that used for multilayer ceramic substrates. Very thin sheets of titanate dielectric are produced by tape casting, and a pattern of metal electrodes is thick-film printed onto one side. Many layers of tape are then stacked on top of one another and laminated together. Individual "chips" are diced out of this laminate and are fired to mature the ceramic-metal sandwich. These tiny chip capacitors can be soldered directly onto printed circuitry.

A number of ceramic materials are electrical insulators with respect to the movement of electrons, nevertheless they exhibit measurable electrical conductivities because of the ability of certain ions to move through the material when an electric field is applied[②]. Such materials are called ionic conductors. If the conductivity is relatively high, they are called *fast ion conductors* or *solid electrolytes*. The most important fast ion conductors are AgI (Ag is the conducting ion), CaF_2 (F is the conducting ion), the so-called beta-aluminas (having roughly the formula $M\ Al_{11}O_{17}$, where M is silver or an alkali such as sodium, the M ion being the one responsible for conduction), zirconia (ZrO_2) doped with lime or yttrium oxide (with O being the conducting ion), and a number of special glasses (usually with alkali ions imparting conduction). Generally, the conductivity of ionic conductors increases rapidly with an increase in temperature, so they are almost always utilized at temperatures above room temperature, and sometimes at quite high temperatures. Their behavior as purely ionic conductors allows their use as solid electrolytes in high-temperature batteries and fuel cells, and the fact that only one particular type of ion moves in an electric field makes them useful as ion-specific sensor materials (an example is the use of stabilized zirconia as an oxygen sensor in automobile exhaust systems to sense the efficiency of the combustion process and activate changes in fuel-to-air ratios).

Although silicon, germanium, and gallium arsenide are the most utilized semiconductor materials, a number of other ceramic materials also are employed for semiconductor applications. Among the most used for these applications are various doped or slightly reduced oxides (especially ZnO) and doped silicon carbide. Such materials are commonly used as varistors (resistance changes with applied voltage) and thermistors (resistance changes with temperature). Varistors are commonly used to protect devices from damage by line surges (such as may be caused by lightning) or by shunting current around the device when the varistor becomes highly conductive due to a voltage spike. Thermistors can be used as temperature measurement devices, and, if they are doped so as to have a positive temperature coefficient of resistance (their resistance increases with increasing temperature), they can be used as self-limiting heater elements in a variety of applications, including to rapidly heat automatic chock elements in automobile engines so that the chock quickly closes after start-up③. When fabricated into single crystal form, ceramic semiconducting materials can be used to form pn junction diodes, and these can be used as power transistors, as light-emitting diodes (LEDs), and even as semiconductor laser diodes.

Selected from: "Ceramics: industrial processing and testing", J. T. Jones and M. F. Berard, Iowa State University Press, Ames, Iowa, 1993

Words and Expressions

1. enumerate [i'nju:məreit] *vt.* 数，计点，列举
2. paramount ['pærəmaunt] *a.* 最高的，高过，优于 (to)
3. stringent ['strindʒənt] *a.* 严格的，精确的
4. exotic [eg'zɔtik] *a.* 奇异的，外国产的；*n.* 舶来品
5. beryllia ['beriliə] *n.* 氧化铍
6. dielectric constant 介电常数
7. polarize ['pouləraiz] *v.* (使) 极化，(使) 偏振化
8. circuitry ['sə:kitri] *n.* 电话，线路，电路学
9. chip ['tʃip] *n.* 薄片，基片，集成电路片
10. hybrid ['haibrid] *n.* 杂化物；*a.* 混合的，杂化的
11. laminate ['læmineit] *v.* 分层，成薄片，层叠
12. dissipation [disi'peiʃən] *n.* 消耗，散失，
13. heat sink 散热片
14. encapsulate [in'kæpsjuleit] *v.* 密封，封装
15. capacitor [kə'pæsitə] *n.* 电容器
16. titanate ['taitəneit] *n.* 钛酸盐
17. dice [dais] *vt.* 切割，切成小片
18. mature [mə'tjuə] *v.* 老化，陈化，成熟

19. sodium [ˈsoudjəm] *n*. 钠（Na）
20. zirconia [zəːˈkouniə] *n*. 氧化锆
21. lime [ˈlaim] *n*. 石灰，氧化钙
22. impart [imˈpɑːt] *v*. 给与，分给
23. germanium [dʒəːˈmeiniəm] *n*. 锗（Ge）
24. gallium [ˈgæliəm] *n*. 镓（Ga）
25. arsenide [ˈɑːsinaid] *n*. 砷化物
26. varistor [væˈristə] *n*. 压敏电阻，可变电阻
27. thermistor [θəːˈmistə] *n*. 热敏电阻
28. diode [ˈdaioud] *n*. 二极管

Notes

① 本句为主从复合句，many of which 引出的是非限制性定语从句，修饰名词 shapes；此从句中还包括一个 so…that 代表的结果状语从句。参考译文：由先进的陶瓷绝缘材料可制得各种形材，其中许多材料的形状是如此之复杂，以致于必须用喷射模制成形或以等静压、再机械加工和抛光的方法来制备。

② with respect to：此词组的意思为“关于，就……而论”；nevertheless：连词，然而，不过。参考译文：就电子运动而言，许多陶瓷材料是电绝缘体；然而当施加电场时，某些离子因为在材料中有迁移的能力，这些陶瓷材料就具有可测量的电导率。

③ 本句由 and 组成二个并列句。在后半句中，if 引出的是假设从句；so as to＋inf. 是词组意为“以便，以致……”；including 引出的独立分词结构作非限制性定语，修饰其前面的名词 application，起补充说明作用。参考译文：热敏电阻能用作为温度测量装置，并且如果进行掺杂以便使它们具有正的温度电阻系数（它们的电阻随温度升高而增加）的话，那么在各种应用中它们可用作为自限制加热元件，包括用作为在汽车发动机中快速加热的自动塞块，以使汽车启动后塞块会快速关闭。

Exercises

1. Translate the underlined sentences in the text into Chinese.
2. Translate the following phrases into English or Chinese：
   ① 介电常数、介电强度、介电损耗
   ② 钛酸钡陶瓷电容器
   ③ 快离子导体和固体电解质
   ④ 离子导体的导电率随温度上升而增加
   ⑤ 压敏电阻和热敏电阻
   ⑥ advanced ceramic electrical insulator materials suitable for more exotic applications
   ⑦ smooth substrates for thick film and thin film deposition of circuitry
   ⑧ the material placed between the plates of a capacitor to serve as the charge storage medium
   ⑨ tiny chip capacitors with ceramic-metal sandwich structure
   ⑩ a positive temperature coefficient of resistance

Reading Material 8

Superconductors, Ferrites and Piezoelectric Ceramics

A tremendous amount of interest has been focused on a group of special ceramic materials that function as superconductors at "high" temperatures. Superconductors have the unusual characteristics that they exhibit no electrical resistance and that they completely repel magnetic fields. (This latter effect is called the Meissner effect.) The first characteristic promises replacement of ordinary conductors to provide for much more efficient electrical power transmission and also the capability of building much more powerful magnets (which is the principal use of superconduductors today). The Meissner effect has drawn great interest as a possible means of magnetic levitation of vehicles, especially trains, to virtually eliminate rolling friction and thereby allow for higher speeds and greatly reduced power consumption. All superconductor materials revert to "ordinary" behavior above a certain critical temperature. Between the discovery of the superconductivity phenomenon in 1911 and 1986, a number of metallic elements and compounds had been verified to show superconducting behavior, but all of them have extremely low critical temperatures, thus requiring cooling by liquified hydrogen (or even liquified helium) in order to remain superconducting; this requirement for bulky and expensive cooling systems have greatly limited the utilization of superconducting materials for practical applications.

Then, in 1986, a ceramic materials (actually a complex oxide of copper, barium, and lanthanum) was discovered with a critical temperature as high as 40K. The tremendous surge of interest in investigating similar ceramic compositions resulted in the discovery in 1987 of a material with a critical temperature as high as 90K. Since that time, a number of superconducting ceramic oxides have been produced, most of which contain copper, an alkaline earth (such as Sr or Ba), and a rare earth (such as Y or La). Such "high-temperature" superconductors offer the possibility of cooling with inexpensive liquified nitrogen.

The pace of these discoveries has given hope that one day a superconductor material might be found with a critical temperature as high as room temperature (about 300K), which would require no cooling at all to remain superconducting. Much research continues toward producing materials with higher and higher critical temperatures, but room temperature is still far above the highest critical temperature known at this writing. Most of the major potential uses of supercondutor materials require that they be available in the form of fine wires, a form in which it is quite difficult to produce a brittle oxide material. Consequently, a great deal of the research on these new ceramic superconductors today is concentrated on novel fabrication technologies.

There are three families of advanced ceramics that find application because of their special magnetic properties; these materials are called *ferrites*. The *spinel ferrites* are known as "soft" magnetic materials, meaning that it is easy to reverse their magnetization direction with a small applied magnetic field. The spinel ferrites have the general formula $MO \cdot Fe_2O_3$, where M is a divalent transition metal ion such as Ni, Zn, Mg, Mn, Fe, or Co. Soft ferrites are usually used for very-low-loss transformer cores or inductors, where their low electrical conductivity inhibits heating by induced eddy currents, which commonly leads to losses with metallic materials. An especially important use of a spinel ferrite is as the particles dispersed in magnetic recording media such as magnetic tapes and computer memory disks. The *magnetoplumbite* or *hexagonal ferrites* are known as "hard" or permanent magnetic materials because they are magnetized by a very strong applied field during manufacture, and they will retain this strong magnetization permanently thereafter. Magnetoplumbite ferrites have the general formula $MO \cdot 6Fe_2O_3$, where M is primarily Ba, but with other divalent alkaline earth ions also substituting for some of the Ba. Hard magnetic materials are used for magnetic latches, for electric motors, for loudspeaker magnets, and for magnetic elements in ore separation processes. There is also some interest in hexagonal ferrite particles for high-density computer disk media. A third class of ceramic magnetic materials are known as the *garnet ferrites*. These materials have the general formula $3\ M_2O_3 \cdot 5Fe_2O_3$, where M is a rare earth such as Y or Gd; however, extensive substitution of other ions for M and for Fe lead to an ability to widely tailor the magnetic properties, a capability that has made these materials important in low-loss microwave applications. The most common composition in this series of materials is yttrium iron garnet, also called YIG.

A special group of ceramic insulator materials find application because they exhibit the *piezoelectric effect*-that is, when they are elastically strained, they generate a voltage, and when a voltage is applied, they undergo an elastic deformation. Such materials can be used for various electro-mechanical transducers, including sonar generators and detectors, ultrasonic cleaners, fixed-frequency resonators, photograph and microphone pickups, and solid-state spark generators and igniters. While many materials are known to show the piezoelectric effect in single crystal form (quartz being a common example), only the special group of ceramic materials called *ferroelectrics* can readily be made show this type of behavior in polycrystalline (sintered) form. The most important ferroelectric ceramic materials are barium titanate ($BaTiO_3$), lead zirconate titanate (various alloys of $PbTiO_3$ and $PbZrO_3$, also designated PZT ceramics), and lanthanum-doped lead zirconate titanate (also designated PLZT ceramics).

Selected from: "Ceramics: industrial processing and testing", J. T. Jones and M. F. Berard, Iowa State University Press, Ames, Iowa, 1993.

Words and Expressions

1. ferrite [ˈferait] *n.* 铁氧体，磁性瓷
2. piezoelectric [paiˌiːzouiˈlektrik] *a.* 压电的
3. levitation [leviˈteiʃən] *n.* 漂浮，悬浮
4. eddy [ˈedi] *n.* 涡流，旋涡，螺旋

5. magnetoplumbite [ˌmægnitouˈplʌmbait] *n.* 磁铅石，磁铁铅矿
6. latch [ˈlætʃ] *n.* 阀钮，插销
7. sonar [ˈsounɑː] *n.* 声纳，声波，定位仪
8. resonator [ˈrezəneitə] *n.* 谐振器，共振器
9. igniter [igːˈnaitə] *n.* 发火装置，点火器
10. ferroelectric [ferouiˈlektrik] *a.*，*n.* 铁电体（性，的）
11. zirconate [ˈzəːkəneit] *n.* 锆酸盐
12. lanthanum [ˈlænθənəm] *n.* 镧（La）

Unit 9 Optical Ceramics

The word *photonics* has been coined to describe the collective optical properties of materials and the application of these properties to make useful devices. This section begins with a brief description of some of the more important photonic properties of materials.

Wide band-gap materials, such as ceramics insulator materials, are inherently transparent to light in the range of wavelengths near to or including the visible range, provided that they do not contain internal inhomogeneities which can serve as scattering sites and which will reduce the transparency to translucency or even opacity①. Consequently, ceramic single crystals, pore-free glasses and even pore-free single phase polycrystalline ceramics can be utilized for photonic applications requiring transmission of light beams.

Even though a material is transparent, that does not mean that the material does not interact with light that passes through it. For example, the velocity with which light waves propagate varies from material to material, having its highest possible value in vacuum (this velocity being the universal constant $c = 3.00 \times 10^8$ m/second). In all other media, light travels slower than c, with the ratio of c to the actual velocity in the material being called the *index of refraction* of the material. On passing from one material into another having a different index of refraction, a light beam will bend; this principle is used when lenses cause light beams to focus or to diverge. In most materials, the index of refraction varies with the wavelength of the light; this behavior is called *dispersion*, and it underlies the separation of different wavelengths from a mixed light beam because of differing amounts of bending.

The electromagnetic waves that constitute a beam of light oscillate perpendicular to the direction of propagation of the beam. Under normal conditions, the oscillations are randomly oriented around the direction of propagation. However, some materials are able to modify the passing light beam so that only certain oscillation directions occur. This is called *polarization*, and many important applications of light require or take advantage of the polarization phenomenon. For example, if a light beam of a given polarization is incident on a material that will only transmit light of a different polarization, then that material will effectively block the passage of the beam.

Stress-free glass and many crystals are optically isotropic, meaning that the index of refraction is the same regardless of the direction of a light beam. However, certain types of crystals will split an incident light beam into two separate beams, each of which is polarized. Glass containing residual stresses will also show this type of behavior. This phenomenon is called *birefringence*, and materials exhibiting this behavior are said to be double refracting or optically active. This phenomenon is the basis for a number of types of optical devices and also as a means for revealing residual stresses in otherwise optically isotropic materials.

No material is perfectly transparent; some of the light entering a material will be absorbed and converted into heat or other forms of energy. Materials that do not absorb more strongly at one wavelength than at another appear to be colorless, but many transparent materials do show selective absorption and therefore appear to be colored.

Applied electric and magnetic fields can modify the refractive indices of materials to some degree; these effects are called the *electro-optic effect* and the *magneto-optic effect*. A particularly interesting ancillary effect of these phenomena is that an applied field can cause a normally optically isotropic material to display birefringence, which disappears when the field is removed②. In certain materials, these effects are sufficiently large that optical devices can be built that take advantage of them.

The photonic applications of ceramic materials depend on one or a combination of the properties just described. For example, windows require simple transmission of light beams without alteration. On the other hand, filters are required to be transparent at certain wavelengths and to be strongly absorbing at others. A single material with the appropriate absorption characteristics can serve as a selective filtering window. Lenses are somewhat like windows except that they are made with surfaces that are not parallel to one another.

An especially important photonic application of glass occurs in optical fibers. The function of these fibers is to carry a beam of light from one point to another without appreciable attenuation due either to absorption or to escape from the sides of the fiber. The most frequent application is in communications, where information is encoded in the form of modulations of the light beam, usually using a diode laser. Special glasses are most often used for optical fibers. To insure very low absorption, the glass must be extremely pure and free from inclusions. To prevent escape of the light beam from the sides, the fiber is usually made to have a central core of glass with low index of refraction, surrounded by a cladding of higher-index glass. The difference in index will cause perfect reflection of any portions of the beam that encounter the interface, thus insuring that all light launched within the core remains there no matter how the fiber may be curved.

Lasers are devices capable of producing highly energetic beams of light having all waves in phase and of the same wavelength. Very-high-intensity lasers can be used for localized heating and melting, but certain types of lasers can also be used to produce very pure, modulated light signals and so are suitable for generating encoded beams used in optical fiber communications. To function, lasers must be "pumped" -that is, an input of energy is required to produce the unstable energy situation necessary for laser action to occur. Pulse lasers are usually pumped by means of an extremely bright flash of light; these lasers are often made from specially doped glasses or single crystals such as Cr-doped Al_2O_3 (ruby lasers) or Nd-doped yttrium aluminum garnet (YAG lasers). Other laser types can provide continuous output and so must be continuously pumped, often with electrical energy. An especially interesting type of continuous laser can be made from a semiconductor or insulator crystal that has been selectively doped so as to produce a pn junction. When a dc electrical voltage is applied across this junction in a direction that tends to force electrons toward the p side and holes toward the n side, recombination of excess electrons and holes in the junction region will release light energy, causing the junction to glow. When the electrical input is small, the light waves generated are not in phase, and the glowing junction is called a light-emitting diode (LED). LEDs are popular for constructing all sorts of electronic displays. When the electrical energy input is large, and certain other geometric requirements are met, the light emitted by the junction will be intense and in phase, the junction will behave as a laser. In lasing mode, the magnitude of the light emitted varies with the magnitude of the applied electrical signal, and the lasing behavior also "switches off" sharply when the pumping signal drops below a threshold level. Consequently, diode lasers are particularly well-suited for converting electrical signals into modulated light beams, and thus are especially valuable as signal generators in optical fiber communications systems.

Transparent polycrystalline electro-optic materials, such as PLZT ceramics, can be used for a variety of devices in which transmission of a polarized light beam is throttled by changing the optical characteristics of the material with an applied electric field③. The uses include rapidly darkening windows to shield pilots or other personnel from the intense flash of a nuclear explosion or a laser weapon, goggles for welders, shutters for optical devices, optical displays, and even image storage devices. Whenever a polycrystalline ceramic is intended for use as a transparent material, very careful processing is necessary from starting powder through forming and firing in order to eliminate light-scattering pores and inclusions. It is not unusual to hot-press such ceramics in order to ensure the absence of porosity.

Selected from: "High Tech Ceramics", P. Vincenzini, Elsevier, 1987.

Words and Expressions

1. photonic [ˈfoutɔnik] *a.* 光子的，光电子的
2. opacity [ouˈpæsiti] *n.* 不透光性，浑浊度，不透明度
3. propagate [ˈprɔpəgeit] *v.* 传播，传导，扩散
4. index of refraction 折射率
5. diverge [daiˈvəːdʒ] *v.* 分离，逸出，散射，偏离
6. dispersion [disˈpəːʃən] *n.* 色散，分散
7. oscillate [ˈɔsileit] *v.* 振荡，振动，
8. polarization [pouləraiˈzeiʃən] *n.* 极化，偏振
9. birefringence [bairiˈfrindʒəns] *n.* 双折射，二次光折射
10. ancillary [ænˈsiləri] *a.* 辅助的，附属的，次要的
11. attenuation [ətenjuˈeiʃən] *n.* 变细（薄），冲淡，减少，衰减
12. inclusion [inˈkluːʒən] *n.* 夹杂（物），掺杂
13. modulate [ˈmɔdjuleit] *v.* 调整，调制
14. ruby [ˈruːbi] *n.* 红宝石
15. threshold [ˈθreiʃhould] *n.* 限度，界限，阈
16. goggles [ˈgɔgls] *n.* 护目镜

Notes

① provided that 为连词，意思为：只要，如果，假如，以……为条件；其中 which 引导的两个并列的定语从句均修饰 inhomogeneities。参考译文：宽能带材料，如陶瓷绝缘体，对于可见光附近或包括可见光区波长范围的光具有固有的透明性，只要这些材料不含有能作为散射位和会将透明性降至半透明性或甚至不透明的内在不纯物。

② 本句中 that 引导的是表语从句；由 which 引导的定语从句修饰 birefringence。参考译文：这些现象中的一个很有趣的附属效应是一个外加电场能够使一种普通的光学上各向同性的材料显示出双折射，当电场移掉时，此种双折射现象即消失。

③ PLZT：P 代表元素铅，L 代表元素镧，Z 代表元素锆，T 代表元素钛。参考译文：透明的多晶电光材料，如 PLZT 陶瓷，能用于许多装置中；在这些装置中，通过改变随电场变化的材料的光学特性，可以调节极化光束的透过率。

Exercises

1. Translate underlined sentences in the text into Chinese.
2. Translate the following phrases into English or Chinese：
   ① 折射率和色散
   ② 晶体的光学上的各向同性
   ③ 电光效应和磁光效应
   ④ 无夹杂物的低吸收玻璃
   ⑤ 根据施加的电场改变材料的光学特性
   ⑥ transparency，translucency，opacity
   ⑦ transmission of light beams
   ⑧ a beam of light oscillate perpendicular to the direction of propagation of the beam
   ⑨ a central core of glass with low index of refraction surrounded by a cladding of higher-index glass
   ⑩ to eliminate light-scattering pores and inclusions

Reading Material 9

Ceramic Materials for Sensors

The need for sensors has grown rapidly in recent years for industrial and automotive applications and consumer uses. The primary variables in sensing include：temperature，pressure and gas compositions. Other variables are force，speed and position. In general，electrical and magnetic properties of ceramic materials can be utilized in these applications. Materials suitable for these applications include：(1) ionic and electronic conductors；(2) ferroelectric and piezoelectric；(3) magnetic and (4) electro-optic materials.

Electrical conduction of ceramic materials can be used to measure temperature and gas concentrations. Pressure cannot be measured by either electrical conductivity of ceramics or by piezoelectrics. Piezoelectric materials can be used to measure pressure changes such as acceleration and vibration. The only commercial pressure sensors utilize the capacitance change of ceramic bellows.

Under equilibrium conditions, the electrical conductivity of a non-stoichiometrical compound is described by the equation

$$\sigma=(P_{O_2}^{m} A/T)\exp[-BkT] \quad (4.1)$$

where A and B are a constant, and the exponent m has a positive value for p-type semiconducting metal oxides and a negative value for n-type semiconducting metal oxides.

When the temperature is held constant, the electrical resistance of these non-stoichiometric compounds is a function of oxygen partial pressure under equilibrium conditions. The conductivity in the low oxygen partial pressure region is n-type. A slope change was observed in the higher oxygen pressure region which was caused by the presence of cation vacancies owing to the Al^{3+} ions acting as acceptors in the TiO_2 lattice.

TiO_2 has been used as an automotive exhaust gas sensor or equilibrium oxygen sensors to measure and control the air-to-fuel (A/F) ratio of internal combustion engines. When the A/F mixture entering an internal combustion engine is at the stoichiometric ratio, combustion can be described by the reaction

$$CH_x+yO_2+3.76yN_2 \longrightarrow CO_2+0.5xH_2O+3.76yN_2 \quad (4.2)$$

If there is excess fuel (rich), CO will be the main residue product of combustion; but if there is excess air (lean), free oxygen will be present in the exhaust gas. The oxygen partial pressure of the exhaust gas will thus be determined by the free oxygen concentration in the lean region and by the CO/CO_2 ratio in the rich region. The theoretical equilibrium oxygen partial pressure of the exhaust gas as a function of A/F at 700℃ is shown by solid line in a figure, with the negative of the log of the partial oxygen pressure being shown at the left vertical axis. At the right-hand vertical axis, the resistance of the device is shown. The experimentally measured resistance of a TiO_2 sensors as a function of the A/F ratio at 700℃ is shown on the curve as dots. The agreement is excellent.

For automotive exhaust gas sensor applications, it is required that the sensor be operated at low temperatures and the response time be 100 milliseconds or shorter at operating temperatures. It is necessary that the sensors should be porous and fine grained. For improved sensitivity of the sensors, catalysts are always used. Sensors without catalyst can only be operated at high temperatures. The catalysts help to bring the gas-gas and gas-solid reactions into equilibrium at lower temperatures. Thin film and porous tin oxide and zinc oxide sensors have been developed by many investigators for CO and other reducing gas measurements.

The best-known humidity sensor is a p-type semiconducting $MgCr_2O_4$-TiO_2. This sensor operates as follows. On the surface, water molecules dissociate into protons and hydroxyl groups. The hydroxyl groups combine with the surface oxygen ions forming water and the protons become positive charge carriers, hence the conductance of the p-type semiconductor increases in air of higher humidity. Phase relationships in the system MgO-Cr_2O_3-TiO_2 have been studied by Somiya *et al*. They reported that 31 mol% TiO_2 forms solid solutions in $MgCr_2O_4$ spinel. It is very possible that the spinel has a formula (Mg_6V_{Mg2})($Cr_4^{2+}Cr_8^{3+}Ti_4^{4+}$)$O_4$, which is mixed-valency semiconductor.

Selected from: "Ceramics: industrial processing and testing", J. T. Jones and M. F. Berard, Iowa State University Press, Ames, Iowa, 1993.

Words and Expressions

1. stoichiometrical [stɔikiə'metrikəl] *a*. 化学计量的
2. catalyst ['kætəlist] *n*. 催化剂
3. humidity [hju(:)'miditi] *n*. 湿气，湿度
4. hydroxyl group 羟基基团
5. dissociate [di'souʃieit] *v*. 分解
6. valency ['veilənsi] *n*. 价，原子价

Unit 10 Bioceramics: Medical Applications of Ceramics

The materials that are used in medicine, i. e. as surgical implants, include metals, plastics, textiles, rubber and ceramics. Biomaterials, in general can be defined as: (1) materials for long-term implantation in human tissue, such as arterial and dental prostheses, prostheses of organs (heart, blood vessels), and artificial joints (hip, knee); (2) products for prolonged contact with vessels and tissue or bone; (3) products for short-term contact with tissue or bone such as probes or instruments for tests and inspection; (4) materials for obtaining and storing blood and blood plasmas; (5) products used as instruments and tools during surgery.

Ceramic materials to be used in this context have therefore to fulfill some or all of the following requirements: high chemical inertness; absence of adverse effects on surrounding tissue; long-term life expectancy; strength/fatigue strength; absence of effects on free metabolic processes.

These requisites can be summarized under the term 'biocompatibility'. Biocompatible ceramics, also termed bioceramics, include pure oxides (alumina, zirconia); complex oxides (hydroxy apatite, calcium phosphates); carbon; fiber-reinforced carbon composites; and glasses (so-called bioglasses). They can be used in load-bearing and non-load-bearing functions, as resorbable or non-resorbable biomaterials; as structured parts or coatings on surgical implants made of other materials.

Load-bearing applications which are in general non-resorbable include, among others, knee and hip implants; dental implants, bone plates; artificial heart valves; artificial tendons and, to some extent, coatings on metal prostheses.

Non-loading-bearing applications are primarily temporary space fillers which can be penetrated and resorbed by the reconstructed natural tissue. They are used to treat maxillo-facial defects; or as composite bone plates. The ceramic materials will, in the course of the healing process, dissolve in the surrounding matrix and display ingrowth into the supporting tissue or bone. Materials can be fast or slow degrading, depending on the required functions.

Biomaterials can be principally classified into three groups: bio-inert, resorbable and bio-active. Examples of bio-inert materials are oxide ceramics such as Al_2O_3 and ZrO_2-TZP (tetragonal zirconia polycrystals) and biocarbons. Calcium phosphstes are examples of resorbable materials, and hydroxy apatite and bioglasses are instances of bio-active materials. Bio-inert materials are used mostly in load-bearing applications. Resorbable materials are conceptually favored, as the host tissue will replace them, but these will also gradually deteriorate as they are chemically dissolved or disintegrated[①]. Therefore they cannot be applied under load-bearing conditions. Bio-active materials are those which tend to form an interfacial chemical bond between the tissue and the implant. These materials can be used in either load-bearing or non-loading-bearing applications (e. g. coatings on metallic implants).

Bioactive glass and glass-ceramic implants have been used for more than 10 years to replace the small bones of the middle ear damaged by chronic infection. Survivability of the bioactive glass implants for middle-ear replacements is considerably longer than occurs when bioinert implants are used for the same purpose. Bioinert implants do not bond to the eardrum and, therefore, gradually erode through the tissue and are extruded through the eardrum within 2～3 years. In contrast, highly bioactive glasses form a bond with the collagen of the eardrum and also bond firmly to the remaining bone of the stapes footplate and, thereby, are anchored on both ends, which prevents extrusion. Sound conduction is excellent, and there is no fibrous tissue growth to impair sound transmission.

The clinical application of bioactive glasses that is most important is in the form of a particulate that is placed around teeth that have had periodontal (gum) disease, a clinical problem that affects tens of millions of people. The 45S5 bioactive glass material rapidly leads to new bone formation around the bioactive glass particles. Because of the speed of formation of the new bone, the epithelial tissues are stopped from migrating down the tooth, a common problem if nothing is used to fill the space between the tooth and repairing bone②. The junction between the tooth and the periodontal membrane is stabilized by use of bioactive glass particulate, and the tooth is saved.

An especially important clinical application of bioactive implants is the use of A/W bioactive glass-ceramic with high strength and fracture toughness in the repair of the spine. The material is made by densifying 5-μm-sized glass powders into the desired shape, then precipitating oxyfluorapatite ($Ca_{10}(PO_4)_6(O,F_2)$) and wollastonite (CaO-SiO_2) phases to yield a crack- and pore-free, dense, homogenous glass-ceramic. The high compressive and bend strengths, 1080 MPa and 215 MPa, respectively; high fracture toughness, 2.0 MPa · $m^{1/2}$; high interfacial bond strength to bone; and excellent resistance to degradation of properties when exposed to physiological loading conditions provide confidence in the use of this material to replace surgically removed vertebrae③.

Selected from: "Medical High-Tech Ceramics: Viewpoints and Perspectives,"
Gernot Kostorz, Academic Press Ltd., London, 1989.

Words and Expressions

1. implant [im'plɑːnt] *n.* 植入物，移植物
2. arterial [ɑː'tiəriəl] *a.* 动脉的，主干的
3. prosthesis [prɔs'θisis] *n.* ([复] prostheses) 修复术，修补物，假体
4. inertness [i'nəːtnis] *n.* 惰性
5. expectancy [iks'pektənsi] *n.* 期望，期待
6. metabolic [metə'bɔlik] *a.* 变化（形）的，同化作用的，（新陈）代谢的
7. biocompatibility [baikəmpætə'biliti] *n.* 生物相容性
8. hydroxy apatite [hai'drɔksi] ['æpətait] *n.* 羟基磷灰石
9. resorbable [ri'sɔːbəbl] *a.* 可重新吸收的
10. tendon ['tendən] *n.* 腱
11. degrade [di'greid] *v.* 降（裂，分）解，降低，衰变
12. disintegrate [dis'intigreit] *n.*, *v.* (使) 崩溃，(使) 分裂，(使) 分解

13. deteriorate [di'tiəriəreit] *v*. 劣（退）化，变坏，损耗
14. erode [i'roud] *v*. 腐蚀，受侵蚀
15. collagen ['kɔlədʒən] *n*. 骨胶原
16. periodontal [periou'dɔntəl] *a*. 牙周的
17. epithelial [epi'θiːliəl] *a*. 上皮的，皮膜的
18. membrane ['membrein] *n*. 薄膜，膜片
19. fracture toughness *n*. 断裂韧性
20. vertebra ['vəːtibrə] *n*.（[复] vertebrae）椎骨，脊椎

Notes

① 第一个 as 引出的是原因状语从句，第二个 as 引出的是伴随时间的状语从句。参考译文：基本上可吸收材料是受欢迎的，因为原来的基组织将会取代它们；但随着它们被化学溶解或裂解，这些可吸收材料也会逐渐劣化。

② a common problem 为同位语；stop from（+*ing*）：词组，意为“阻止……”。此句参考译文：由于新骨的形成速度，阻止了皮膜组织迁移在牙齿上；这原本是一个常见的难题，如果在牙齿和修复骨之间的空隙没有东西填充的话。

③ 此句谓语是 provide。参考译文：高达 1080 MPa 的抗压强度和 215 MPa 的抗弯强度、高达 2.0 MPa · $m^{1/2}$ 的断裂韧性、高的与骨结合的界面键强，以及在生理承重条件下优异的抗降解性能，这些均不容置疑地证明这种材料可在外科手术上用于取代缺损的脊椎骨。

Exercises

1. Translate first paragraph into Chinese.
2. Translate the following phrases into English or Chinese：
   ① high chemical inertness and long-term life expectancy
   ② load-bearing bioglass
   ③ resorbable or non-resorbable biomaterial
   ④ the reconstructed natural tissue
   ⑤ a chemical bond between the collagen of the eardrum and the bioglass
   ⑥ 羟基磷灰石和磷酸钙陶瓷
   ⑦ 生物惰性、可吸收性和生物活性材料
   ⑧ 在金属植入体上的生物活性涂层
   ⑨ 生物惰性的四方氧化锆多晶体
   ⑩ 优异的抗降解性能

Reading Material 10

Calcium Phosphate Ceramics

Calcium phosphate-based bioceramics have been in use in medicine and dentistry for 20 years. Different phases of calcium phosphate ceramics are used depending upon whether a resorbable or bioactive material is desired. The stable phases of calcium phosphate ceramics depend considerably upon temperature and the presence of water, either during processing or in the use environment. At body temperature, only two calcium phosphates are stable in contact with aqueous media, such as body fluids: at pH < 4.2, the stable phase is $CaHPO_4 \cdot 2H_2O$ (dicalcium phosphate, C_2P), whereas, at pH>4.2, the stable phase is $Ca_{10}(PO_4)_6(OH)_2$ (hydroxy apatite, HA). At higher temperatures, other phases, such as $Ca_3(PO_4)_2$ (β-tricalcium phosphate, C_3P, TCP) and $Ca_4P_2O_9$ (tetracalcium phosphate, C_4P) are present. The unhydrated, high-temperature calcium phosphate phases interact with water, or body fluids, at 37℃ to form HA. Sintering of calcium phosphate ceramics usually occurs at 1000～1500℃, following compaction of the powder into a desired shape.

Hydroxy apatite as the main mineral constitute of bone can be used to prepare material which is biocompatible, demonstrates no reaction to foreign bodies and is integrated into bone. According to investigations carried out by Jarcho *et al.* and Dennisen *et al.*, it appears that the size and volume of pores in HA are important with respect to the degradability of HA. If the density of the material is low, a high degree of degradation is observed, whereas with reduced microporosity, degradation slows down. An explanation for this behavior could be the lack of available sites for cellular or chemical attack in pore-free HA.

Hydroxy apatite is used as implant material in various forms; as a solid body with little porosity, as granular particles, as a porous structure, or as coating on metallic implants. The implantation of solid, preformed HA bodies seems to be less successful (fitting problems) than the use of granular particles of size 20～60μm. These particles are used, for example, for alveolar ridge augmentation, when injected into tooth sockets. A macroporosity of 150～250μm has been proposed by Klein *et al.*, who showed bony ingrowth into the macropores and along the surface of the materials. The pores are filled with connective tissue.

The research on HA blocks and granules has concentrated on preventing resorption of alveolar bone after premature loss of teeth. A variety of shapes and sizes of HA blocks is used; anatomically shaped implants maintain the stability of the alveolar contour. After 6 weeks, new prosthetic appliances such as fixed bridge work can be inserted. The functional and aesthetic results seem to be better than with the previous methods.

Sintered HA powder can be formed into various shapes with macroporous structure, for use as bone replacement and for bony ingrowth. However, load-bearing applications seem to be less successful except for tooth implants or in middle-ear channel wall prostheses.

Coatings of HA on metal implants are increasingly used to facilitate acceptance of implants and fixations in the osseous surrounding by bony ingrowth. Coatings are applied by plasma spraying techniques, preferably by vacuum plasma spraying. In a wide sense, the parts thus produced can be classified as metal-ceramic composites. The coating thickness is 50μm and an intermediate layer of titanium is applied to enhance the adherence strength.

Another technique developed recently is a coating of a HA-alumina compound which is plasma sprayed on dental implants made of titanium. The product is expected to function as a tooth root material and as a base for the subsequent attachment of a crown.

It is still too early to decide on the long-term behavior of HA-coated implants; yet HA coatings seem to stimulate the direct chemical bonding of tissue to prostheses, and/or bone ingrowth.

To summarize, next to TCP, HA shows the highest rate of new bone formation. If compared to metallic implants, the rate of new bone formation is four to five times higher than for titanium or PMMA bone cement.

Examples of other bone mineral-related materials proposed for use as bone substitutes are 'true bone ceramic' (TBC), which is produced by the sintering of cattle bone at high temperatures; flour apatite for dental implants; porous phosphate glass ceramics for bone implants; fluoride-containing bio-active glasses; glass ceramics toughened by tetragonal zirconia; SiC-reinforced bioglass for tooth roots.

Selected from: "Bioceramics", L. L. Hench, J. Am. Ceram. Soc., 81 [7] 1705-28 (1998).

Words and Expressions

1. dentistry ['dentistri] *n*. 牙科学，牙科
2. cellular ['seljulə] *a*. 细胞的，由细胞组成的，多孔的
3. alveolar [æl'viələ] *a*. 牙槽的，小泡的
4. ridge ['ridʒ] *n*. 脊，螺纹
5. augmentation [ɔːgmen'teiʃən] *n*. 扩大，增加，增长，增加物
6. socket ['sɔkit] *n*. 窝，穴，孔，床
7. premature [premə'tjuə] *a*. 早熟的，不成熟的，过早的
8. anatomically [ænə'tɔmikəli] *a*. 解剖的，解剖学上的
9. contour ['kɔntuə] *n*. 轮廓，外形
10. appliance [ə'plaiəns] *n*. 应用，器具，器械，装置
11. aesthetic [iːs'θetik] *a*. 美学的
12. osseous ['ɔsiəs] *a*. 骨（状）的

Unit 11 Advanced Structural Ceramics

Structural components derived from engineering ceramics are used as monoliths, coatings and composites in conjunction with or as replacements for metals when applications rely on mechanical behavior of the ceramics and their refractory properties, that is chemical resistance to the working environment[①]. Nickel superalloys are currently the main high-temperature materials for components such as combustors in gas turbine engines. They have melting points around 1573 K and a maximum working temperature near 1300 K. Compared with metals, ceramics are generally more resistant to oxidation, corrosion, creep and wear in addition to being better thermal insulators. They have higher melting points and greater strength than superalloys at elevated temperature so that a major potential application, particularly for silicon nitride, is in gas turbine and reciprocating engines where operating temperatures higher than attainable with metals can result in greater efficiencies[②]. This enhanced strength is shown in figure for hot-pressed silicon nitride (HPSN), hot-pressed silicon carbide (HPSC), hot isostatically pressed silicon nitride (HIPSN), sintered silicon nitride (SSN), sintered silicon carbide (SSC), reaction-bonded silicon nitride (RBSN) and reaction-bonded silicon carbide (RBSC). Although ceramics offer improvements in engine efficiency, incorporation of silicon nitride over the past three decades has been slow, mainly because of the difficulty in reproducible fabrication of dense components to close dimensional tolerances.

Silicon nitride occurs in two phases, the α and the β forms. The β form consists of SiN_4 tetrahedra joined together by sharing corners in a three-dimensional network. It is possible to replace silicon by aluminum and maintain charge neutrality in the crystal lattice by substitution of nitrogen with oxygen. The resulting solid solutions in the Si-Al-O-N system are known as β'-sialons whose structures are identical with β-Si_3N_4 over the composition range $Si_{6-b}Al_bO_bN_{8-b}$ $(0<b<4)$. They exhibit mechanical behavior similar to β-Si_3N_4 and have some features of aluminum oxide. However, in contrast with Al_2O_3, which consists of six-coordinated Al, β-Si_3N_4 contains Al that is four-coordinated by oxygen and this results in an enhanced Al-O bond strength compared with the oxide. Unlike Si_3N_4, β'-sialons can be densified readily by pressureless sintering and they have been put into commercial production by Lucas Cookson Syalon Limited. Syalon components include automotive parts such as valves, valve guides and seats, tappets, rocker inserts and precombustion chambers in addition to weld shrouds, location pins, extrusion dies, tube drawing dies and plugs.

As far as material properties are concerned, the ceramic is assumed to provide very good thermal shock resistance. Aluminum titanate, for example, with its extremely low thermal expansion coefficient, develops outstanding thermal shock resistance. Aluminum titanate is used as port liners in some automobile engines because its low thermal conductivity

($2\ Wm^{-1}K^{-1}$) reduces heat flow to the cylinder block and hence the amount of cooling required. Glass ceramics have applications in cooking utensils, tableware, heat exchangers, vacuum tube components and missile radomes. Partially stabilised zirconia was developed in 1975 and is particularly suited for withstanding mechanical and thermal shock because of its high fracture toughness. Examples are dies for extrusion of copper and aluminum tubes, diesel engine cam follower faces, valve guides, cylinder liners and piston caps, wear and corrosion-resistant nozzles in papermaking equipment, wear resistant inserts such as tabletting dies as well as scissors and knives.

Not all ceramic components require high-temperature strength. The high Young's modulus (550 GPa) of titanium diboride, TiB_2, makes it useful for armour plating whereas ceramics are suitable materials in seals because of their chemical resistance. Hence sintered silicon carbide is used for mechanical seals and sliding bearings whereas boron nitride, which is not wetted by glass and liquid metals, constitutes break rings in the horizontal continuous casting process for steels. Boron carbide, a harder ceramic than SiC, is suited to wear-resistant applications such as grit blasting nozzles whereas Si_3N_4 is also used as ball bearings.

An established industrial use for engineering ceramics is as cutting tools for steels where high-temperature hardness of sialons and zirconia toughened alumina together with their low reactivity towards metals are desirable properties. Cutting tools are subject to high mechanical, chemical and thermal loads on their cutting edges during machining operations. On average, 45kW power is transferred to an in-attack cutter with a contact surface of only $2mm^2$. Particularly in the first cut, any interruptions and change in cutting depth give rise to a complex dynamic force that can reach a level of some 5000N. At high cutting speeds, the temperature of the cutting edge may exceed 1000℃. Obviously, metals are liable to undergo plastic deformation, diffusion phenomena between tool and workpiece, and oxidation-induced scaling at such temperatures. Ceramic cutting tools experience no such problems and are therefore insensitive to high cutting speeds and accordingly high cutting-edge temperatures.

The latest material development is aimed at further increasing the strength of such ceramics through the incorporation of fibers or whiskers. Whisker-reinforced ceramic composites hold the promise of quasi-ductile strength behavior. The whisker reinforcing principle is based on activation of the following mechanisms: transfer of stress from the matrix material to the high-strength reinforcing components through the introduction of whiskers with high Young's moduli, generating compressive stresses in the matrix by introducing whiskers with higher thermal expansion coefficients, impeding crack propagation through the whiskers, diverting the cracks along the whisker-matrix interface, and inducing microcracking by differences in the mechanical and thermal properties of the whiskers and the matrix[3]. However, the bonding forces between the whiskers and matrix should be kept low enough to ensure that dynamic stress will only pull the whiskers out of the matrix instead of tearing them apart. In whisker-reinforced ceramics, the mechanisms described may occur in superimposition.

Selected from: "High Tech Ceramics", P. Vincenzini, Elsevier, 1987.

Words and Expressions

1. superalloy [sjuːpəˈælɔi] *n*. 超耐热不锈钢
2. reciprocate [riˈsiprəkeit] *v*. 往复运动，上下移动，来回
3. utensil [juːˈtensl] *n*. 器皿（具），用具
4. shroud [ʃraud] *n*. & *v*. 覆盖，罩
5. thermal shock resistance 抗热震（性）
6. radome [ˈreidoum] *n*. 雷达天线罩，整流罩
7. cam [kæm] *n*. 凸轮
8. corrosion-resistant *a*. 抗腐蚀的
9. armour [ˈɑːmə] *n*. 盔甲，装甲
10. grit [ˈgrit] *n*. 磨料
11. whisker [ˈhwiskə] *n*. 晶须
12. ductile [ˈdʌktail] *a*. 可延展的，易变形的
13. impede [imˈpiːd] *v*. 阻碍，阻止
14. superimposition [sjupəˈimpəziʃən] *n*. 重叠，添加，附加物

Notes

① derived from：来源于，取自，由……派生而来；in conjunction with：和……一起，连同；that引出的定语从句说明前面的名词。参考译文：当材料的应用性依赖于陶瓷的机械性能和它们的耐熔性—即陶瓷对工作环境的化学抵抗能力时，由工程陶瓷组成的结构部件可用作为与金属组合或取代金属的块片状材料、涂层和复合材料。

② 参考译文：在高温下它们比超耐热不锈钢具有更高的熔点和强度，因此尤其对氮化硅而言，主要且潜在的应用是用在汽轮机和往复式发动机方面：陶瓷比金属能承受更高操作温度，能使这些机械达到更大的能效。

③ 参考译文：晶须增强原理是基于下列机理的活化作用，通过采用高杨氏模量的晶须，将应力由基材上转移到高强的增强介质上；通过引入高热膨胀系数的晶须使基体中产生压应力；由晶须阻止裂纹的扩散；使裂纹沿晶须-基体的界面转移；和通过晶须与基体的机械和热性能的差异产生微裂纹化。

Exercises

1. Translate underlined sentences in the text into Chinese.
2. Translate the following phrases into English or Chinese：

   ① 抗氧化
   ② 热等静压的氮化硅
   ③ 在晶格中由氧取代氮
   ④ 断裂韧性
   ⑤ 晶须-基材界面
   ⑥ tetrahedra joined together by sharing corners
   ⑦ good thermal shock resistance

⑧ high Young's modulus of the structural ceramics
⑨ impeding crack propagation through the whiskers
⑩ whisker-reinforced ceramics

Reading Material 11

Research on Aerospace Ceramics

Ceramics are currently vital to a broad range of aerospace applications ranging from the thermal protection system on the space shutter to ceramic coatings used in the combustors of gas turbine engines. Ceramics are attractive high temperature structural materials because of their strength, low density, environmental resistance, abundant supply of non-strategic raw materials, and net shape fabricability. However, the brittle nature of ceramics make these materials sensitive to minute flaws and defects that can be ignored in metals. The wide range of flaw sizes and spatial distributions tends to make ceramic strength unreliable. Thus narrower strength distribution and improved fracture toughness are prerequisites to wider use of ceramics.

The use of ceramic materials in heat engines eliminates the need for cooling even at temperatures in the range of 2500℉.

Research emphasis is being placed on improvement of monolithic ceramic reliability via elimination of process derived flaws in the 10 to 100 micrometer range or by toughening the ceramic to make it more forgiving of flaws. Such flaws are failure origins and cause scatter in ceramic strength. As a result, current ceramic components are less reliable than comparable metal parts. Also, ceramics generally fail in a catastrophic brittle manner. Thus, higher strength and reliability through a thorough understanding of the series of processing steps involved in the preparation of dense toughened ceramic materials is one current focus while fiber reinforcement to toughen, strengthen and provide for graceful fiber controlled fracture is a second.

The different processing techniques that are being used to prepare silicon nitride (Si_3N_4) and silicon carbide (SiC) specimens for evaluation typically consist of the formation of a "green" body (~60 percent theoretical density) comprised of fine SiC or Si_3N_4 powder and various sintering aids, followed by sintering (densification) at high temperatures in argon (for SiC) or a high nitrogen pressure environment (for Si_3N_4) or by hot isostatic pressing (HIP).

Research in the processing of powders involved the characterization of high purity SiC and Si_3N_4 powders, the evaluation of particle size reduction through comminution in SiC and Si_3N_4 milling hardware, and the comparison of samples formed using "wet" and "dry" consolidation techniques. A fine, pure starting powder is desirable for obtaining good sinterability and minimizing defects. The understanding and control of particle size reduction is necessary to processes in which the particle size distribution is a critical processing parameter. Results of the comminution of Si_3N_4 by various techniques are shown that attrition milling gave fastest particle size reduction and least contamination.

Densification of Si_3N_4 powder is accomplished through the addition of sintering aids. These additives lead to the formation of a liquid phase which enhances densification during heating at high temperatures (liquid phase sintering). The heating is performed in a high nitrogen pressure (25～50atm) furnace in order to prevent dissociation of the Si_3N_4. Various sintering aids such as Y_2O_3, La_2O_3, Sm_2O_3 and GeO_2 have been evaluated. Sintering aid choice influences strength and microstructure. The sintered material containing Y_2O_3 has flexural strength superior to sintered material containing La_2O_3 at 1000℃ and displays a microstructure richer in high aspect ratio grains. Sintering aid choice also has a profound influence on oxidation resistance with optimum Y_2O_3 containing material being superior.

Enhancement of ceramic toughness via additions of particles or whiskers to deflect and arrest cracks, and toughening and strengthening of ceramics via fabrication of continuous ceramic filament reinforced ceramics are approaches to permit ceramic parts to be more forgiving of flaws and to exhibit stress versus strain behavior comparable to ductile metals. The primary materials of interest here are: (1) silicon carbide fibers reinforcing silicon nitride or carbide; and (2) various ceramic oxide, carbide or nitride whiskers or particulates in silicon carbide or silicon nitride matrices. Particulate and whisker reinforcements lend themselves to conventional ceramic processing methods which use powder processing methods to form green compacts prior to firing. Thus, besides offering three-dimensional toughening, these reinforcements also offer economic advantages, and as such, are well suited for future large volume production, such as for automotive engine application.

Use of continuous fibers can strengthen as well as toughen ceramics. An approach that shows promise for yielding strong and tough high temperature composites is the formation of reaction-bonded Si_3N_4 matrices reinforced by continuous SiC fibers. Commercially available, large diameter (140 micrometer) SiC monofilament fibers are uniformly distributed within a Si_3N_4 matrix with fiber content up to 40%. Stress-strain curves for this material show the development of multiple matrix cracks before the composite ultimately fails due to fiber fracture. When compared to the current state-of-the art monolithic, the high fiber content composites display an equivalent strength for matrix cracking, but a significantly greater fiber-controlled ultimate strength. Most importantly, the composites fail in a controlled stable manner as compared to catastrophic fracture of monolithics.

Selected from: "High Tech Ceramics", P. Vincenzini, Elsevier, 1987.

Words and Expressions

1. prerequisite [priː'rekwizit] *n.*, *a.* 前决条件（的），必要条件，前提
2. scatter ['skætə] *n.* 散布，散射，分散
3. catastrophic [kætə'strɔfik] *a.* 大变动的，灾变的，不幸的

4. particle size distribution 粒径分布
5. contamination [kəntæmiˈneiʃən] *n.* 污染，杂质
6. filament [ˈfiləmənt] *n.* 细丝，长纤维
7. particulate [pɑːˈtikjuleit] *n.*，*a.* 粒子，细粒（的）
8. attrition [əˈtriʃən] *n.* 摩擦，消耗

PART Ⅲ GLASS

Unit 12 Structure of Glass

1. The Structure of Glass

In spite of the world wide development of glass technology we still have found no definite answer to the question: what is glass? The following three different definitions are given to demonstrate how to describe the state of glass:

- Glass is an inorganic product of a melt which solidifies without crystallizing;
- Glass is an undercooled liquid with a very high viscosity;
- Glass is an intermediate substance between the liquid and crystalline states. It consists of a crystal-like network combined with each other randomly.

An early idea of the structure of glass was based on the concept of the term supercooled liquid. Molten glass was regarded as a solution of one oxide within another oxide, or rather a mutual solution of constituents[1] within each other. The molten liquid is cooled without crystallization to form a rigid body at room temperature.

2. The Network Theory

In recent years, the theory of the atomic structure of glass advanced by Zachariasen has become widely accepted. His random network theory assumes unit building blocks placed together in a random network manner. Our understanding of the constitution and the behavior of glasses is based on the descriptions of the structures of oxide glasses and on the conditions of glass formation as interpreted by a few pioneers in glass research. Tammann began to explore systematically the phenomena of the glassy state stating that the rate of cooling is most important for the understanding of the glassy state. Glasses are rigid solids and not liquids. In 1926, Goldschmidt presented his ideas on modern crystal chemistry.

A glass may resemble the crystal of the same composition with respect to the short range order, but its typical glass properties are the result of the lack of long range order. The ability of a molten substance to solidify on cooling without crystallization was explained on the basis of the geometry of the polyhedra, in particular of the ratio of the sizes of anions and cations. Thus, Goldschmidt introduced crystal chemical concepts into the field of glass technology. A decisive step in the development of glass structures was made by Zachariasen in 1932 who presented a picture of the atomic structure of vitreous silica in which the silicon atoms are surrounded by four oxygens in the same way as in the different structures of crystalline silica and silicates. The only difference between glass and crystal was the absence of periodicity. The continuous, random, three-dimensional structure shows the same short range order as the crystalline modifications of silica but without their long range order[②].

The introduction of alkali oxides into vitreous silica loosens its structure by decreasing the number of corners which each tetrahedron has to share with others[③]. This feature could account for the lower viscosity of an alkali silicate glass as compared to pure silica. The classification of the constituents of a glass into network forming oxides and those which modify the network was simple and useful. The "intermediates" were introduced years later. There was a nearly universal acceptance of Zachariasen' rules concerning glass formation. Warren and his school using X-ray techniques for determining the atomic structures of glasses agreed with Zachariasen's picture. The application of X-rays made by for the most important contribution to the present concept of the constitution of glass.

The network formers belong to a group of elements having an energy of the element-oxygen bond of 340 to 500 KJ/mol. The network-modifiers, for example Mg, Ca, Li, K, Na, Cd, and Cs have an ionic oxygen bond with a bonding energy of 40 to 250kJ/mol. Their rates of diffusion are higher especially for the Me^+ ions. They break the continuous Si-O-Si network decreasing the viscosity of the melt at all temperatures. Me^{2+} ions act as a bridge between two oxygen atoms. They also break the network structure, but are less movable, influencing the flow of the melt less than Me^+ ions.

The main difference between a crystal and a glass is the kind of linkage of the tetrahedra. The crystalline structure repeats itself continuously in three dimensions, while in silica glass the tetrehedra are linked in a random network without an orderly repetition. In this network the SiO_2 units are called glassformers. Such a glassformer determines the overall structure of the network. Commercial soda-silica and soda-lime-silica glasses contain other materials added to the silica glass. These materials are called network-modifiers, because they open the network up and introduce into it a number of oxygens larger than can be contained in the structure where all oxygens are bridges between two silicons. This produces some non-bridging oxygens which are connected to only one silicon and cause a breaking of the structure.

Selected from "Process Mineralogy of Ceramic Materials", W. Baumgart, A. C. Dumham, G. C. Amstutz, Heidelberg and Hull, May 1984

Words and Expressions

1. solidify [sə'lidifai] *v.* 固化
2. undercooled *a.* 过冷的
3. supercooled *a.* 超冷的
4. rigid body *n.* 刚性体
5. short range order 近程有序
6. Long range order 长程有序
7. be surrounded by 被包围

8. periodicity [piriə'disiti] *n.* 周期律
9. account for 是……原因
10. net work former 网络形成体
11. net work-modifier 网络调整体

Notes

① mutual solution of constituents：组成的互溶体，把玻璃看成是过冷的液体。

② The continuous, random, three-dimensional structure shows the same short range order as the crystalline modifications of silica but without their long range order：连续，随机和三维的结构具有和二氧化硅晶体相同的近程有序性，只是不具备相同的长程有序性。

③ The introduction of alkali oxides into vitreous silica loosens its structure by decreasing the number of corners which each tetrahedron has to share with others：桥氧位于四面体的顶角，所以 corners 在这里指桥氧，整句可译成：玻璃态的二氧化硅中引入了碱金属之后，由于降低了由各个四面体共享的桥氧数，使结构变得松散。

Exercises

1. Find the missing words in the following paragraph.

   A decisive step in the development of glass structures was made by Zachariasen in 1932 who______a picture of the atomic structure of vitreous silica in which the silicon atoms are______by four oxygens in the same way as in the different structures of crystalline silica and silicates. The only difference between glass and crystal was the absence of______. The______, ______, ________structure shows the same short range order as the crystalline modifications of silica but without their______ ______order.

2. Put the following phrases into Chinese.

universal acceptance	in spite of	be based on
random network theory	on the basis of	be regarded as
in particular of	as compared to	act as

3. Put the following Chinese into English

互溶体	玻璃态的	玻璃组成	网络结构
网络调整体	中间体	学说	四面体
说明，解释	刚性体	碱金属	缺乏

Reading Material 12

A Hierarchical Model of the Glass Structure

1. Introduction

The history of the amorphograghy (vitrography) is strongly influenced by the struggle of two classical concepts - the random network model (RNM) and the model of the inhomogeneous glass structure (MIGS). After the works of Zachariasen and Warren for a long period the RNM was the dominant concept for the structure of glasses. Different cluster and molecular MIGSs have been proposed even before RNM but their empirical proof came with some delay.

The present state of knowledge confirms the Marinov's suggestion that no one structural model, neither RNM nor different MIGSs, can describe by itself the abundance of all possible glass structures. The claim of the supporters of these models for exhaustive description of all glass structures is inadequate. A useful structural model must combine the RNM with the different MIGSs, rather than contradict them.

The best way to merge RNM with MIGS is to create an enhanced hierarchical model of the glass structure. Each range of order in such a model has to be represented by its specific structural units. The model has to lay emphasis on the chemical, topological, geometrical, etc parameters of this structural units (SUs). The bridging parameters of the SUs, i. e. the parameters showing how a given SU is embedded in the glass network, have to be highlighted too. Information about the theoretical and/or empirical methods for determination of these parameters is also essential. Last but not least the model has to point out the connection between glass properties and type, concentration and linkage of the different SUs. The model has to be able to catalog the main features in the glass structure.

2. The Present Day Hierarchical Model

A basic hierarchical model may be regarded the RNM itself. It contains only two hierarchical levels - the Short Range Order (SRO) and the Long Range Order (LRO). The latest, however, is characteristic only for crystals. The SUs of the SRO are geometrically well defined network - forming polyhedrons. The glass network, formed by corner shared polyhedrons, is both geometrically and topologically random. The properties of the glasses are determined by the type and concentration of different polyhedrons. The geometrical parameters of the polyhedrons and topological ones can be determined by diffraction and spectroscopic methods, molecular dynamics simulations, etc.

The requirement for comprehensiveness is the only one, which the RNM does not satisfy. Indeed there are structural features below SRO like chemical bonds and above SRO like rings, Krogh-Moe complexes, "pseudophases", etc which can not be classified in the frame of the RNM.

The term intermediate RO (IRO) is often used to classify all structural features above SRO. In fact some of this features are too different to be classified in only one hierarchical level. In borate glasses, for example, it has been observed two qualitatively different types of IRO structural features - Krogh-Moe complexes and "pseudophases". The Krogh-Moe complexes are both chemically and topologically well defined molecular complexes. The "pseudophases" are three-dimensional fluctuations of density or concentration. The nanometer dimensions of the "pseudophases" are independent on the thermal treatment. It is interesting to note that a hierarchical subordination has been found between the structural features considered: in some glasses the "pseudophases" are build up by clustering of Krogh-moe complexes.

Several hierarchical models have been proposed in order to catalog comprehensively the different features in the glass structure. These models have been briefly reviewed in.

In the model of Connell & Lucovsky special attention has been paid to the point defects in the glass structure. These defects are important for the spectroscopic properties of the glasses in the UV-VIS spectral region. A special, Local RO has been introduced to catalog the point defects. The Local RO is a more fundamental hierarchical level than the Short RO. The electronic structure of glasses, however, is represented only partially by the point defects. In our viewpoint a more general RO, Electron RO, have to be introduced to catalog thoroughly all features in the electronic structure of the glasses.

An attempt to separate different IRO structural features into different ROs has been made in the models proposed by Galeener, Wright et al. This models, however, does not clarify the difference between some SUs. For example, in the model of Wright, Galeener et al. only the network-forming polyhedrons are called "structural units". Some well-defined combinations of polyhedrons, "superstructural units" (in our term-molecules), are also considered. Both "structural units" and "superstructural units" are classified together in Range I of the model.

A three-ranged hierarchical model of the glass structure has been proposed by White. The different hierarchical levels are represented by network polyhedra, "basic structural units" and "clustered units" "…each with its own contribution to the overall disorder of the bulk glass".

With the purpose to evolve the above mentioned models and to meet the requirements announced in previous chapter a new five ranged model of the glass structure will be discussed below.

3. The New Hierarchical Model

The electron range of order (ERO) is considered as a basic structural level in model presented. The constituents of the electronic structure of glasses i. e. the chemical bonds as well as the atomic and molecular orbitals (in terms of the valence-bond and molecular orbital theories respectively) may be regarded as SUs of this basic RO. The parameters of this SUs are symmetry, type, coefficients, energy and occupation of molecular orbitals, distributions of different valence distances and angles, distribution of the ionic-covalence character of the bonds etc. The methods to determine this parameters are quantum chemical calculations, ESCA (UPS & WPS), Auger ES, XAS& EXAFS, positron annihilation, etc. The ERO predetermines all glass properties, e. g. electrical, optical (refractive index, spectral transmittance), mechanical (through the bending and stretching force constants), etc. Unfortunately a comprehensive description of the electronic structure of glasses is at present unachievable. Therefore, in order to forecast the properties of glasses some additional information about the ionic structure of glasses is also necessary. Being basic, the ERO is labelled as level zero.

Selected from "PROCEEDINGS OF XVII INTERNATIONAL CONGRESS ON GLASS VOL. 2 Glass Formation and Structure", Gong Fangtian, International Academic Publishers, 1995

Words and Expressions

1. Hierarchical [haiə'rɑːkikəl] *a*. 体系的
2. Amorphogragphy [ə'mɔːfəgrɑːfi] *n*. 无定形网络
3. Vitrography [vitrigrɑːfi] *n*. 玻璃网络
4. Topological [tɔpə'lɔdʒikəl] *a*. 拓扑学的
5. Spectroscopic method 光谱学方法
6. Molecular dynamics simulation 分子动力学模拟
7. Pseudophase [psjuːdoufeis] *n*. 伪相
8. borate glass 硼酸盐玻璃
9. Krogh-Moe complex Krogh-Moe 螯合物
10. three-dimensional fluctuation 三维波动
11. UV-VIS spectral region 紫外到可见光光谱范围
12. superstructural unit 超结构
13. ESCA 化学分析电子能谱
14. UPS 紫外光电子能谱
15. Auger ES 俄歇电子能谱
16. XAS X-射线吸收谱
17. EXAFS 扩散 X-射线吸收谱
18. positron ['pɔzitrɔn] *n*. 正电子
19. annihilation [ənaiə'leiʃən] *n*. 湮灭

Unit 13 Glass Formation

Diezel introduced into the structural concepts of the alkali silicate glasses a new viewpoint, by considering the distribution of the alkalies. The structure of an alkali silicate glass is described as a random, continuous, three-dimensional network. A distinction is made between two kinds of oxygen ions, the bridging oxygens and the non-bridging oxygens. The addition of alkali oxides to silica leads to a breakage of a Si-O-Si chain. The alkali ions are placed near the broken bridge oxygen ions and are surrounded by a certain number of bridged oxygen ions. This allows a more or less random distribution of the non-bridging oxygen ions among the bridging oxygen ions.

Sodium oxide or calcium oxide enter the holes in the network as ions. Fundamentally, glass becomes ionic in nature and this ionic nature gives it conduction at high temperature. However, at room temperature the ions are so restricted in their movements that glass is an insulater. With increasing thermal energy the number of bonds which can break increases. Thus, glasses have no specific melting point, but are characterized by a softening range.

The relationships between the liquid, the crystalline and the glassy states of a material are best explained in a volume-temperature diagram for a glass forming substance shown in Fig. 3. 1 The volume of a substance decreases on cooling steadily along the line ab. At a sufficiently slow cooling rate with nuclei present in the melt, crystallization will take place at the temperature T_f accompanied by a decrease in volume following be. On further cooling, the crystalline substance contracts along cd. No crystallization will take place at T_f, if the rate of cooling is sufficiently rapid. The volume of the now supercooled liquid decreases on further cooling along the line be. At a certain temperature T_g, the volume-temperature curve of the supercooled liquid undergoes a marked change in direction and continues almost parallel to the contraction curve of the crystalline form. The temperature T_g, at which the bend occurs, is called the transformation or glass transition temperature. Only below T_g it is correct to describe the substance as a glass. Between T_g and T_f the substance is a supercooled liquid. At T_g the viscosity is extremely high, about 10^{12} Pa • s. If the temperature of the glass is held constant at T, the volume decreases slowly until it reaches a point on the dotted line. This process, by which the glass reaches a more stable condition, is known as stabilization. Other properties of the glass also change with time near the transition temperature. The properties of a glass depend to a certain extent on the rate at

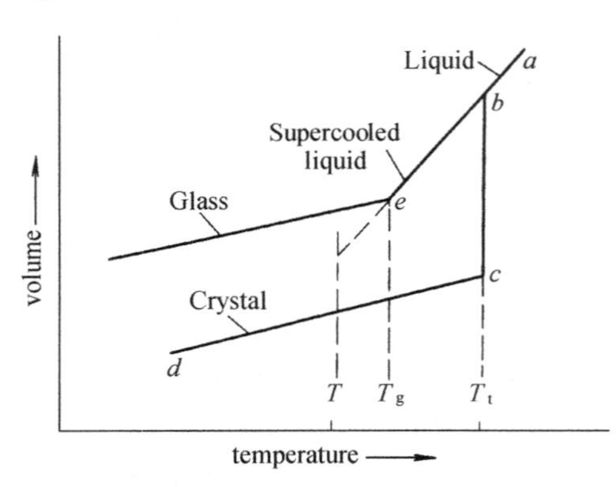

Fig. 3. 1 relation between the glassy, liquid and solid states (JONES, 1956)

which it has been cooled, particularly through the temperature range near T_g. Also the exact value of T_g depends on the rate of cooling being lower the smaller the rate of cooling.

Alumina does not form a glass. When the phase diagram CaO-Al_2O_3 was determined in 1909, it was found that in a small composition range around the compound $12CaO$-$7Al_2O_3$ the liquidus temperature drops to approximately 1400℃ and a glass formation was observed, having an Al_2O_3 composition range of 38%～65%. While pure calcium-aluminate glasses have to be cooled rather quickly, their stability can be raised by adding about 5% SiO_2. Glasses based upon calcium-aluminate became of interest when the optical industry searched for glasses with good infrared transmissions.

For the production of technical glasses the ternary system Na_2O-CaO-SiO_2 is of great importance. The main composition of glasses belonging into this system covers the area of the NC_3S_6-βCS border. Devitrite, Na_2O-$3CaO$-$6SiO_2$, decomposes at 1045℃ forming wollastonite (CS) and a liquid. A homogeneous liquid is formed at 1325℃. Devitrite is the primary phase which crystallizes from a large number of commercial glasses.

Thuringian glass enjoyed a particularly good reputation with respect to its workability① . The sands found in this part of Germany contained some feldspar which introduced a few percent of alumina into the glass. Al_2O_3 suppresses the tendency of the glass to devitrify and improves its chemical resistance②.

A soda-lime-silica glass of the composition of devitrite has a liquidus temperature of 1325℃, but some of its O^{2-} ions are still mobile 700℃ below this temperature. The alkali ions are still mobile 1000℃ below the liquidus temperature. The alkali and alkaline earth ions do not seem to remain randomly distributed.

The following single oxides form glasses: SiO_2, GeO_2, B_2O_3, P_2O_5, As_2O_3. Each of these oxides may be melted with a second oxide or mixture of oxides. Usually, however, there are limits to percentages of other oxides which may be added. In addition to the group of the five glass-forming oxides, there exists a second group including TiO_2, SeO_2, MoO_3, WO_3, Bi_2O_3, Al_2O_3, Ga_2O_3, and V_2O_5 of which none will form a glass itself, but each will do so when melted with a suitable quantity of a second oxide or mixture of oxides③. The oxides of the second group will be distinguished from the first single glass-forming oxides by calling them: conditional glass-forming oxides. A third group, called intermediate oxides, contains oxides such as ZnO, BeO, PbO, ZrO_2, Sb_2O_3.

Selected from "Process Mineralogy of Ceramic Materials", W. Baumgart, A. C. Dunham, G. C. Amstutz, Heidelberg and Hull, 1984

Words and Expressions

1. bridging oxygen 桥氧
2. non-bridging oxygen 非桥氧
3. transition temperature 转变温度
4. Liquidus [ˈlikwidəs] *a.*, *n.* 液相线，液相的

5. Approximately [ə'prɔksəmeitli] *adv*. 大约地
6. calcium-aluminate glass　钙铝酸盐玻璃
7. Infrared ['infrə'red] *a*. 红外的
8. Transmission [trænz'miʃən] *n*. 透射
9. Ternary ['təːnəri] *a*. 三元的
10. Devitrite [diː'vitrait] *n*. 失透石
11. Decompose [diːkəm'pouz] *v*. 分解
12. Thuringian　（德国的）图林根州的

Note

① Thuringian glass enjoyed a particularly good reputation with respect to its workability. with respect to：在某方面，workability：可操作性，可加工性。

② Al_2O_3 suppresses the tendency of the glass to devitrify and improves its chemical resistance. to devitrify：是 suppresses 的宾语补足语。

③ In addition to the group of the five glass-forming oxides, there exists a second group including TiO_2, SeO_2, MoO_3, WO_3, Bi_2O_3, Al_2O_3, Ga_2O_3, and V_2O_5 of which none will form a glass itself, but each will do so when melted with a suitable quantity of a second oxide or mixture of oxides. Which：指 a second group，即 none of the second group. 整句句子可译作：除了五种玻璃形成氧化物，还有第二类氧化物，包括 TiO_2，SeO_2，MoO_3，WO_3，Bi_2O_3，Al_2O_3，Ga_2O_3 和 V_2O_5，它们本身都不能形成玻璃，但只要和适量的另一种氧化物或混合氧化物一起熔化，就可以形成玻璃。

Exercises

1. Classify the following oxides into three groups according to their behavior of forming a glass.

   SiO_2, As_2O_3, TiO_2, SeO_2, MoO_3, WO_3, GeO_2, B_2O_3, Bi_2O_3, Al_2O_3, Ga_2O_3, V_2O_5, ZnO, BeO, PbO, ZrO_2, P_2O_5, Sb_2O_3.

Glass forming oxides	Intermediate oxides	Conditional glass forming oxides

2. Complete the following sentences by filling in the blanks with correct temperature.

   a) Devitrite, Na_2O-$3CaO$-$6SiO_2$, decomposes at______forming wollastonite and a liquid.

   b) A homogeneous liquid of devitrite is formed at______.

   c) A soda-lime-silica glass of the composition of devitrite has a liquidus temperature of 1325℃, but some of its O^{2-} ions are still mobile at______. The alkali ions are still mobile at______.

3. Put the following Chinese into English.

碱金属硅酸盐玻璃	热能	熔点	软化范围
三元系统	钠钙硅玻璃	钙铝酸盐玻璃	冷却速率
初晶相	液相温度	相图	红外透射

Reading Material 13

Atomistic Hypotheses of Glass Formation

1. Atomistic Hypotheses of Glass Formation

Glass formation is a kinetic phenomenon; any liquid, in principle, can be transformed into glass if cooled sufficiently quickly and brought below the transformation range. A good glass-forming material is then one for which the rate of crystallization is very slow in relation to the rate of cooling. As discussed in the earlier section, with conventional rates of cooling, some melts produce glass more easily than others. These facts lead many workers to postulate different atomistic hypotheses correlating the nature of the chemical bond, and the geometrical shape of the groups involved, with the ease of glass formation. It should be pointed out that, although these empirical hypotheses explain glass formation in some allied liquid systems, a unified hypothesis capable of explaining the phenomenon of glass formation in all the known systems has yet to be developed.

2. Goldschmidt's Radius Ratio Criterion for Glass Formation

According to Goldschmidt for a simple oxide of the general formula $A_m O_n$, there is a correlation between the ability to form glass and the relative sizes of the oxygen and A atoms. Glass-forming oxides are those for which the ratio of ionic radii R_A/R_O lies in the range 0.2 to 0.4. For ionic compounds the coordination number is often dictated by the radius ration rule. From simple geometrical considerations of the maximum number of spherical anions packed around a cation maintaining anion-cation contact, the results set out in Table3.1 can be calculated. Thus according to Goldschmidt, a tetrahedral configuration of the oxide is a prerequisite of glass formation. However, it should be pointed out that in glass-forming oxides the anion-cation bonding is far from purely ionic. Besides, as discussed earlier in the case of $9TeO_2$: PbO the coordination number of Te is six and not four. BeO with $R_{Be}/R_O \sim 0.221$ does not form glass.

Table3.1 Limiting radius ratios for various coordination polyhedra

Polyhedron	Coordination number	Minimum radius ration	Polyhedron	Coordination number	Minimum radius ration
Equilateral triangle	3	0.155	Square pyramid	5	0.414
Tetrahedron	4	0.225	Octahedron	6	0.414
Trigonal bipyramid	5	0.414	Cube	8	0.732

3. Smekal's Mixed Bonding Hypothesis

According to Smekal pure covalent bonds have sharply defined bond-lengths and bond-angles and these are incompatible with the random arrangement of the atoms in glass. On the other hand, purely ionic or metallic bonds completely lack any directional characteristics. Thus the presence of "mixed" chemical bonding in a material is necessary for glass formation. According to Smekal, glass-forming substances with mixed bonding may be divided into three classes as follows:

a) inorganic compounds, e. g. SiO_2, B_2O_3, where the A-O bonds are partly covalent and partly ionic.

b) Elements, e. g. S, Se having chain structures with covalent bonds within the chain and Van der Waals' forces between the chains.

c) Organic compounds containing large molecules with covalent bonds within the molecule and Van der Waals' forces between them.

4. Kinetic Approach to Glass Formation

Whether or not a given liquid will crystallize during cooling before T_g is reached is strictly a kinetic problem involving the rate of nucleation and crystal growth on the one hand and, on the other, the rate at which thermal energy can be extracted from the cooling liquid. In recent decades there have been several treatments of the conditions of glass formation, based on considerations of crystallization kinetics, and a good review is contained in the article "Under what condition can a glass be formed?" By Turnbull. This author pointed out that there are at least some glass-formers in every category of material, based on bond type (covalent, ionic, metallic, Van der Waals, and hydrogen). Cooling rate, density of nuclei and various material properties like crystal-liquid surface tension, and entropy of fusion etc. were suggested as significant factors which affect the tendency of different liquids to form glasses. This approach naturally raises the question not whether a liquid will form a glass on cooling, but rather how fast must a given liquid be cooled in order to avoid any detectable crystallization?

Uhlmann, developing Turnbull's idea, has provided some useful guidelines for glass formation by using theoretical time-temperature-% transformation (T-T-T) curves to specify critical cooling rates in terms of material constants. In the case of single-component materials or congruently melting compounds, if the nucleation frequency and rate of crystal growth are constant with time, then the volume fraction X crystallized in a time t may be expressed as:

$$X \sim \pi I_V \mu^3 t^4 / 3 \text{ (for small value of X)}$$

where I_V is the nucleation frequency per unit volume, and μ is the rate of advance of the crystal-liquid interfaces per unit area of the interfaces. Both nucleation frequency I_V and rate of advance μ are inversely proportional to the viscosity of the liquid.

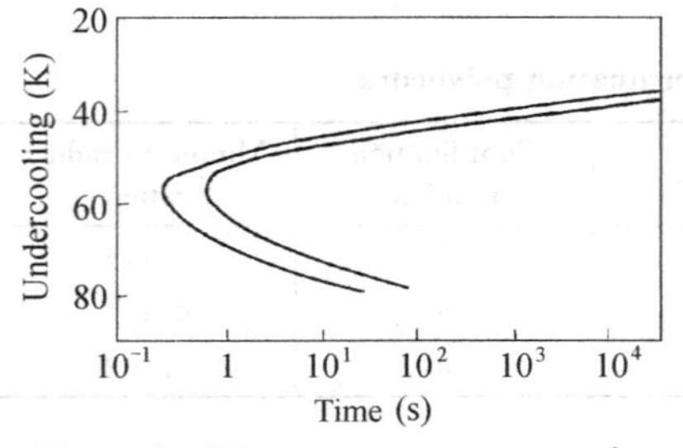

Fig. 3. 2 Time-temperature transformation curves for salol corresponding to volume fractions crystallized of (A) 10^{-6} and 10^{-8}

The cooling rate required to avoid a given volume fraction crystallized may be estimated from equation by the construction of T-T-T curve, an example of which is shown in Fig. 3. 2 for two different volume fractions crystallized. In constructing these curves, a particular fraction crystallized is selected, the time required for that volume fraction to form at a given temperature is calculated, and the calculations are repeated for other temperatures. The nose in a T-T-T curve, corresponding to the least time for the given volume fraction to crystallize, results from competition between the driving force for crystallization (which increases with decreasing temperature) and the atomic mobility (which decreases with decreasing temperature). The transformation times t_i are relatively long in the vicinity of the melting point as well as at low temperatures. The cooling rate required to avoid a given fraction becoming crystallized can be approximately represented by the relationship as follows.

Selected from "CHEMISTRY OF GLASSES", A. PAUL, 2nd edition, Chapman and Hall, 1990

Words and Expressions

1. atomistic [ætə'mistik] *a.* 原子论的
2. postulate ['pɔstjuleit] *v.* 假定，以……出发点
3. hypothesis [hai'pɔθəsis] *n.* 假设，(pl. Hypotheses)
4. radius ratio criterion 原子半径比准则
5. equilateral triangle 等边三角形
6. trigonal bipyramid 三方双锥
7. square pyramid 方锥，四方锥
8. crystal growth 晶体生长
9. hydrogen 文中指：氢键
10. entropy ['entrəpi] *n.* 熵
11. congruently ['kɔŋgruəntli] *adv.* 相应地，适合地
12. congruently melting compoumd 一致熔化合物

Unit 14 Manufacture of Glass: Present Trend in Industrial Glass Melting

1. Introduction

The objective of industrial glass making is to produce the required quality at the lowest possible global cost. This has been achieved in the past by continuous evolution ever since the invention of the Siemens tank furnace. Technical innovations such as the fusion cast refractory and the substitution of oil or natural gas for producer gas simply accelerated progress and the trends were always in the same direction. What is new is that the cost of glass now includes the price of preserving the environment and, because of the uncertainty as to the most economical solutions to the environmental problems, there is also uncertainty about future trends.

Although these problems are the center of much attention the industry will continue to evolve by integration of technical developments and in reply to commercial requirements. This short review will begin with products and quality. A chapter on environmental considerations will then be proceeded by remarks on refractories and followed by a paragraph on modeling.

2. New Products

New products may require new compositions and in this case new or modified methods of melting may also be needed. The three following examples illustrate the range of the problems involved.

Anti-Solar Glass

New colours for automobile or architectural glazing have in general been produced with little difficulty. However, when the product is required to be as opaque as possible to near infrared radiation it follows that melting and tank behavior will be disturbed by the reduced radiant heat transfer through the molten glass①.

Another difficulty is that to reach the required ferrous iron level, a reducer must be used and the usual sulfate additions limited. This entails the risk of inadequate silica digestion. In addition, a high ferrous iron content may be accompanied by the formation of traces of sulfide and unwanted amber coloration. The fact that it is not easy to obtain the desired characteristics in a normal furnace inspired the conception of an entirely new glass melting process: refining is carried out under reduced pressure which also removes the traces of sulfide②. This technology remains, for now, the exception that proves the rule that progress in glass making has usually been achieved by evolution rather than revolution③.

Zero-Expansion Transparent Glass Ceramics

Glass ceramics designed to resist thermal shock are based on the lithia-alumina-silica system whose thermal expansivity, after ceramisation, is almost zero. The basic problems in the elaboration of the parent glass are its high viscosity, which is close to 400 poises at 1600℃, and the digestion of the nucleant. Techniques for melting such glasses have however been developed over the last 40 years. Four products have been successively commercialized: opaque cooking-ware, opaque cooker tops, transparent cooking-ware and, more recently, the transparent cooker tops. Each of these new products has given rise to significant progress in glass quality. The transparent cooker top in particular implies not only absence of visible macroscopic defects but also the absence of even smaller inclusions that might prevent the mechanical shock resistance from reaching the particularly high level required.

Glass for Active-Matrix Liquid-Crystal Display Panels

For this application, thin sheets of glass are required containing no seed bigger than a few hundreds of a millimeter and with perfectly flat surfaces obtained with as little polishing as possible after forming. These two basic requirements imply unusually high degrees of refining and of homogeneity. Other properties are also essential: a high strain point (to avoid "compaction" during the heat treatments associated with the production of the grid of transistors) absence of alkali (which might diffuse into the liquid crystal and transistor layers) low expansivity (to match the amorphous silicon used) and resistance to acids (used during the process). The absence of alkali and relatively low expansion leads to the use of B_2O_3 which, being somewhat volatile, may eventually complicate the attainment of the required homogeneity.

In spite of these difficulties, such substrates are being produced in quantities sufficient for the expanding market for portable computers. Even more rapid expansion is expected in the future as the cathode ray tube gives way to the flat screen in new generations of television receivers.

3. Electric Melting

The cold-top electric furnace is essentially non-polluting and is chosen for melting glasses such as fluoride opal or lead crystal. Its greatest handicap is the cost of electric power which in Europe is more expensive than gas by a factor that varies from 3 in Switzerland to 10 in Spain. Electric melting is not likely to be adopted simply to avoid dust, NO_X and SO_X emission. On the other hand, because the thermal efficiency of electric melting is less sensitive to furnace size, small electric furnaces can be used economically in countries where electricity is not too expensive.

In spite of the growing attention to emissions, global electricity consumption by the glass industry in Europe is probably decreasing. As the gap widens between electricity costs and fuel costs it has become more profitable to increase furnace size than to use electric boosting. This is particularly true for furnaces making containers, which represent 65% of all glass produced.

Selected from "PROCEEDINGS OF ⅩⅦ INTERNATIONAL CONGRESS ON GLASS VOL. 1 Invited Lecture", Gong Fangtian, International Academic Publishers, 1995

Words and Expressions

1. global [ˈgloubl] *a.* 综合的，全面的
2. anti-solar glass 热反射玻璃
3. glazing [ˈgleiziŋ] *n.* 上釉，玻璃窗
4. reducer [riˈdjuːsə] *n.* 还原剂
5. entail [inˈteil] *v.* 使……承担
6. digestion [diˈdʒestʃən] *n.* 消化力，领悟
7. amber [ˈæmbə] *n.* 琥珀
8. lithia-alumina-silica system 锂铝硅系统
9. ceramisation [sirəmaiˈzeiʃən] *n.* 陶瓷化
10. elaboration [ilæbəˈreiʃən] *n.* 精制，精品
11. poise [pɔiz] *n.* 泊
12. nucleant [ˈnjuːkliənt] *n.* 核化剂
13. active-matrix 活化构造
14. seed [siːd] *n.* 小气泡
15. refine [riˈfain] *v.* 澄清
16. homogeneity [houmədʒəˈniːiti] *n.* 均化
17. grid [grid] *n.* 栅极
18. volatile [ˈvɔlətail] *a.* 可挥发的
19. attainment [əˈteinmənt] *n.* 获得
20. cold-top electric furnace 冷炉顶电炉
21. handicap [ˈhændikæp] *n.* 不利条件，缺陷
22. producer gas 发生炉煤气

Notes

① However, when the product is required to be as opaque as possible to near infrared radiation it follows that melting and tank behavior will be disturbed by the reduced radiant heat transfer through the molten glass. It 作形式主语，主语为 that 引导的从句。

② The fact that it is not easy to obtain the desired characteristics in a normal furnace inspired the conception of an entirely new glass melting process: refining is carried out under reduced pressure which also removes the traces of sulfide. The fact 引导同位语从句，inspired the conception 激发了灵感。全句译作：在普通的窑炉中难以获得要求的特性激发了创造一种全新的玻璃熔化工艺的灵感：降压澄清，如此还可以除去熔融玻璃中微量的硫化物。

③ This technology remains, for now, the exception that proves the rule that progress in glass making has usually been achieved by evolution rather than revolution. for now：插入语，the exception that proves the rule：the exception of the rule，全句译作：玻璃制造方面的进步通常是进化而不是革命，然而这项技术却是一个例外。

Exercises

1. Translate the following Chinese into English.

零膨胀	透明微晶玻璃	热震	母体玻璃
乳白色锅子	乳白色锅盖	氟化物乳白玻璃	应变点
铅晶质玻璃	阴极射线管	液晶显示板	纯平显示器
环境保护	未来趋势	注意焦点	熔融玻璃

2. Make sentences by using following phrases.
   give rise to——
   prevent…from——
   give way to——
   in reply to——
3. Put the underlined paragraph into Chinese.

Reading Material 14

Environmental Considerations in Glass Manufacturing

The recycling of container glass was inspired by the idea of conserving raw materials and energy. Acid rain confirmed the need to reduce SO_x emissions while smog and the hole in the ozone layer motivated the drive to control emissions of NO_x. The glass industry is also affected by the increasingly severe regulation of land-fill which will lead to a more complete recycling of used products, scrap and waste.

Recycling

About 50% of the container glass produced in western Europe is at present recycles. The main advantage to the glass maker is the economy in specific energy consumption which may now be less than 1 kWh/kg of glass when very high proportions of cullet are used. There is also revived interest in pre-heating which is simpler with cullet than with loose batch.

The recuperated cullet might also have been expected to increase maximum furnace output as is the case when cullet from the same furnace is used. This has not been found possible in France no doubt because of the higher foam levels that are observed and which can be attributed to the mixture of oxidized and reduced glasses in cullet that is not colour sorted.

Another disadvantage of this lack of sorting is that all of the recycled containers must be consumed by the limited number of furnaces producing green glass.

The principal difficulties however are caused by the presence of non-vitreous materials. In spite of the various systems that remove most of the metals and ceramics, there are still problems due to lead, aluminium and porcelain. The lead problem is in recession because of improved construction techniques and legislation eliminating lead from wine bottle capsules.

Aluminium from closures, is still producing silicon spherules by reduction of SiO_2 in the molten glass. Even though not always visible they can seriously weaken glass containers. Extension of container glass recycling would be greatly facilitated by separate collection of three bottle colours and removal, by the public, of all metal closures.

As to the recycling of other glass products, from scrapped automobiles in particular, the problems to be solved are more evident than the solutions.

Scrap

In flat glass and container manufacturing, all trimmings, sub-standard on broken products become "cullet" and are a welcome adjunct to the batch. In glass wool or reinforcement fiber production any unsaleable output becomes "scrap" difficult to recycle in the furnace not only because of handling difficulties but also because of the chemically reducing nature of the sizing or binder. With the rapidly rising cost of disposing of fiber scrap as land-fill, recycling techniques are being explored involving combinations of chopping, grinding, calcining and melting.

Waste

Beside the problem of scrap there is also that of non-glass waste: filter residues, regenerator deposits and used refractories. The practice of disposing of such material as land-fill is bound to be replaced by recycling or valorization.

The quantities of regenerator "condensates" are small compared with the output of the furnace: of the order of 20 tons per year for an end-fired furnace producing 400 tons per day. Nevertheless, recycling implies storage, grinding and redox adjustments. The mass of electro-filter dust will be very roughly 10 times greater than the condensates if natural gas is used but could be 50 times greater in the case of heavy oil containing 3.5% sulfur. As this latter quantity exceeds considerably the sulfate required in the batch, it is obvious that high-sulfur fuel is incompatible with the recycling of filter dust.

Increasing proportion of used Cr_2O_3 based refractories are now being recuperated by the producers. The high Cr_2O_3 refractories are recycled to give a lower grade and less expensive product whereas lower chrome AZS finds use in other agglomerated materials. Finding solutions for all the other used refractories will require imagination as there is certainly no single treatment valid for the various materials in very different states of purity or contamination. Any brick that can be ground to a fine powder might be used in the glass batch. This has already been done with a silica crown.

Emissions

The wisps of white smoke from glass works' chimneys contribute, in Europe, from 0.4% to 0.8% to the total of the man-made emissions of dust, SO_x, NO_x and CO_2. The regulations that now exist in western Europe are progressive and are in general less severe for existing furnaces than for new furnaces or furnaces after repair. The following are the present limitations in Germany expressed in mg/Nm^3 (with the range in untreated emissions indicated in parentheses): dust, 50 decreasing to 20 (80 to 400); SO_x, 500 (gas), 1500 (oil) (500 to 4000); NO_x, 1200 to 3500 (depending on fuel and furnace type) decreasing to

500 (800 to 4000).

Dust and SO_x

The cost and performance of techniques for simultaneously removing SO_x and dust are already well known: dry or semi-dry scrubbing with lime, quicklime, sodium hydroxide or carbonate, followed by filtering in a bag-house or with an electrostatic filter.

The repercussions on furnace design may be the introduction of an exhaust gas cooling system (in the form of a boiler) and the use of an extractor instead of natural draught. The traditional 65 meter high chimney can then be replaced by a shorter one whose height depends on local or national regulations (around 40 m in France).

The NO_x Problem

In contrast with SO_x abatement there is no simple and generally accepted technique for the attenuation of NO_x emissions.

A radical solution is to replace pre-heated air by oxygen. This technique, already being used for special glasses, presents a number of virtues: installation on existing furnaces with or without shut-down, possibility of increased temperatures, quality and pull, decreased consumption, exhaust gas volume reduced to 1/4, steady operation (no inversions) reduced cost and space required for a new furnace. On the other hand, the cost of oxygen is high, depends of the price of electricity, the pressure required, the means of delivery and on the size and type of the production unit. As a result, in the USA alone, prices of oxygen for glass-making have been observed varying by a factor of three.

The CO_2 Question

Ever since the 1992 summit meeting in Rio de Janera when it was decided to take measures to combat the planetary glass-house effect, industry in general is living with the perspective of an incitation to reduce CO_2 emissions. Whatever form this incitation takes, its effect will no doubt be to increase the price of fossil fuels and also, one might think, of electricity as long as even a fraction of electric power is generated in thermal power stations. There is little reason to incite glass makers to use electricity rather than gas because the thermal efficiency of a regenerative furnace is usually higher than that of a thermal power station.

The effect of a CO_2 constraint will be the necessity to improve the thermal efficiency of all furnaces. This will mean a return to the situation existing at the height of the fuel crisis when it became economical in Europe to build furnaces with double and even triple-pass regenerators. The difference is that the higher air temperatures, this time, will aggravate the NO_x problem.

The use of oxygen for combustion reduces CO_2 emission by the economy of fuel. However, because of the electricity required to produce the oxygen, a global decrease is obtained only in the conversion of furnaces of low thermal efficiency or when the electricity is mostly from sources other than fossil fuels.

Selected from "ROCEEDINGS OF ⅩⅤⅡ INTERNATIONAL CONGRESS ON GLASS VOL. 1 Invited Lectures", Gong Fangtian, International Academic Publishers, 1995

Words and Expressions

1. cullet [ˈkʌlit] *n*. 碎玻璃
2. revive [riˈvaiv] *v*. 复活，苏醒
3. recuperate [tiˈkjuːpəreit] *v*. 回复，再生
4. legislative [ˈledʒislətiv] *a*. 立法的
5. spherule [ˈsferuːl] *n*. 小球体
6. trimming [trimiŋ] *n*. 修剪，打理
7. adjunct [ˈædʒʌŋkt] *n*. 附属品
8. sizing [ˈsaiziŋ] *n*. 胶料
9. land-fill *n*. 回填
10. redox [riˈdɔks] *n*. 氧化还原
11. wisp [wisp] *n*. 一缕
12. scrub [skrʌb] *v*. 洗涤
13. quicklime [ˈkwiklaim] *n*. 生石灰
14. repercussion [riːpəˈkʌʃən] *n*. 影响
15. extractor [iksˈtraktə] *n*. 分离器
16. abatement [ˈəbeitmənt] *n*. 减少，缓和
17. incitation [insaiˈteiʃən] *n*. 激励
18. aggravate [ˈægrəveit] *v*. 使恶化

Unit 15 Glass Properties

1. Density

The thermal history of a glass determines its properties. For example, the density of most glasses is dependent upon its thermal history and decreases with temperature. The density of glasses covers a range from 2.2 to 8.0 g/cm^3. Glasses cooled at various rates from above the annealing point will differ in density with the more rapidly cooled glasses having a lower density①. As the thermal conductivity and the specific heat can be calculated from the oxide composition, so can the density according to HUGGINS and SUN.

Glass technologists have determined empirically for a certain composition field how additions or substitutions affect the different properties of a glass②. This method of calculating a property of a glass on the basis of additivity cannot be applied to glasses which contain boric oxide. The density of glasses was among the first properties that was calculated on the basis of composition. Density measurements are widely used for quality control.

2. Thermal Expansion

The thermal expansion of glasses from room temperature into the softening range has been used for many years in order to determine the transformation temperature, the temperature at which the supercooled liquid changes into a glass. Even in a fully annealed glass the thermal expansion is not uniform over a large temperature range. The coefficient alpha represents the change in length per unit of length per degree rise in temperature within a given temperature region. The increase in thermal expansion of well annealed glasses in their softening range is attributed to the formation of defects such as vacant anion sites of incomplete coordination. Defects introduce asymmetries into the short range order of glasses and increase the thermal expansion by raising the thermal vibrations. This explanation applies equally well to silicate glasses with their ionic networks and to organic or molecular glasses.

The mean coefficient of linear thermal expansion generally is expressed in units of 10^{-7}cm/cm/K. For catalogue purposes, glass manufacturers quote the value for the range 0℃ to 300℃, but other ranges, such as 20℃ to 100℃, are not uncommon.

Since thermal expansion is an important consideration in sealing glass to another material, another useful coefficient is from 25℃ to the setting point of the glass. The setting point is that temperature at which the glass on cooling becomes a rigid elastic body, and numerically is defined as 5℃ above the strain point. The largest changes of thermal expansion occur in the transformation range. This range generally is about 100℃ in width and is centered near the strain point of the glass. The expansion coefficient of glass also depends on its composition. Alkalies raise the coefficient markedly, silica or boric oxide generally lower the coefficient, the other oxides act intermediate. The expansion coefficient of glass can be calculated with fair accuracy from the composition by use of appropriate factors. The most generally applicable are those of ENGLISH and TURNER.

The weight percentage of each component of the glass is multiplied by the corresponding factor for the component. The sum of the products is the linear expansion coefficient per degree C for the glass. As an example, the glass with the composition SiO_2 76%, Na_2O 12%, CaO 12% shows the following calculation:

$$SiO_2\ 76\times0.05\times10^{-7}=3.80\times10^{-7}$$
$$Na_2O\ 12\times4.32\times10^{-7}=51.84\times10^{-7}$$
$$CaO\ 12\times1.63\times10^{-7}=\frac{19.56\times10^{-7}}{75.20\times10^{-7}}$$

This calculated expansion coefficient refers to the temperature range of 25 to 90℃.

3. Thermal Conductivity

The thermal conductivity of a glass is the rate of heat flow per unit area under existence of a temperature gradient in the glass. Glass is a poor conductor of heat and this property is inherent in the random structure of glass. The thermal conductivity of glasses ranges from 0.0042 to 0.0126 J/cm·s℃. They can be calculated according to the RATCLIFFE oxide factors from the chemical analysis of the glass.

The thermal conductivity of glasses decreases with decreasing temperature in contrast to crystals. The thermal conductivity is more influenced by the structure of a glass than by its chemical nature. It responds strongly to defects and heterogeneities in the structure. The free path of a phonon as an unit of vibrational thermal energy in a glass is much smaller than that in a crystal, because of the lack of long range order in the glass. Glasses have much lower thermal conductivities than crystals.

Selected from "Process Mineralogy of Ceramic Materials", W. Baumgart, A. C. Dunham, G. C. Amstutz, Heidelberg and Hull, 1984

Words and Expressions

1. thermal conductivity 热传导率
2. additivity [ædi'tiviti] *n*.加和性
3. be attributed to 归因于
4. asymmetry [ei'simitri] *n*.不对称性
5. quote [kwout] *v*.引用，举证
6. sealing glass 封结玻璃
7. setting point 固化点
8. strain point 应变点
9. inherent [in'hiərənt] *a*.固有的
10. heterogeneity [hetərədʒi'ni:iti] *n*.异质，不同成分

11. phonon [ˈfounɔn] *n*. 声子
12. in contrast to 与……比较

Notes

① Glasses cooled at various rates from above the annealing point will differ in density with the more rapidly cooled glasses having a lower density. 全句译作：玻璃在退火点以上的温度下以不同的速率冷却具有不同的密度，冷却速率越快，密度越低。

② Glass technologists have determined empirically for a certain composition field how additions or substitutions affect the different properties of a glass. How 引导的宾语从句。全句译作：玻璃工艺学家根据经验在某些组成范围内确定了添加剂或替代物对于玻璃各种性能的影响。

Exercises

1. Put the following Chinese into English.

热历史	比热	热膨胀系数	软化范围
转变温度	退火玻璃	不完整的配位	阴离子位空穴

2. Answer the following question according to the text.

   How to define setting point of a glass?

   How to define transformation range of a glass?

   How to define strain point of a glass?

   How to calculate the expansion coefficient of a glass?

3. Read the text and the reading material and complete the following table.

Glass Properties	Definition
Density	
Thermal expansion	
Thermal conductivity	
Hardness	
Strength	

Reading Material 15

Glass Properties

1. Hardness

Glass is generally placed between apatite and quartz on MOHS hardness scale. The mean value is 6.5. A few heavy lead glasses are softer than apatite, some boro-silicate glasses are slightly harder than quartz. Glasses are brittle in a macroscopic scale, but they can flow under shear stresses in a microscopic scale. The flow and the mutual compatibility of glasses makes it impossible to compare the hardness of glasses among themselves by the scratch test. Abrasion is not only a matter of the structure, but also involves mechano-chemistry. The most promising tool for studying the hardness of crystalline and amorphous solids seems to be the indentor. Hardness is a property closely related to the mechanical strength of a glass and to its low temperature viscosity. The different experimental ways for testing the hardness of glasses have been compiled by MOREY.

2. Strength

It is well known that the measured mechanical strength of glass is much lower than the theoretical strength. A great deal of work has been done in attempting both to explain this discrepancy and to bring the practical strength near to the theoretical limit. GRIFFITH put forward the theory that the difference was largely due to minute cracks acting as stress concentrators.

It is not possible to state definite strength values because of the brittle behaviour of glass and the effect of flaws or defects which are created on glass surfaces in the process of manufacture or in use. Most glasses show a reduction of strength with increasing temperature, except glasses with higher silica content. Generally, the high lead glasses have the weakest strength and the alumino-silicate glasses the highest. All other glasses must be considered approximately equal in strength.

3. Chemical Stability

The chemical durability of silicate glasses results from the inert nature of silica itself. Water and acids extract the alkali oxides at the surface, but have little effect on silica except to weaken its structure. Alkaline solutions or hydrofluoric acid attack all constituents including silica. All types of glasses are affected in some degree by such agents as water, acids, alkalies, and salt solution. It is suggested that two types of reaction may occur when a liquid attacks a glass: ion exchange and network breakdown. One or the other process will predominate with rates and duration of attack.

Moisture attack of glass surfaces occurs under atmospheric conditions in humid environments. Water vapour combines with the chemical constituents of the glass forming visible reaction products that appear on the surface as either a light haze or a heavy accumulation. This type of surface activity is described in literature as scaling and staining of glass. Deterioration of the surface is due to solvent action between the condensed moisture and the alkali that has migrated to the surface from the glass network.

4. Optical Properties

The refractive index depends upon the wavelength of light, the density, temperature, thermal history, stress, and composition of the glass. The change of index with wavelength is called dispersion. It is because of this change that the various colours are dispersed by a prism. Glasses of higher refractive index have greater dispersion, the higher the index, the more the dispersion tends to increase with decreasing wavelength. Glasses with a relatively low ABBE value are called optical flints, with a relatively high ABBE value are called optical crowns.

The refractive index of a glass and its change with the composition and heat treatment are of primary importance for optical glasses, but it cannot be related directly to structural changes because the refractive index n_D depends upon two properties, the molar refractivity R and the molar volume V. R does not give information on structural details, because it integrates over the whole system. For most glasses the refractive index increases with increasing temperature up to the softening range. Above this range the volume of glasses expands more rapidly on heating and the refractive index of all glasses decreases.

5. Electrical Nature of Glass

When light, which is considered an electromagnetic vibration with surrounding electric fields, enters a metal it is immediately stopped on its way by the conduction of the metal. The waves connot maintain themselves because their electrical components are altered by the free electrons of the metal. Metal cannot support an electrical potential, they tend to equalise such potential by free electron conduction. Glasses do not have free electrons because of their bonding nature. Their electrons are bound within the solid structure of their ions or atoms. They connot move freely and, therefore, do not equalise an electrical current.

The electrical nature of glass which lacks electronic conductivity is such that it can support electric potential without free electron movement. Because the electrons are tightly held to positions within the structure by the type of bonding in glass, they cannot move greater distances to neutralize the electrical nature of light. Basically, there are no interactions of a permanent nature between the electric components of the mass and the light. Thus, alteration of light is minor and the glass is transparent. The transparency is explained by two properties: first, it has no surface of internal structure which give reflection, refraction, or scattering and, second, it has no free electrons which can interact with the electromagnetic nature of wave motion including visible light.

Many glasses are electrolytic conductors at elevated temperatures and they behave like an aqueous solution of an electrolyte at room temperature. At sufficiently high temperatures the O^{2-} ions in glasses and crystalline oxides become mobile and carry electrical charges. The transfer of O^{2-} ions from one state of polarization to another is a characteristic process of acid-base reactions. In silicates, the acid-base transition consists of the breaking of an oxygen bridge (strongly polarized O^{2-}) and the formation of a pair of more polarizable nonbridging O^{2-} ions. The bridging O^{2-} which are exposed to two Si^{4+} ions are bound more tightly and, therefore, they are less polarizable than the nonbridging ones. The stability of the O^{2-} ions in a glass can be measured by a galvanic cell and compared with the stability of O^{2-} ions in other systems at the same temperature. The polarizability of the O^{2-} ion can be used as a measure of the basicity of an oxide on the basis of comparison with related glasses.

Electrical conductivity of glass

Glasses are electrolytic conductors at all temperatures, but a tremendous change in resistance occurs when the temperature of the glass changes. From 25 to 1200℃ the resistivity may change from 10^{19} ohms to 1 ohm. Thus, at room temperature glass is a good electrical insulator while at high temperatures it becomes a good conductor. Specific resistance or resistivity is the resistance in ohms of a cm-cube measured across two opposite faces. Conductivity is the reciprocal of the specific resistance.

Dielectric properties

Alkali ions are an important factor in the relationship between dielectric properties and glass composition. They move about more easily inside the material than the other constituents. The structrue which the other constituents and these alkali ions assume determines the mobility of the alkalies. The dielectric constant is determined by the number of heavier ions and the crystalline phases, if present.

Selected from "Process Mineralogy of Ceramic Materials", W. Baumgart, A. C. Dunham, G. C. Amstutz, Heidelberg and Hull, 1984

Words and Expressions

1. apatite [ˈæpətait] *n.* 磷灰石
2. MOHS hardness scale 莫氏硬度表
3. indentor [inˈdentə] *n.* 压痕计
4. compile [kəmˈpail] *v.* 编纂
5. discrepancy [disˈkrepənsi] *n.* 不相符
6. stress concentrator 应力集中
7. ion exchange 离子交换
8. predominate [priˈdɔmineit] *v.* 掌握，支配
9. haze [heiz] *n.* 薄雾
10. optical flint 火石光学玻璃
11. optical crown 冕牌光学玻璃
12. equalise [iːˈkwɔlaiz] *v.* 使相等
13. electrolyte [iˈlektrəlait] *n.* 电解质
14. galvanic cell [gælˈvænik] 电流表
15. basicity [bəˈsisiti] *n.* 碱性度

Unit 16 Special Glass

1. Advanced Biomedical Materials Derived from Glasses

Since the discovery of Bioglass by Hench et al in early 1970s, various kinds of glasses and glass-ceramics have been found to bond to living bone, and some of them are already clinically used. For example, Bioglass in the system Na_2O-CaO-SiO_2-P_2O_5 is extensively used as periodontal implants, artificial middle ear bones etc. in U. S. A., because of its high bioactivity. Glass-ceramic A-W① containing apatite ($Ca_{10}(PO_4)_6(O,F_2)$) and wollastonite ($CaO \cdot SiO_2$) is extensively used as artificial vertebrae, intervertebral discs, iliac crests etc. in Japan, because of its high mechanical strength as well as high bioactivity. Over 5000 patients received glass-ceramic A-W as their bone substitutes during the last 3 years.

Even glass-ceramic A-W, however, can not substitute for highly loaded bones such as femoral and tibial bones, since its fracture toughness of 2.0 $Mpam^{1/2}$ at maximum. Some attempts have been made to reinforce the bioactive glasses and glass-ceramics with metal fibers, metal particles or ceramic particles. Even an apatite- and-wollastonite-containing glass-ceramic reinforced with $ZrO_2(Y_2O_3)$ particles, which shows highest toughness of 3.0 $Mpam^{1/2}$ among them, however, can not substitute for the highly loaded bones. Metallic materials coated with bioactive glasses and glass-ceramics can substitute for them. The coated layer is, however, not stable for a long period in the body environment.

Fundamental understanding of factors governing bioactivity of glasses and glass ceramics have been greatly progressed. This enable us to design novel tough bioactive materials such as bioactive metals and organic polymers by utilizing glasses.

It has been also shown that glasses and glass-ceramics can play an important role in hyperthermia treatment and radiotherapy of cancers. A chemically durable Y_2O_3-Al_2O_3-SiO_2 glass microsphere, which can be activated to β-emitter by neutron bombardment, is already clinically used for treatment of liver tumors in Canada. It was recently shown that ion implantation technique is useful for obtaining glasses for this purpose.

2. Materials for Hypertermia Treatment

Luderer et al first reported that a ferromagnetic glass-ceramic containing lithium ferrite ($LiFe_5O_8$) in a Al_2O_3-SiO_2-P_2O_5 glassy matrix is useful as thermoseeds② for hyperthermia treatment of cancer, since it heats the cancer locally by magnetic hysteresis loss under an alternately magnetic field, and cancer cells are destroyed above 43℃. Later the present authors showed that bioactive and ferromagnetic glass-ceramic containing magnetite (Fe_3O_4) in a CaO-SiO_2-based matrix is useful as the thermoseeds especially for bone cancers. Glass-ceramics capable to generate a heat more efficiently below 50℃ and to cease the generation above 50℃ are now being searched by choosing an appropriate ferromagnetic or ferromagnetic phase having Curie temperature around 50℃ as the crystalline phase③.

3. Materials for Radiotherapy

Ehrhardt et al first reported that a chemically durable Y_2O_3-Al_2O_3-SiO_2 glass is useful for radiotherapy of cancer. When microspheres 20 to 30μm in size of this glass are injected to liver tumor through the hepatic artery, after Y-89 in the glass is activated to β-emitter Y-90 with half-life time of 64. 1 hour by neutron bombardment, they are entrapped in the capillary bed of liver tumors and give large local radiation dose of the short-ranged, highly inonizing β-ray to the tumors, with little irradiation to neighboring organs④. The radioactive Y-90 is hardly released from the glass because of its high chemical durability. Radioactivity of the glass decays to a negligible level in 21 days because of short half-time of Y-90.

The short half-life for Y-90, however, may result in the substantial decay of radioactivity before the cancer treatment. P-31 with 100% natural abundance can be activated to β-emitter P-32 with a little longer half-life time of 14. 3 days by the neutron bombardment. The biological effectiveness of P-32 is about four times as large as that of Y-90. Preparation of a chemically durable glass with high P_2O_5 content is, however, difficult by the conventional melting technique.

Such glass could be prepared by ion-implantation technique. The silica glass implanted with P^+ ion by more than $1\times10^{17}/cm^2$ at 50 keV released appreciable amounts of the silicon and phosphorus into a pure water at 95℃, since the phosphorus was distributed up to the glass surface and oxidized there, giving maximum concentration at a depth of 50nm. The same glass implanted with P^+ ion by the same dose rate but at 200 keV, however, hardly released both the silicon and phosphorus, since the phosphorus was not distributed up to the glass surface, giving maximum concentration at a depth of 200 nm. This indicates that ion implantation at high energy can give a new kind of glass useful for radiotherapy of cancer.

Selected from "PROCEEDINGS OF ⅩⅤⅡ INTERNATIONAL CONGRESS ON GLASS VOL. 1 Invited Lectures", Gong Fangtian, International Academic Publishers, 1995

Words and Expressions

1. bioglass [ˈbaiəglɑːs] *n.* 生物玻璃
2. clinical [ˈklinikl] *a.* 临床的
3. bioactivity [baiəæktiviti] *n.* 生物活性
4. intervertebral disc [intəˈvəːtəbrəl disk] 脊椎骨间盘
5. iliac [ˈiliæk] *a.* 肠骨的
6. femoral [ˈfemərəl] *a.* 大腿骨的
7. tibial [ˈtibiəl] *a.* 胫骨的
8. hyperthermia [hipəˈθəːmiə] *a.* 高热症
9. radiotherapy [reidiouˈθerəpi] *n.* 放射线疗法
10. hysteresis [histəˈriːsis] *n.* 磁滞现象

11. β-emitter [imitə] β射线源
12. Lithium ferrite 铁酸锂

Notes

① Glass-ceramic A-W：磷灰石和钙灰石的微晶玻璃。
② thermoseeds：热弹。指文中 ferromagnetic glass-ceramic congtaining lithium ferrite 如同高热法治疗癌症的热弹。
③ Glass-ceramics capable to generate a heat more efficiently below 50℃ and to cease the generation above 50℃ are now being searched by choosing an appropriate ferromagnetic or ferromagnetic phase having Curic temperature around 50℃ as the crystalline phase：to cease the generation means to cease the generation of heat，Curic temperature：居里温度。
④ When microspheres 20 to 30μm in size of this glass are injected to liver tumor through the hepatic artery，after Y-89 in the glass is activated to β-emitter Y-90 with half-life time of 64.1 hour by neutron bombardment，they are entrapped in the capillary bed of liver tumors and give large local radiation dose of the short-ranged，highly inonizing β-ray to the tumors，with little irradiation to neighboring organs. When 和 after 引导的都是状语从句，they 是主语，以下有两个并列句。

Exercises

1. Put the following Chinese into English.

现代生物医学材料	人工中耳骨	载荷骨	断裂韧性
生物活性金属	玻璃微珠	中子轰击	离子植入技术
玻璃态构造	铁磁体微晶玻璃	磁场	半衰期

2. Put the underlined sentences into Chinese.
3. Complete the following table by filling in the appropriate contents

Glasses	Introduced by	Glass system	Usage
Biaglass			
Ferromagnetic glass-ceramic			
Glass microsphere			

Reading Material 16

Glasses for Electronic Applications

1. Introduction

Both oxide and non-oxide glasses have long played important roles in electronic applications as active and non-active components. Recently glass-like solids derived from oxide gels and metal-organic precursors are also used in photonic applications.

The most common definition of a glass is that it is a product of fusion which has solidified without crystallization. For this report, however, the word glass will not be limited to melt-derived disordered solids. It will include glass-like solids obtained from chemical precursors in solution at room temperature. These will include gel-based oxides, gel-based organically modified silicates, the so-called ORMOSILS, and metal organic derived amorphous covalent solids. The words electronic applications will include electrical as well as optical applications.

2. Electronic Conduction in Oxide Glasses

Approximately 30 years ago, it was discovered that transition metal oxides such as vanadium pentoxide and iron oxide are electronic conductors. The conductivity mechanism is termed a hopping process. It was soon shown that this process is primarily governed by short-range order and not by long-rang order. Thus, transition metal ions dispersed in a glassy matrix will provide electronic conduction so long as they exist in two valence states such as ferrous and ferric and they are sufficiently near one another. The theory for this process has been developed by N. F. Mott. Since the 1960's, many semiconducting oxide glasses have been discovered. Unlike covalent electrical resistivities, the lowest electrical resistivity at room temperature for these glasses is only about 100 ohm-cm. They are thus a special class of semi-insulators. For any applications involving the use of oxide glasses, ionic conduction can be a negative factor because of electrolysis effects under an electric field. The use of these electronically conducting glasses is much preferred because conduction does not involve mass transport. These glasses in thin-film forms have been successfully used in various image tubes in which the image transfer element must have relatively high electrical resistivity and non-ionic conduction. Typical examples are V_2O_5-P_2O_5, Fe_2O_3-P_2O_5 and silicates containing transition metal and, because of their relatively high activation energy for conduction, can be fairly good infrared detecting solids.

3. Electronic Conduction in Chalcogenide Glasses

The most common non-oxide inorganic glasses are the so-called chalcogenides. These are mainly based on sulfur and selenium as glass-formers. Unlike the semiconducting oxide glasses, which are ionic, these glasses are covalent semiconductors, or really covalent semi-insulators since their lowest room-temperature resistivity are also around 100 ohm-cm. These glasses are also photoconductive. Their high resistivity, photoconductivity, ease of fabrication and good chemical durability make them ideal for use as the optical elements in copying machines. Perhaps, however, these glasses are best known for their electrical switching behaviors through the pioneering work of Stanford Ovshinsky. Under applied electric field, these glasses initially would show ohmic behavior. However, when the field reaches some critical value, the normally high resistivity sample would rapidly switch over to become a conductive element. This is known as threshold switching. Depending on the chemical composition of the glass, some would exhibit non-reversible behavior after switching. These are known as memory switches. The threshold switch is believed to be the result of a form of dielectric breakdown whereas the memory switch is probably due to some form of phase transformation. These glasses have been shown to be radiation resistant. Thin films form of these chalcogenide glasses are used in electronic calculators and copying machines.

4. Secondary Emission and Microchannel Plates

Another interesting device which makes use of the fabricability of glasses, and their secondary electron emission is the so-called microchannel plate. When a solid surface is bombarded in a vacuum by high energy electrons, secondary electrons are emitted. The yield of secondaries is typically two to three for each primary. The secondaries can also be accelerated by an electrical potential to give new secondaries. Thus if the device is a glass tube under an electric field, an electron multiplier is formed.

A single glass tube multiplier operates in the following way: Primary electrons from a photo-cathode impinges on the inner surface of the tube and generates secondaries. One electron can create as many as 10^6 output electrons on the far right. The tube is typically based on a lead silicate glass. The surface of the glass is reduced in hydrogen to produce lead globules, partially contacting one another. This then permits the replenishment of electrons from the depletion due to the emission of secondaries and the low electronic conductivities required for the operation.

In the fabrication process for MCP's glass rods of poor acid resistance are placed inside lead glass tubes and drawn down. The drawn tube-rod pairs are then packed and sintered to form large composite rods. Thin elements are then sliced to form discs and the central rod etched away with acids. The multichannel pale is then reduced in hydrogen gas to cause the onset of small electronic conduction through the small clusters of lead atoms formed. Microchannel plates have been successfully developed into the form of goggles for night vision devices. The uniqueness of glass is very clearly illustrated here. After all, how many materials are easily fabricated into microchannel plates which must also have the correct electronic conductivity as well as an acceptable secondary emission coefficient.

5. Glass-Ceramics

Glass-ceramics are fairly widely used in electronic packaging because of their ease of fabrication, vacuum tightness, chemical durability, mechanical strength and high electrical resistivity. Perhaps the most ingenious use of glass ceramics is in the chemical machining of glass to form components in various electronic devices. In this process, a glass is first melted to contain Ce^{3+} ions and Ag^{+} ions. A sample is then selectively masked and exposed to UV radiation. The Ce^{3+} ions in the exposed part of the glass are oxidized by radiation. The ejected electrons are captured by the surrounding silver ions to form silver atoms. The silver atoms so formed aggregate to form silver clusters which become nucleating agents. On heat treatment, the exposed parts of the glass are nucleated and crystallized. The unexposed party remained glassy. The crystallized regions can then be preferentially removed by etching with acids. Depending on the mask used, very fine patterns can be formed.

Selected from CERAMIC TRANSACTIONS VOLUME 20 "Glass for Electronic Application",
K. M. Nair, The American Ceramic Society, Inc., 1991

Words and Expressions

1. oxide gel [ɔksaid gel] *n.* 氧化物胶体
2. precursor [ˌpriːˈkəːsə] *n.* 前驱物
3. photonics [foutəˈniks] *n.* 光子学
4. vanadium pentoxide [vəˈneidiəm penˈtɔksaid] *n.* 五氧化二钒
5. electrical resistivity 电阻
6. chalcogenide [kælˈkɔgnaid] *n.* 硫属化物
7. photoconductive [ˌfoutəˈkəndʌktiv] *n.* 光电导的
8. memory switch [meməri switʃ] *n.* 记忆开关
9. microchannel plate [maikrəˈtʃanəl pleit] *n.* 微通道板
10. electron multiplier [ˈilektrɔn mʌltiplaiə] *n.* 电子放大器
11. globules [ˈglɔbjuːl] *n.* 液滴，水珠
12. replenishment [riˈpleniʃmənt] *n.* 补充
13. depletion [diˈpliːʃən] *n.* 耗尽
14. ingenious [inˈdʒiːnjuəs] *a.* 有独创性的，巧妙的

Unit 17 Glass Ceramics

1. Introduction

The emergence of synthetic ceramics as a prominent class of materials with a unique combination of properties has been an important part of the materials-science scene over the past 20 years. These high-technology ceramics have varied applications in areas utilizing their exceptional mechanical, thermal, optical, magnetic or electronic properties. A notable development of the 1970s was that of Si-based ceramics as high-temperature engineering solids. More recently the zirconia-based ceramics have evolved as a class of material with significant improvements in fracture-toughness. In the 1980s we are on the threshold of development of ceramic-matrix composites with the promise of overcoming major limitations in engineering design with brittle ceramics and the development of novel properties unattainable with monolithic microstructures①. Throughout this period there have been significant but less well-publicized developments in the field of glass-ceramics and glasses. It is the purpose of this publication to review selected topics within this important area of materials science.

2. Devitrification

Glass-ceramics are derived from the controlled crystallization of glasses to give a material consisting of one or more crystal phases plus some residual glass depending on the starting composition and the heat treatment given.

During the crystallization process, molecular rearrangements occur to produce the appropriate crystalline structures. These structures are often themselves metastable polymorphs which under further heat treatment can transform to the thermodynamically stable crystal phases. These molecular rearrangements present a changing environment for the various nuclei in the glass and MAS NMR② provides a technique for observing these various environments and following the crystallization process.

Several papers have been published in which the glassy and crystalline environments have been compared.

3. Volume Nucleation in Silicate Glass

The last twenty-five years or so have seen steady advances in the science and technology of glass-ceramics, materials prepared by the controlled crystallization of glass. Peter McMillan made many outstanding contributions to these advances and the publication of the first edition of his new classic textbook in 1964 remains a landmark in the development of the field.

The preparation of a glass-ceramic involves several stages. First, a glass is melted and formed into the appropriate shape. The glass article is then given a heat treatment schedule to nucleate and grow crystals in its volume until a material with the desired degree of crystallinity is produced. The kinetics of crystal nucleation and growth are thus critical in determining those compositions which can be cored into glasses reasonable stable towards devitrification, and which subsequently can be economically converted into fine-grained glass-ceramics by suitable heat treatment.

This chapter is concerned with crystal nucleation in glass, although no attempt is made to present a comprehensive discussion of the whole subject. Rather, certain topics, which are believed to be of particular interest, are highlighted. Throughout, the emphasis is on studies of simple silicate systems involving quantitative measurements of volume nucleation kinetics. However, such studies are considered helpful in identifying the various factors influencing nucleation behaviour in glasses in general. Moreover, these factors also apply to the more complex compositions used in glass-ceramic manufacture.

After a general outline of the relevant theories, experimental studies of volume nucleation in various systems, in which the crystallizing phase has the same composition as the parent glass, are discussed. Both steady state and non-steady state nucleation are considered. The results form a remarkably consistent pattern and indicate that the nucleation in these systems is predominantly homogeneous. The more complex case when the crystallizing phase has a different composition from that of the parent glass is then discussed. Studies of heterogeneous nucleation on metallic particles and the roles of non-metallic nucleation agents are described. Finally, recent investigations of the effects of amorphous phase separation on crystal nucleation kinetics are reviewed.

Selected from GLASSES AND GLASS-CERAMICS, M. H. Lewis, Chapman and Hall, 1988

Words and Expressions

1. unattainable [ʌnə'teinəbl] *a*. 不能获得的，难以达到的
2. devitrification [diːvitrifi'keiʃən] *n*. 失透，析晶
3. metastable [metə'steibl] *a*. 亚稳的
4. polymorph ['pɔlimɔːf] *n*. 同质多形体
5. landmark ['lændmɑːk] *n*. 里程碑

Notes

① In the 1980s we are on the threshold of development of ceramic-matrix composites with the promise of overcoming major limitations in engineering design with brittle ceramics and the development of novel properties unattainable with monolithic microstructures: threshold 后接两个 development，指两个关键时刻，即 development of ceramic-matrix composites and the development of novel properties. with the promise of overcoming major limitations in engineering design with brittle ceramics 修饰 composites. unattainable with monolithic microstructures 修饰 novel properties。

② MAS NMR：magic-angle-spinning nuclear magnetic resonance 幻角自旋核磁共振。

Exercises

1. Translate the underlined passage in text into Chinese.
2. Translate the following phrases into English.

氧化硅陶瓷	氧化锆陶瓷	断裂韧性	热力学稳定晶相
体积核化	受控结晶	母体玻璃	异质核化

Reading Material 17

US5591682 Low expansion transparent glass-ceramic

Applicant (s)：Kabushiki Kaisya Ohara，Japan

News，Profiles，Stocks and More about this company

Issued/Filed Dates：Jan. 7，1997 / June 2，1995 CC

Application Number：US1995000458345

IPC Class：C03C 10/14；

ECLA Code：C03C10/00E2；

Class：Current：501/004；501/007；501/063；501/070；

Original：501/004；501/007；501/063；501/070；

Field of Search：501/4，7，63，70

Priority Number (s)：Sept. 13，1994 JP1994000244683

Oct. 26，1994 JP1994000285920

Legal Status：Gazette date Code Description (remarks) List all possible codes for US

Nov. 18，1997 CC Certificate of correction

Jan. 7，1997 A Patent

June 2，1995 AE Application data

June 2，1995 AS02 Assignment of assignor's interest (KABUSHIKI KAISHA OHARA 1-15-30，OYAMA，SAGAMIHARA-SHI KANAGAWA-KEN，JAPAN * GOTO，NAOYUKI：19950509)

Oct. 26，1994 AA Priority

Abstract：A low expansion glass-ceramic which has a coefficient of thermal expansion ($\alpha \times 10^{-7}$/℃.) within the range of from -5 to +5 within a temperature range of from −60℃. to +160℃.，has a remarkably reduced variation of 10 ppm or below in relative length of. DELTA. 1/1，has an excellent optical homogeneity owing to reduced melting temperature in the base glass，and has an improved transparency is obtained by restricting the ratio in weight of P_2O_5 to SiO_2 within the range of from 0.08 to 0.20，and adding Li_2O，MgO，ZnO，CaO and BaO of specific content ranges as essential ingredients in a base glass of a SiO_2-P_2O_5-Al_2O_3-Li_2O system containing TiO_2 and ZrO_2 as nucleating agents，and As_2O_3 as an optional ingredient.

Attorney, Agent, or Firm: Hedman, Gibson & Costigan, P. C. ;

Primary/Assistant Examiners: Group; Karl;

Family: Patent Issued Filed Title

US5591682 Jan. 7, 1997 June 2, 1995 Low expansion transparent glass-ceramic

JP8133783A2 May 28, 1996 Oct. 26, 1994 LOW EXPANSION TRANSPARENT GLASS CERAMIC

JP2668057B2 Oct. 27, 1997 Oct. 26, 1994 TEIBOCHOTOMEIGARASUSERAMITSUKUSU

3 family members shown above

U. S. References: Show the 5 patents that reference this one Patent Issued Inventor (s) Applicant (s) Title

US3928229 12/1975 Neuroth Janaer Glaswerk Schott & Gen. Transparent glass-ceramic laserable articles containing neodymium

US4755488 7/1988 Nagashima Nippon Sheet Glass Co. , Ltd. Glass-ceramic article

US4835121 5/1989 Shibuya et al. Nippon Electric Glass Company, Limited Infrared transparent glass ceramic articles with beta-quarts solid solution crystals without any other crystals

US5064460 11 /1991 Aitken Corning Incorporated Blue transparent glass-ceramic articles

US5336643 8 /1994 Goto et al. Kabushiki Kaisha Ohara Low expansion transparent crystallized glass-ceramic

CLAIMS:

What is claimed is:

1. A low expansion transparent glass-ceramic formed by subjecting to heat treatment a glass consisting in weight percent of: $SiO_2+P_2O_5$ 55%～70% in which SiO_2 50%～62%, P_2O_5 6%～10%, Al_2O_3 22%～26%, Li_2O 3%～5%, MgO 0.6%～1%, ZnO 0.5%～2%, CaO 0.3%～4%, BaO 0.5%～4%, TiO_2 1%～4%, ZrO_2 1%～4%, As_2O_3 0～2%. wherein the ratio in weight of P_2O_5 to SiO_2 is between 0.08 and 0.02, said glass-ceramic containing β-quartz solid solution as a main crystalline phase, said glass-ceramic having a coefficient of thermal expansion of $0\pm5\times10^{-7}$/°C. within a temperature range of from −60℃. to+160℃. , and a maximal variation of . DELTA. 1/1 curve (variation in relative length) of 10ppm or less.

2. A low expansion transparent glass-ceramic as defined in claim 1, consisting in weight percent of: $SiO_2+P_2O_5$ 56%～65% in which SiO_2 50%～60% P_2O_5 6%～10% Al_2O_3 22%～26% Li_2O+MgO+ZnO 4.5%～6.5% in which Li_2O 3%～5% MgO 0.6%～2% ZnO 0.5%～2% CaO+BaO 1%～5% in which CaO 0.3%～4% BaO 0.5%～3% TiO_2+ZrO_2 2.5%～5% in which TiO_2 1%～4% ZrO_2 1%～4% As_2O_3 0～2%. where in a ratio in weight of P_2O_5 to SiO_2 is between 0.10 and 0.17.

3. A low expansion transparent glass-ceramic as defined in claim 1, consisting in weight percent of: $SiO_2+P_2O_5$ 60%～65% in which SiO_2 53%～57% P_2O_5 7%～9% Al_2O_3 23%～25% Li_2O+MgO+ZnO 5.0%～6.0% in which Li_2O 3.7%～4.5% MgO 0.7%～1.4% ZnO 0.5%～1.5% CaO+BaO 1.5%～2.5% in which CaO 0.5%～2.5% BaO 0.5%～

1.5% TiO_2 + ZrO_2 3.5%～5.0% in which TiO_2 1.5% ～3.0% ZrO_2 1.0%～2.5% As_2O_3 0～2%. where in a ratio in weight of P_2O_5 to SiO_2 is between 0.13 and 0.17.

4. A low expansion transparent glass-ceramic as defined in claim 1 which is prepared by melting, forming, and annealing said glass raw material, and thereafter subjecting to heat treatment the resulting base glass under such heat-treating conditions that the nucleation temperature is between 650℃. and 750℃., and the crystallization temperature is between 750℃. and 840℃.

Background/Summary:

BACKGROUND OF THE INVENTION

1. Field of the Invention

2. Description of the Related Art

Words and Expressions

1. Applicant (s) *n.* 专利申请人
2. News, Profiles, Stocks *n.* 信息披露，公司概况，股份
3. Issued/Filed Dates *n.* 公布/建档日期
4. Application Number *n.* 申请号
5. IPC Class *n.* 国际专利分类
6. Class: Current *n.* 类别：当前
7. Field of Search *n.* 搜索领域
8. Priority Number *n.* 优先号
9. Legal Status: Gazette date Code *n.* 法定状态：公布日期编码
10. Certificate of correction *n.* 更正证书
11. Assignment of assignor's interest *n.* 专利转让人权益委托

PART Ⅳ CEMENT AND CONCRETE

Unit 18 Portland Cement

Portland cement is made by heating a mixture of limestone and clay, or other materials of similar bulk composition and sufficient reactivity, ultimately to a temperature of about 1450℃. Partial fusion occurs, and nodules of clinker are produced. The clinker is mixed with a few per cent of calcium sulfate and finely ground, to make the cement. The calcium sulfate controls the rate of set and influences the rate of strength development. It is commonly described as gypsum, but this may be partly or wholly replaced by other forms of calcium sulfate. Some specifications allow the addition of other materials at the grinding stage. The clinker typically has a composition in the region of 67% CaO, 22% SiO_2, 5% Al_2O_3, 3% Fe_2O_3 and 3% other components, and normally contains four major phases, called alite, belite, aluminate and ferrite. Several other phases, such as alkali sulfates and calcium oxide are normally present in minor amounts. Hardening results from reactions between the major phases and water.

Alite is the most important constituent of all normal Portland cement clinkers, of which it constitutes 50%~70%. It is tricalcium silicate (Ca_3SiO_5) modified in composition and crystal structure by ionic substitutions. It reacts relatively quickly with water, and in normal Portland cements is the most important of the constituent phases for strength development; at ages up to 28 days, it is by far the most important.

Belite constitutes 15%~30% of normal Portland cement clinkers. It is dicalcium silicate (Ca_2SiO_4) modified by ionic substitutions and normally present wholly or largely as the β polymorph. It reacts slowly with water, thus contributing little to the strength during the first 28 days. But substantially to the further increase in strength that occurs at later ages. By one year, the strengths obtainable from pure alite and pure belite are about the same under comparable conditions.

Aluminate constitutes 5%~10% of most normal Portland cement clinkers. It is tricalcium aluminate ($Ca_3Al_2O_6$), substantially modified in composition and sometimes also in structure by ionic substitutions. It reacts rapidly with water, and cause undesirably rapid setting unless a setcontrolling agent, usually gypsum, is added.

Ferrite makes up 5%~15% of normal Portland cement clinkers. It is tetracalcium aluminoferrite (Ca_2AlFeO_5), substantially modified in composition by variation in Al/Fe ratio and ionic substitutions. The rate at which it reacts with water appears to be somewhat variable, perhaps due to differences in composition or other characteristics, but in general is high initially and low or very low at later ages[①].

Types of Portland Cement

The great majority of Portland cements made throughout the world are designed for general constructional use. The standard specifications with which such cements must comply are similar, but not identical, in all countries and various names are used to define the material, such as Class 42.5 Portland cement in current European and British standards (42.5 is the minimum 28-days compressive strength in MPa), Type Ⅰ and Ⅱ Portland cement in the ASTM (American Society for Testing and Materials) specifications used in the USA, or Ordinary Portland Cement (OPC) in former British standards[②]. Throughout this book, the term 'ordinary' Portland cements is used to distinguish such general-purpose cements from other types of Portland cement, which are made in smaller quantities for special purposes.

Standard specifications are, in general, based partly on chemical composition or physical properties such as specific surface area, and partly on performance tests, such as setting time or compressive strength developed under standard conditions. The content of MgO is usually limited to 4%~5%, because quantities of this component in excess of about 2% can occur as periclase (magnesium oxide), which through slow reaction with water can cause destructive expansion of hardened concrete. Free lime (calcium oxide) can behave similarly. Excessive contents of SO_3 can also cause expansion, and upper limits, typically 3.5% for ordinary Portland cements, are usually imposed. Alkalis (K_2O and Na_2O) can undergo expansive reactions with certain aggregates, and some specifications limit the content, e.g. to 0.6% equivalent Na_2O ($Na_2O + 0.66\ K_2O$). Other upper limits of composition widely used in specifications relate to matter insoluble in dilute acid, and loss ignition. Many other minor components are limited in content by their effects on the manufacturing process, or the properties, or both, and in some cases the limits are defined in specifications.

Rapid-hardening Portland cements have been produced in various ways, such as varying the composition to increase the alite content, finer grinding of the clinker, and improvements in the manufacturing process, e.g. finer grinding or better mixing of the raw materials. The alite contents of Portland cements have increased steadily over the one and a half centuries during which the latter have been produced, and many cements that would be considered ordinary today would have been described as rapid hardening only a few decades ago[③]. In ASTM specifications, rapid-hardening Portland cements are called high early strength or Type Ⅲ cements. For both ordinary and rapid-hardening cements, both lower and upper limits may be imposed on strength at 28 days, upper limits being a safeguard against poor durability resulting from the use of inadequate cement contents in concrete[④].

Destructive expansion from reaction with sulfates can occur not only if the latter are present in excessive proportion in the cement, but also from attack on concrete by sulfate solutions. The reaction involves the Al_2O_3-containing phases in the hardened cement, and in sulfate-resisting Portland cements its effects are reduced by decreasing the proportion of the aluminate phase, sometimes to zero. This is achieved by decreasing the ratio of Al_2O_3 to Fe_2O_3 in the raw materials. In the USA, sulfate-resisting Portland cements are called Type

Ⅴ cements.

White Portland cements are made by increasing the ratio of Al_2O_3 to Fe_2O_3, and thus represent the opposite extreme in composition to sulfate-resisting Portland cements. The normal, dark colour of Portland cement is due to the ferrite, formation of which in a white cement must thus be avoided. It is impracticable to employ raw materials that are completely free from Fe_2O_3 and other components, such as Mn_2O_3, that contribute to the colour. The effects of these components are therefore usually minimized by producing the clinker under slightly reducing conditions and by rapid quenching. In addition to alite, belite and aluminate, some glass may be formed.

The reaction of Portland cement with water is exothermic, and while this can be an advantage under some conditions because it accelerates hardening, it is a disadvantage under others, such as in the construction of large dams or in the lining of oil wells, when a cement slurry has to be pumped over a large distance under pressure and sometimes at a high temperature. Slower heat evolution can be achieved by coarser grinding, and decreased total heat evolution by lowering the contents of alite and aluminate. The ASTM specifications include definitions of a Type Ⅱ or 'moderate heat of hardening' cement, and a more extreme Type Ⅳ or 'low heat' cement. The Type Ⅱ cement is also suitable for conditions exposed to moderate sulfate attack, and is widely used in general construction work. Heating evolution can also be decreased by partially replacing the cement by flyash (pulverized fuel ash; pfa) or other materials, and this is today a widely used solution. The specialized requirements of oil well cements are discussed in Section 11. 8.

Selected from "Cement Chemistry." H. F. W. Talor, 2nd Edition. Thomas Talford Publ. 1997

Words and Expressions

1. Portland Cement 波特兰水泥，普通水泥，硅酸盐水泥
2. clinker [ˈkliŋkə] *n.* 熟料
3. calcium sulfate [ˈkælsiəm ˈsʌlfeit] 硫酸钙
4. gypsum [ˈdʒipsəm] *n.* 石膏
5. alite [ˈeilait] *n.* 阿利特，硅酸三钙石 (C_3A)
6. belite [ˈbiːlait] *n.* 比利特，二钙硅酸盐 (C_2S)
7. ferrite [ˈferait] *n.* 菲利特，铁铝酸四钙
8. tricalcium silicate 硅酸三钙
9. standard specification 标准规范
10. comply [kəmˈplai] *vt.* 遵照，根据
11. specific surface area 比表面积
12. setting time 凝结时间
13. compressive strength 抗压强度
14. periclase [ˈperikleis] *n.* 方镁石
15. destructive expansion 破坏性膨胀

16. concrete [ˈkɔnkriːt] *n*. 混凝土
17. aggregate [ˈægrigeit] *n*. 骨料 *vt*. 集结，使聚集
18. exothermic [ˌeksəuˈθəːmik] *a*. 放热的

Notes

① at which 引导的定语从句修饰主语 the rate，谓语有两个 appears 和 is，为 but 连接的并列复合句，appears to be 是科技文章中常用的一种表达方式，比较婉转和客观属于这类的词还有 seem、look 等。参考译文：非利特与水的反应显得有些易变，也许是由于组成和其它特征的不同，但是总的说来前期速度很高而后期低甚至很低。

② 此句较长为带有一个定语从句的用 and 连接的并列复合句。第一句到 in all countries。参考译文：在所有国家中波特兰水泥必须遵照的标准是相似的，但是不完全等同，使用各种名字来定义。例如在现行的欧洲和英国共同标准中称为 42.5 号波特兰水泥（42.5 是用 MPa 表示的 28 天抗压强度的最小值），用在美国的是 ASTM 标准（美国测试与材料学会）的Ⅰ号与Ⅱ号水泥，如同原先的英国标准则命名为普通波特兰水泥（OPC）。

③ 这是用 and 连接的并列复合句，前半句中 during which 引导的定语从句修饰 centurie，后半句有一个 that 引导的定语从句修饰 many cements。从上下文看，文中的 the latter 指的是 rapid hardening Portland cement，对应的 the former 应该是前面提到的 ordinary Portland cements。后半句中谓语部分多了一个 would，这是科技文章较常用的虚拟语气，比较婉转、客观。参考译文：在过去的一个半世纪中波特兰水泥中的阿利特含量稳定上升，在这期间制造了快硬波特兰水泥，在今天看来很普通的许多种类水泥，仅在几十年以前被当作快硬水泥。

④ 本句中 upper limits 为 being 开始的现在分词短语的逻辑主语这种形式往往用来使句子意思更完整。参考译文：对普通水泥与快硬水泥来说，都规定了 28 天强度的上限与下限；上限是一种保护措施，防止混凝土中掺加水泥量不当引起的耐久性差。

Exercises

1. Translate the following into Chinese or English.

   partial fusion　gypsum　alkali sulfate　ionic substitution　standard specification
   destructive expansion　sulfate-resisting　reducing condition　lining of oil wells
   cement slurry　pulverized fuel ash
   波特兰水泥　熟料　阿利特　贝利特　非利特　比表面积　凝固时间　抗压强度
   混凝土　骨料　快硬水泥　快速淬冷　放热反应

2. Answer the following questions in full sentences.

   ① What is alite? What important role does it play in normal Portland cement?
   ② Why should the contents of alkali be limited?
   ③ What measures can we take to accelerate the hardening of Portland cement?
   ④ In which case is the exothermic reaction of cement with water a disadvantage? How can we decrease its negative influence?

3. Translate the following into Chinese.

   Modern Portland cement originated in Britain in the nineteenth century when high temperatures were first used in the preparation of cements. The strongly cementitious calcium silicates, C_2S and C_3S were produced during the high temperature reactions

Reading Material 18

Manufacture of Portland Cement

Raw Materials and Fuel

The raw mix for making Portland cement clinker is generally obtained by blending a calcareous material, typically limestone, with a smaller amount of an argillaceous one, typically clay or shale. It may be necessary to include minor proportions of one or more corrective constituents, such as iron ore, bauxite or sand, to correct the bulk composition. On the other hand, some argillaceous limestone and marls have compositions near to that required, making it possible to use a blend of closely similar strata from the same quarry.

Many limestones contain significant amounts of minor components, either as substitutes in the calcite or in accessory phases, some of which are deleterious if present in amounts exceeding a few per cent (e. g. MgO, SrO), a few tenths of a per cent (e. g. P_2O_5, CaF_2, alkalis) or even less (some heavy metals).

Suitable shales and clays typically have compositions in the region of 55%~60% SiO_2, 15%~25% Al_2O_3 and 5%~10% Fe_2O_3, with smaller amounts of MgO, alkalis, H_2O and other components. Mineralogically, their main constitutes are clay minerals, finely divided quartz and, sometimes, iron oxides. In place of clays or shales, other types of siliceous rocks, such as schists or volcanic rocks of suitable compositions, are sometimes used.

Pulverized coal, oil, natural gas and lignite have all been widely used as fuels, but due to pressing environmental and economic requirements are increasingly being supplemented by waste materials. In addition to conserving non-renewable fossil fuels and in some cases lowering CO_2 emissions, the use of waste materials as fuels can provide a means of safe and environmentally acceptable disposal. The contribution of the fuel to the clinker composition must be taken into account, especially with coal or lignite, which produce significant quantities of ash broadly similar in composition to the argillaceous component. Some fuels also contribute sulfur.

The Dry Process

The raw materials first pass through a series of crushing, stockpiling, milling and blending stages, which yield an intimately mixed and dry raw meal, of which typically 85% passes through a 90 μm sieve. With automated, computer-controlled procedures, the LSF [lime saturation factor=$CaO/(2.8SiO_2+1.2Al_2O_3+0.65Fe_2O_3)$], SR[silica ratio=$SiO_2/(Al_2O_3+Fe_2O_3)$] and AR (alumina ratio=$Al_2O_3/Fe_2O_3$) can be maintained constant to standard deviations of 1%, 0.1 and 0.1, respectively.

The raw meal passes through a preheater and frequently also a precalciner before entering a rotary kiln. A preheater is a heat exchanger, usually of a type called a suspension preheater in which the moving powder is dispersed in a stream of hot gas coming from the kiln. Heat transfer takes place mainly in co-current; the raw material passes through the preheater in less than a minute, and leaves it at a temperature of about 800℃. These conditions are such that about 40% of the calcite is decarbonated. It is possible to introduce a proportion of the fuel into a preheater, with a corresponding reduction in the quantity fed to the kiln; a precalciner is a furnace chamber introduced into the preheater into which 50%～65% of the total amount of fuel is introduced, often with hot air ducted from the cooler. The fuel in a precalciner is burned at a relatively low temperature; heat transfer to the raw meal, which is almost entirely convective, is very efficient. The material has a residence time in the hottest zone of a few seconds and its exit temperature is about 900℃; 90%～95% of the calcite is decomposed. Ash from the fuel burned in the precalciner is effectively incorporated into the mix.

Because less heat is supplied to the kiln, precalcination allows the rate at which material can be passed through a kiln of given size to be greatly increased, thus saving on capital cost. Alternatively, the rate of providing heat can be reduced, which lengthens the life of the refractory lining.

The Rotary Kiln

The rotary kiln is a tube, sloping at 3%～4% from the horizontal and rotating at 1～4 rev/min, into which the material enters at the upper end then slides, rolls or flows counter to the hot gases produced by a flame at the lower or 'front' end. In a system employing a precalciner, the kiln is typically 50～100m long and its ratio of length to diameter is 10～15. The maximum material temperature, of about 1450℃, is reached near the front end of the kiln in the 'burning zone', also called the clinkering or sintering zone, in which the material spends 10～15 minutes. The kiln is lined with refractory bricks, of types that vary along its length in accordance with the varying gas and material temperatures. The bricks become coated with a layer of clinker, which plays an essential part in the insulation and in extending their life.

Nodules of clinker, typically 3～20 mm in diameter, are formed in a semi-solid state in the burning zone, and solidify completely on cooling, which begins in a short cooling zone within the kiln, and continues in a cooler. In modern plants, when the nodules leave the kiln, their internal temperatures are around 1350℃, but their surface temperatures are considerably lower.

Liquid or pulverized solid fuels are blown into the kiln through a nozzle with 'primary' air. Additional, 'secondary' air is drawn into the kiln through the clinker cooler. The flame in the rotary kiln must meet several requirements. The clinker must be correctly burned, so as to minimize its content of free lime, with the least expenditure of fuel. The ash from a solid fuel must be uniformly absorbed by the clinker. For normal Portland cements, the conditions must be sufficiently oxidizing that the iron is present in the cooled clinker almost entirely as Fe^{3+}; however, for white cements, mildly reducing conditions may be preferable. Proper flame control also extends the life of the refractory lining of the kiln. Computer-aided or fully automated control of kiln operating conditions is increasingly used.

Cooling and Grinding of Clinker

The clinker cooler is essentially a heat exchanger that extracts heat from the clinker for return to the system; also, a cooled clinker is more readily transported, ground or stored. Rapid cooling from the clinkering temperature down to 1100℃ produces a better quality clinker, and the clinker should be effectively air-quenched as soon as it leaves the burning zone. When the clinker enters the grinding mill, its temperature should preferably be below 1100℃.

To produce Portland cement, the clinker is ground together with gypsum. Portland cement clinker has a long storage life, and while it may be ground immediately, there are often good reasons for grinding it intermittently, and not necessarily in the same plant. Compositional and other variations in the clinker can be much reduced by using storage systems in which blending occurs. To make interground composite cements, widely varying proportions of granulated blastfurnace slag, flyash or other materials are added.

Selected from "Cement Chemistry." H. F. W. Taylor 2nd edition. Thomas Taylor Talford Publ. 1997

Words and Expressions

1. calcareous [kæl'kæriəs] *a.* 石灰质的
2. argillaceous [ɑ:dʒi'leiʃəs] *a.* 粘土质的
3. marl [mɑ:l] *n.* 灰泥，泥灰岩
5. accesary [ək'sesəri] *n.* 辅助设备；*a.* 附加的
6. schist [ʃist] *n.* 片岩
7. lignite ['lignait] *n.* 褐煤
8. stockpile ['stɔkpail] *n.* 储备，蕴藏量
9. standard deviation 标准偏差
10. decarbonate [di:'kɑ:bənait] *vt.* 去除二氧化碳
11. convective [kən'vektiv] *a.* 迁移的，传送性的
12. slope [sləup] *n.* 斜坡
13. expanditure [iks'penditʃə] *n.* 消费，支出
14. granulate ['grænjuleit] *vt.* 使粒化

Unit 19 Hydration of Portland Cement

The silicates and aluminates present in cement react with water to form products of hydration and in time, these set to a hard mass. The different anhydrous phases have very different cementitious properties, C_3S hydrates rapidly and develops high early strength whereas β-C_2S hardens more slowly. Hydration products of C_3A and C_4AF have very little strength. The hydration of commercial cement can be represented approximately by the summed hydration of the components. C_3S is the phase mainly responsible for the initial hardening; C_3S and β-C_2S give set cement and concrete its long time strength.

Hydration of cement is a complicated process and part of the difficulty in studying it is that the main products of hydration are either gelatinous or poorly crystalline, thus making conventional X-ray diffraction studies extremely difficult. The main product and the most important one for high strength is a poorly crystalline calcium silicate hydrate (C—S—H), sometimes called C—S—H gel or, incorrectly, tobermorite gel. The composition of this material is uncertain and is probably variable both in lime to silicate and in silica to water ratios; it may also contain Al^{3+}, Fe^{3+} and SO_4^{2-} ions. In addition to C—S—H gel, hardened cement contains unreacted clinker, $Ca(OH)_2$, aluminate hydrates, aluminosulphate hydrates and water.

Many of the physical and mechanical properties of hardened cement and concrete seem to depend on the physical structure of the hydration products on a colloidal scale, rather than on their chemical composition①. Advances in understanding the hydration processes are currently being made by using various techniques, including electron microscopy combined with microanalysis of the phases present. Hydration appears to involve at least two stages. First, a coating of C—S—H gel forms rapidly on the surface of the anhydrous cement particles. Second, this coating thickens by both growing outwards and eating into the anhydrous cement particles. The coatings subsequently begin to join up within a few hours and products stiffens or sets.

The water to cement ratio affects the properties of cement. Once cement paste has set its apparent volume stays approximately constant; this final volume increases with increasing water to cement ratio in the original mix. Set cement is porous and contains both very small water-filled holes, ~10 to 20Å across (gel pores), and much larger channels, ~1μm across (capillary pores). Interconnected capillary pores are mainly responsible for the permeability of set cement and its vulnerability to frost damage. The absence of interconnected capillary pores is clearly desirable. It may be attained after a sufficiently long time of moist curing, i. e. hydration in a moist atmosphere and by using a sufficiently low water to cement ratio. Thus, for water to cement ratios of ~0. 4, about three days are needed before the capillaries are no longer connected, whereas for a ratio of ~0. 7 at least one year is needed.

The problem of *flash set* is caused by the very rapid reaction between C_3A and water.

The C_3A appears to dissolve very rapidly, followed by precipitation of calcium aluminate hydrates, and is accompanied by much evolution of heat. Although this reaction is rapid, the mechanical properties of a cement that has undergone flash set are very poor. In practice, flash set are avoided by adding I to 2% gypsum to cement clinker. In a complex reaction, gypsum, in the presence of $Ca(OH)_2$, acts to retard the hydration of C_3A. Instead, aluminosulphate, $Ca_4Al_2(OH)_{12}SO_4 \cdot 6H_2O$, are formed, probably as a protective coating on the surface of the C_3A crystals.

There are several different anhydrous calcium silicates but only two, C_3S and β-C_2S, have cementitious properties suitable for use in hydraulic cements (i. e. they react with water to form an insoluble product which sets to form a rigid mass). The reasons for this are only poorly understood and there are probably several factors which affect cementing ability.

One feature that C_3S and β-C_2S have in common and which distinguishes them from other calcium silicates is their metastability. Below 670℃, β-C_2S is metastable relative to γ-C_2S. At temperatures below 1250℃, C_3S is metastable with respect to the combination $CaO+C_2S$. At room temperature, C_3S is shown as being metastable relative to β-C_2S+lime which, in turn, is metastable relative to γ-C_2S+lime②. Because C_3S and β-C_2S are metastable, the decrease in free energy on their hydration should be greater than for hydration of the corresponding stable phases, i. e. γ-C_2S+CaO and γ-C_2S, respectively③. This, of course, assumes that the products of hydration of β-C_2S and γ-C_2S have the same free energy. However, although C_3S and β-C_2S are thermodynamically metastable, it does not automatically follow that their hydration will be kinectically more rapid than that of the corresponding stable phases. There is an activation energy for hydration. ΔE, whose magnitude is governed by the ease of attack of water molecules on the anhydrous phase and is therefore related to the crystal structure of the anhydrous phase. It has been suggested that C_3S and, to a certain extent, β-C_2S have rather open crystal structures which may facilitate penetration and subsequent attack by water molecules at the surface of the crystals, thereby reducing ΔE for hydration of these phases④. Another factor which may reduce ΔE for hydration of C_3S is the presence in the crystal structure of CaO-like regions which may provide the initial points for attack by H_2O. The problem in comparing the cementing ability of two phases in terms of diagrams is that it is difficult to evaluate the various factors which may influence the values of their hydration activation energies⑤.

Particle size greatly affects hydration kinectics, because with a smaller particle size the surface area of the crystals is greater and so hydration, which is mainly a surface reaction, proceeds more rapidly. In practice, the economics of grinding the cement clinker to a finer size have to be balanced against the more rapid development of strength which is thereby obtained. For ordinary Portland cement in Britain, regulations require a minimum surface area of $225m^2 \cdot kg^{-1}$, although, in practice, $300m^2 \cdot kg^{-1}$ is a more typical value.

Selected from "Solid State Chemistry and Application". Authony. R. West. John Wiley&Sons Ltd. 1984

Words and Expressions

1. anhydrous [æn'haidrəs] *a*. 无水的
2. cementitious [siːmen'tiʃəs] *a*. 水泥质的
3. gelatinous [dʒə'lætinəs] *a*. 胶状的
4. tobermorite [təub'əmɔːrait] *n*. 水化硅酸钙($5CaO \cdot 6SiO_2 \cdot 5H_2O$)
5. aluminosulphate *n*. 硫酸铝，铝硫酸盐
6. vulnerability ['vʌlnerəbiliti] *n*. 弱点，要害
7. capillary pore 毛细孔
8. moist curing 湿养护
9. flash set 瞬凝
10. effringite ['efriŋdʒait] *n*. 钙矾石($Ca_6Al_2(SO_4)_3(OH)_{12} \cdot 26H_2O$)
11. monosulphate *n*. 单硫酸盐
12. assemblage [ə'semblidʒ] *n*. 汇集，组合

Notes

① 谓语为 seem，后面跟一个不定式是实质上的谓语，这是科技英语中经常用的一种表达形式，比较婉转与客观，类似的动词还有 appear、look 等。

② 本句中有一用 which 引导的定语从句，修饰 β-C_2S+lime。按照上下文，可以译作：相对于 β-C_2S+lime，C_3S 是亚稳定的，前者相对于 γ-C_2S+CaO 又是亚稳定的。Relative to 是相对于，与前面一句中的 with respect to 相似，后面都跟名词。

③ 这句的主句为比较句，主语为 the decrease in free energy，than 后面省略了被比较部分 the decrease in free energy，由于这两部分完全一样。

④ suggest 也是科技文章中常用的词，表示建议、启示、认为，为表示论者观点或讨论实验结果的一种常用形式。类似的动词，还有 assume，indicate，imply，deduce，follow，语气有不同，表示肯定程度的差异。参考译文：人们认为，C_3S 和 β-C_2S（一定程度上）具有相当开放的晶体结构，开放结构促进了水分子穿透晶体表面，随后促进了水分子对它的攻击，从而降低了这些晶相的水化能。

⑤ 主从复合句，that 引导的表语从句中又有一个定语从句。参考译文：用图比较二种相的胶凝能力存在着一个问题，即难于评价影响它们的水化活化能的各种因素。

Exercises

1. Translate the following expressions into Chinese or English.
   cementitious properties　silica to water ratio　unreacted clinker　microanalysis of phases　cement paste　vulnerability to frost damage　equilibrium assemblage　hydration kinetics
   水泥的水化　早期强度　后期强度　X 射线衍射　毛细孔　湿气养护　水灰比　速凝　放热　阻缓水化　胶凝能力　自由能　活化能　热力学上亚稳定的　颗粒尺寸
2. Translate the following into Chinese.
   The kinetics and mechanism of β-C_2S hydration are similar to those for C_3S, apart from the much lower rate of reaction, and as noted earlier, the products are similar apart from

the much smaller content of CH. Preparations appear to be more variable in reactivity than those of C_3S; this is partly attributable to differing stabilizers, but could also be due to differing amounts or natures of phases in intergranular spaces or exsolution lamellae.

3. Fill in the blanks with suitable words.

① C_3S hydrates______and develops______ while β-C_2S hardens______, C_3S is mainly responsible for______; both C_3S and β-C_2S make a great contribution to______of set cement and concrete.

② Many______properties of hardened cement and concrete depend not so much on______ as on______of the hydration products on a______scale, in turn they are affected by the ______ratio.

③ Below ______β-C_2S is metastable relative to______; below 1250℃ C_3S is______relative to______+______, in turn______+______is metastable relative to γ-C_2S+lime.

Reading Material 19

Reactivities of Clinker Phases

Effect of Major Compositional Variation

The ability of a substance to act as a hydraulic cement depends on two groups of factors. First, it must react with water to a sufficient extent and at a sufficient rate; γ-C_2S, which is virtually inert at ordinary temperatures, has no cementing ability. Second, assuming that an appropriate ratio of water to cement is used, the reaction must yield solid products of very low solubility and with a microstructure that gives rise to the requisite mechanical strength, volume stability, and other necessary properties. C_3A reacts rapidly and completely with water, but the products that are formed when no other substances are present do not meet these criteria, and its ability to act as a hydraulic cement is very poor. C_3S, in contrast, satisfies both sets of conditions, and is a good hydraulic cement.

In this section, only the factors that control reactivity are considered. Any understanding of them must be based on a knowledge of the mechanisms with water. It is highly probable that these are in all cases ones in which an essential step is transfer of protons to the solid from the water, which is thus acting as a Bronsted acid. As an initial approximation, one may consider the problem purely in terms of the idealized crystal structures. The reactivities of the oxygen atoms towards attack by protons depend on their basicities, i. e. the magnitudes of the negative charges localized on them. Any structural feature that draws electrons away from the O atoms renders them less reactive, the basicity thus depending on the electronegativities of the atoms with which they are associated. In this respect, the nearest neighbours are the most important, but the effects of atoms further away are far from negligible. This hypothesis leads to the following predictions, all of which agree with the facts.

1. O atoms attached only to atoms of a single element will be less reactive as the electronegativity of that element increases. Thus, C_3S and lime both contain O atoms linked only to Ca, and are more reactive than β-C_2S, in which all the O atoms are also linked to Si, while α-Al_2O_3, in which all are linked to Al, is inert. However, the reactivity of lime decreases if it strongly burned; this is discussed below.

2. O atoms forming parts of silicate, aluminate or other anionic groups will be less reactive as the degree of condensation with other such groups increases. β-C_2S, in which the tetrahedra do not share O atoms, is more reactive than any of the C_3S_2 or CS polymorphs, in which they do.

3. O atoms forming partes of anionic groups similar as regards degree of condensation will be less reactive as the central atoms in the groups become more electronegative. In contrast to the C_3S_2 and CS polymorphs, CA, $C_{12}A_7$ and C_3A are all highly reactive, even though the AlO_4 tetrahedra share corners in all cases.

Other hypotheses based on consideration of crystal structure have been proposed, and in varying degrees may account for second-order effects. Thus, Jeffery suggested that irregular coordination of Ca was responsible for the high reactivity of C_3S as compared with γ-C_2S; however, lime reacts with water, but the coordination of its Ca atoms is highly symmetrical. Jost and Ziemer, who noted the weaknesses in this and other earlier hypotheses, considered that high reactivity was associated with the presence of face-sharing polyhedra, but lime contains no such groupings, yet can be highly reactive.

Effects of Ionic Substitutions, Defects and Variation in Polymorph

The considerations discussed in preceding section suffice only to explain the effects on reactivity of major variations in composition. They do not, in general, explain the effects of variations in polymorph or introduction of substituent ions. These effects are often complex, and while in some cases the results appear clear-out, there are many others in which they present a cofusing and sometimes apparently contradictory picture. The probable reason is that many variables are involved, which are difficult or impossible to control independently. These include, besides chemical composition and polymorphic change, concentrations and types of defects; particle size distribution; textural features such as crystallite size and morphology, mechanical stress, presence of microcracks and the monocrystalline or polycrystalline nature of the grains; influences of reaction products, whether solid or in solution. In a cement as opposed to a pure phase, a foreign ion may not only substitute in a particular phase, but also influence the microstructure of the material in ways unconnected with that substitution, e. g. by altering the physical properties of the high-temperature liquid present during its formation. For both microstructural and chemical reasons, the reactivity of a given phase in a cement may not be the same as that observed when it is alone.

Defects play a particularly important role. Sacurai *et al.* noted that C_3S, alite, C_2F and C_4AF could all take up Cr_2O_3 and that this greatly accelerated reaction at early ages. Electron microscopic studies showed that reaction began at grain boundaries and at points of emergence of screw dislocations, the concentration of which was greatly increased by Cr_2O_3 substitution. It was also shown that the substituted materials were semiconductors, and a mechanism of attack based on electron transfer processes was suggested. Fierens and co-workers also found that the influence of substituent ions on the reactivity of C_3S was due to the presence of defects, which could be studied using thermoluminescence, and which could also be introduced by suitable heat treatment.

The complex relations between content of substituent ions, polymorphism, defects and reactivity are well illustrated by the results of Boikova and co-workers on ZnO-substituted C_3S. With increasing ZnO content, triclinic, monoclinic and rhombohedral polymorphs were successively stabilized. Curves in which the extent of reaction after a given time were plotted against ZnO content showed maxima corresponding approximately to the T_2-M_1 and M_2-R transitions, with intermediate minima. As in the work mentioned above, it was shown that these compositions were also ones in which the numbers of defects of a particular type were at a maximum. Reactivity thus depends not so much on the amount of substituent or nature of the polymorph as on the types and concentrations of defects.

Studies on the comparative reactivities of the β-, α'-, and α-C_2S, reviewed by Skalny and Young, have given contradictory results. As these authors conclude, reactivity probably depends on specimen specific factors other than the nature of the polymorph, and in the lower temperature polymorphs may be affected by the exsolution of impurities. This latter hypothesis receives strong support from subsequent observations that attack begins at exsolution lamellae and grain boundaries, and that these may contain phases, such as C_3A, that are much more reactive than the C_2S. Without these lamellae, β-C_2S might be much less reactive than it is.

There is wide agreement that substitution of alkali metal ions retards the early reaction of the aluminate phase, which is thus less for the orthorhombic than for the cubic polymorphs. The effect has been attributed to structural differences, but the early reaction of pure C_3A is also retarded by adding NaOH to the solution, and the OH^- ion concentration in the solution may be the determining factor. The reaction of C_3A is also retarded by iron substitution and by close admixture with ferrite; formation of a surface layer of reaction products may be a determining factor, at least in later stages of reaction, and the retarding effect of such a layer may be greater if it contains Fe^{3+}.

Selected from "Cement Chemistry." 2nd, H. F. W. Taylor. Thomas Telford Publ. 1997

Words and Expressions

1. requisite [ˈrekwizit] *a.* 必不可少的；*n.* 要素
2. initial approximation 初步估算
3. face-sharing 共面的
4. grouping [ˈgruːpiŋ] *n.* 集团，分类
5. textual feature 结构特征

6. microcrack [ˈmaikrəkræk] *n.* 微裂纹
7. points of emergence 出露点
8. screw dislocation 螺旋位错
9. thermoluminescence [ˈθəːməuljuminəsəns] *n.* 热致发光
10. triclinic [traiˈklinik] *a.* 三斜的
11. monoclinic [mɔnəˈklinik] *a.* 单斜的
12. rhombohedral [ˌrɔmbəˈhedrəl] *a.* 菱形的，菱面体的，三角晶系的
13. orthorhombic [ˌɔθəuˈrɔmbik] *a.* 斜方晶系的，正交晶系的
14. cubic [ˈkjuːbik] *a.* 立方晶系的
15. exsolution [eksˈsəluʃən] *n.* 脱熔作用（熔融岩石溶液的冷却分离）
16. lamellae [ləˈmelə] *n.* 薄片，板，层

Unit 20 Oil Well Cementing

General

In oil well cementing a cement slurry is pumped down the steel casing of the well and up the annular space between it and the surrounding rock. The main objects are to restrict movement of fluids between formations at different levels and to support and protect the casing. More specialized operations include squeeze cementing, in which the slurry is forced through a hole in the casing into a void or porous rock, and plugging, in which the casing is temporarily or permanently blocked at a specified depth①.

With current technology, oil wells are typically up to 6000m deep. The temperature of the rock at the bottom of the well ('bottom hole static temperature') at that depth is 100～250℃. The maximum temperature of the slurry during pumping ('bottom hole circulating temperature') is in general lower but may still be as high as 180℃. The pressure experienced by the slurry during pumping is equal to the hydrostatic load plus the pumping pressure, and may be as much as 150Mpa. The entire depth of a deep well would not be cemented in a single operation, but even so, pumping can take several hours. In geothermal wells, the maximum temperatures encountered may exceed 300℃.

Types of Cement and of Admixture

The slurry must remain sufficiently mobile for the pumping operation to be completed and must provide adequate strength, resistance to flow of liquid or gas and resistance to chemical attack after it has been placed. By using a high-temperature, high-pressure consistometer, in which the regime of temperature and pressure during pumping is simulated, it is possible to monitor the changes in consistency and to predict the 'thickening time' during which pumping is practicable②. The thickening time is akin to final set under the simulated well conditions. The American Petroleum Institute has defined various classes of Portland cement, of which G and H are widely used. The specifications of both are typically met by sulfate-resisting Portland cements, coarsely ground to 280～340$m^2 kg^{-1}$ for Class G or to 200～260 $m^2 \cdot kg^{-1}$ for Class H. Free lime is minimized to permit good response admixtures. Both classes are intended to be used as basic cements at depths down to about 2500m, and at greater depths with suitable admixtures. In practice, admixtures of many kinds are used at most depths.

Retarders and dispersants (water reducers) are widely employed, especially in the deeper wells and also to counteract the effects of other admixtures that have incidental accelerating effects. Lignosulfonates, modified lignosulfonates, cellulose derivatives and saturated NaCl are among those used. NaCl is effective up to about 130℃, and modified lignosulfonates to at least 150℃. Accelerators, such as $CaCl_2$ (2%～4% on the mass of cement) or

NaCl (2.0%~3.5%) are also used. In marine locations, sea water is often used for mixing, and act as an accelerator. Sodium chloride may be added to fresh water; in addition to its accelerating or retarding properties, it reduces damages to salt and shale strata and causes the hardened paste to expand.

Various admixtures are used to modify physical properties of the slurry, though some have incidental chemical effects that are countered by the use of further admixtures. It may be necessary to adjust the bulk density, e. g. by adding hematite to raise it, or bentonite (sodium montmorillonite) or sodium silicate to lower it. Bentonite greatly increases the water demand, but may be used together with calcium or sodium lignosulfonate and sometimes NaCl to obtain a desired combination of density, fluidity, w/c ratio and thickening time. The optimum addition of untreated bentonite is 8%, but this is reduced to 2% if the bentonite has been prehydrated, i. e. mixed with water and allowed to swell before being used. Granular, lamellar or fibrous materials are occasionally added to prevent slurry from being lost in rock fissures when lightweight or thixotropic slurries are insufficiently effective. Expanded perlite (a heat-treated vocanic material), walnut shells, coal, cellophane and nylon are examples. Nylon or other fibres have been used to increase shear, impact and tensile strength but sometimes present logistical problems. Cellulose derivatives, water reducers and latex admixtures are among admixtures that reduce loss of solution from the slurry into porous strata.

More specialized admixtures include radioactive tracers, which may be detected by devices lowered down the hole to trace the movement of the slurry. Dyes or pigments may similarly be used to check its emergence. Some of the chemicals added to drilling muds are strong retarders for cement. Proprietary 'spacer fluids' are commonly pumped ahead of the cement slurry to counteract contamination. Admixtures of paraformaldehyde and sodium chromate are sometimes also used. Addition of 5%~10% of gypsum produces a thixotropic slurry, which can be pumped but which gels rapidly when stationary; this can be used to help the slurry to pass permeable formations③. Gypsum, if added in appropriate proportion, also causes expansion, and it or other expansive admixtures may be used to improve the seal with the rock or casing.

Effects of Temperature and Pressure

At the high temperatures encountered in deep wells, pozzolanic admixtures are essential to prevent strength retrogression, as in high-pressure steam curing. Silica flour (finely ground quartz) and silica sand are the most commonly used. There are few data on the effects of prolonged exposure of cement-silica mixes to hydrothermal conditions; pastes cured for 2.5~4 months at 140~170℃ and saturated steam pressures are reported to have similar strengths to those so treated for shorter times, though some replacement of tobermorite by gyrilite and xonotlite was observed. In a deep well, the pressure may be much above that of saturated steam; this alters the equilibria and possibly also the kinetics. At 110℃ or 200℃ and 7~68MPa, mixtures of cement and quartz were shown to give C—S—H (I), which began to change into tobermorite within 32~64h. In hot, geothermal wells, many phases can form in addition to or in place of those found in autoclaved cement materials.

Special problems arise in cementing wells in the Arctic, where permafrost may exist to a depth of 1000m. It is necessary that the cement should set at low temperatures, that the surrounding ground should not be disturbed by melting or erosion during drilling or cementing or in the subsequent life of the well, and that freezable liquids should not be left in the annular space. Calcium aluminate cements, and mixtures based on Portland cement and gypsum, have been used.

Selected from "Cement Chemistry." H. F. W. Taylor, 2nd Edition. Thomas Telford Publ. 1997

Words and Expressions

1. casing [ˈkeisiŋ] *n*. 壳体，外壳
2. annular [ˈænjulə] *a*. 环形的
3. hydrostatic load [haidrəuˈstætik] 液体静压力
4. geothermal [ˈdʒiːəuθəməl] *a*. 地热的
5. consistometer [kənsisˈtəmitə] *n*. 稠度计
6. thickening time 稠化时间
7. akin [əˈkin] *a*. 同类的，同性质的
8. retarder [riˈtaːdə] *n*. 阻滞剂，缓凝剂
9. lignosulfonate [ˈlignəusʌlfəuneit] *n*. 木质素磺酸盐
10. cellulose [ˈseljuləus] *n*. 纤维素；*a*. 含纤维素的
11. superplasticizer [sjuːpəˈplæstisaizə] *n*. 超塑化剂
12. hematite [ˈhemətait] *n*. 赤铁矿
13. bentonite [ˈbentəˌnait] *n*. 膨润土
14. thixotropic [ˈθiksətrəupik] *a*. 触变性的
15. perlite [ˈpəːlit] *n*. 火山岩玻璃
16. walnut [ˈwɔlnət] *n*. 胡桃树
17. cellophane [ˈseləfein] *n*. 塞璐玢，玻璃纸
18. logistical [ləuˈdʒistikəl] *a*. 逻辑的，计算的，后勤的
19. paraformaldehyde [ˌpærəfɔmˈældihaid] *n*. 多聚甲醛
20. retrogression [ˈretrəˈgreʃən] *n*. 衰退
21. pozzolanic [ˈpɔzəuˌlaːnik] *a*. 火山灰的
22. gyrolite [ˈdʒaiərəlait] *n*. 白钙沸石（$4CaO \cdot 6SiO_2 \cdot 5(H,K,Na)_2O$）
23. xonotlite [ˈzəunətˌlait] *n*. 硬硅钙石（$5CaSiO_3 \cdot H_2O$）

Notes

① 此句主语为 operations，谓语为 include，它带有两个并列宾语，squeeze cementing 与 plugging。这两种操作过程分别有一个用 in which 引导的定语从句，说明操作的主要过程，可以分开译。

② 此句为带有两个定语从句的主从复合句，第一个定语从句用 in which 引导，修饰 cosistometer，可分开译。It 为主句的形式主语，它代表的是两个不定式短语。第二个定语从句为 during which 引导，修饰 thickening time。

③ 此句中有两个定语从句，修饰同一个词 slurry，但是由于第二个定语从句中的条件状语 when stationary 只说明 gels 这一动作发生的条件，所以只得分成两个定语从句。

Exercises

1. Translate the following expressions into Chinese or English.

annular space	bottom hole circulating temperature	resistance to chemical attack
modified lignosulfonates	bulk density	fluidity
expanded pertite	drilling mud	sodium chromate
autoclaved cement		
限制液体移动	现有技术	井底静态温度
抗硫酸盐水泥	减水剂	衍生物
加速剂	纤维状物质	轻质泥浆
高压蒸汽养护		

2. Translate the following into Chinese.

Pozzolans can also be mixed with Portland cement to form pozzolanic cement. The Portland cement component reacts as usual and the liberated $Ca(OH)_2$ reacts with the pozzolan to form more C—S—H gel. Removal of the $Ca(OH)_2$ by subsequent reaction with the pozzolan has two advantages: first, pozzolanic cement has good resistance to chemical attack, especially by sulphate; second, the final strength may be higher than that of Portland cement alone, because the mechanically weak $Ca(OH)_2$ is replaced by more C—S—H gel. Pozzolanic cement hardens more slowly than does Portland cement and so, because of the slow rate of heat development, it can be used in massive structures.

3. Fill in the blanks with suitable words.

① In oil well cementing, a cement slurry is ______ the steel casing of the well and up the ______ between ______ and the surrounding rock. The main purpose are ______ movement of fluids between formations at ______ and ______ the casting.

② The cement slurry used in oil well cementing must meet some requirements: such as sufficient mobility ______ ______ ______. Portland cement ______ and ______ are widely used as basic cement at depth down to ______.

③ Due to high temperature in deep well, ______ are essential to prevent ______ retrogression, the most commonly used is ______ and ______.

4. Write an essay (about 150 words) to describe various admixtures and their effects.

Reading Material 20

Very High Strength Cement-based Materials

This section deals with cement-based materials having compressive strengths much above

100MPa or comparable uprating of other mechanical properties. Relatively modest improvements yield materials with potential specialist uses in construction. Larger ones, especially in tensile or flexural strength and fracture toughness, offer the possibility of making low-volume, high-technology materials.

The compressive strength can be increased by lowering the w/c ratio. As the latter decreases, the particle size distribution of the starting material becomes increasingly important. Brunauer *et al*. described the preparation and properties of cement pastes with compressive strengths up to 250MPa. Portland cement clinkers were ground to 600 ~ 900$m^2 kg^{-1}$ using grinding aids and subsequently mixed at w/c 0.2 with admixtures of calcium lignosulfonate and K_2CO_3.

Lime-quartz materials with compressive strengths of up to 250MPa can be made by moulding the starting materials under a pressure of 138MPa before autoclaving. Portland cement pastes have similarly been pressure moulded to allow use of w/c ratios down to 0.06 and development of 28 day strengths up to 330MPa. Roy and co-workers obtained still higher strengths by hot-pressing Portland or calcium aluminate cement pastes, followed by normal curing in water. A Portland cement paste pressed for 1h at 250℃ and 350MPa and then cured for 28 days had a strength of 650MPa. The compressive strengths and total porosities (1.8% in the case mentioned) obeyed the Schiller relation.

Impregnation with an organic polymer of a concrete that has already developed some strength is another way of reducing porosity and increasing strength. The concrete is first dried, and the monomer is then introduced and polymerized in situ by γ-irradiation or by including a catalyst and subsequently heating at 70~90℃. Poly (methylmethacrylate) (PMMA) is possibly the most effective polymer. For maximum uptake of polymer, it is necessary to dry strongly (e.g. by heating at 150℃) and to evacuate, but useful amounts can be introduced without evacuation. Compressive strengths can be approximately doubled, and values around 220MPa have been reported for cement-sand mortars. Vacuum impregnation of cement pastes and autoclaved materials with molten sulfur at 128℃ similarly increased microhardness and elastic modulus by factors of up to 6 and 4 respectively.

In general, XRD and other studies show that the phase compositions of the very high strength materials described above are similar to those of weaker ones of similar types, the proportion of unreacted clinker phases increasing with decreasing in porosity. The microstructures of hot-pressed cements are dense and compact; the major product detected in hot-pressed calcium aluminate cements was C_3AH_6. This is consistent with Feldman and Beaudoin's view that this and similar dense, crystalline phases produce high strengths if sufficiently closely welded together in materials of low porosity. The same applies to unreacted clinker phases. Pastes impregnated with PMMA or sulfur are still sufficiently permeable to water that expansion occurs on long exposure. In polymer-impregnated cement pastes, there is evidence of interaction between Ca^{2+} ions and carboxylate and possibly other groups of the polymer matrix.

DSP Concretes

Very high strength concretes have since been obtained using Portland cements with super plasticizers and silica fume. In so called DSP (densified systems containing homogeneously arranged ultrafine particles) materials, the use of low w/s ratios (0.12～0.22), special aggregates, including fibies, and special processing conditions allows compressive strengths of up to 270MPa to be obtained, with good resistance to abrasion and chemical attack. The properties were attributed to a combination of effects. The particles of silica fume, being much finer than those of the cement, partially fill the spaces between the cement grains, and this, together with the superplasticizer, allows the latter to pack more uniformly. They also provide nucleation sites for hydration products, undergo pozzolanic reaction and improve the paste-aggregate bond.

MDF Cements

The tensile or flexural strengths of the materials described above were, in general, about one-tenth of the compressive strengths, as in normal cement pastes or concretes. In so-called MDF (macro-defect-free) cements, Birchall and co-workers, obtained higher relative values of flexural strength and other mechanical properties. The materials were made by including a water-soluble polymer in a Portland or calcium aluminate cement mix. The polymer [typically PVA, i. e. poly (vinyl alcohol), poly (acrylamide) or methylcellulose] made it possible to achieve mixing at a very low w/c ratio (0.10～0.15). Subsequent high-shear mixing and pressing produced a dough that could be formed by extrusion or other techniques. The highest strengths were obtained using calcium aluminate cements; compressive strengths up to 300MPa, flexural strengths up to 150MPa and Young's moduli up to 50Gpa were obtained.

Kendall *et al.* considered that MDF cements owed their high strength primarily to the absence of large flaws, which they held to be the reason for the relative weakness of normal cement pastes; they regarded the polymer essentially as a processing aid. However, the large volume fraction of polymer and the small extent of hydration of the cement that can occur in view of the low w/c ratio render this unlikely, and later work showed that the polymer plays an essential role in determining the physical properties of the product.

Selected from "Cement Chemistry." H. F. W. Taylor, 2nd Edition. Thomas Telford Publ. 1997

Words and Expressions

1. uprate [ˈʌpreit] *vt.* 改进
2. flexural strength 抗弯强度
3. methylmethacrylate [ˌmeθil meˈθækrileit] *n.* 异丁烯酸甲酯
4. evacuate [iˈvækjuleit] *vt.* 使撤离，转移
5. carboxylate [kɑːˈbɔksileit] *n.* 羧酸盐

6. macro-defect-free 宏观无缺陷的
7. vinylalcohol [ˈvainilælkəhɔl] *n*. 乙烯醇
8. acrylamide [ˌækrəˈlæmaid] *n*. 丙烯酰胺
9. methylcellulose [ˈmeθilˈseljuləus] *n*. 甲基纤维素
10. dough [dəu] *n*. 生面团似的一团；（揉好的）生面

Unit 21 Concrete Chemistry

Cement Paste in Concrete

Concrete can not properly be described as a composite of coarse and fine aggregate in a matrix of cement paste otherwise identical with the aggregate-free material. The microstructure of the paste close to the aggregate differs from that of cement paste in bulk, and much of the paste in a concrete or mortar is in this category. Because the strength and durability of concrete depend in part on features at the cement-aggregate interface, many of the studies on concrete microstructure have concentrated on this aspect. Several reviews exist.

In a study of thin sections of mortars by light microscopy and TEM, Farran and coworkers showed the presence in some cases of an interfacial transition zone, which was up to 35μm wide, the paste was of increased porosity and presumably lower strength. Microhardness measurements confirmed this. Further TEM studies showed that the aggregate surfaces were closely covered with poorly crystalline material, probably C—S—H.

Studies of specimens in which cement paste was cast against glass or polished surfaces of aggregates, and of fracture surfaces, showed the presence of highly oriented layers of CH on the aggregate surfaces. In some cases, duplex films of CH and C—S—H, typically of total thickness 1.0～1.5μm, were reported. Ettringite contents were also shown to increase on approaching the aggregate surface. A TEM study of ion-thinned sections of mortars gave no evidence of either a duplex film or of CH in contact with the aggregate surfaces, though CH was sometimes present near the interface[①]. C—S—H was commonly present in contact with the aggregate.

The Nature of the Paste—Aggregate Bond

In principle, chemical reactions between paste and aggregate could strengthen the bond by corroding the aggregate surface and thereby increasing the area of contact, but they also could weaken the material by creating spaces between paste and aggregate or by producing expansive forces too strong for the bond to withstand[②].

Struble *et al*. reviewed early work on the paste-aggregate bond. Postulated superficial pozzolanic reactions at ordinary temperatures between paste and quartz or other common siliceous aggregates appear to be unsupported by experimental evidence, except for the deleterious alkali-silica reaction. On the other hand, there is considerable evidence that superficial reaction occurs with calcite aggregate and that it strengthens the bond with the paste[③]. From XRD and SEM studies on composites of pastes cast against marble surfaces and on pastes made from cement mixed with finely ground calcite, Grandet and Ollivier (G99) concluded that $C_4AC_{0.5}H_{12}$ was formed initially and that it was later replaced by C_4ACH_{11}. The calcite surfaces were strongly pitted. This reaction, earlier postulated by Lyubimova and Pinus, is noted in Section 9. 6. 3 in connection with the use of calcite as a mineral addition.

Monteiro and Mehta found that the calcite was similarly pitted if alite was substituted for cement and reported the appearance of an XRD peak at 0. 79nm. they considered that the reaction product, either with alite or with cement, was not a carbonate-containing AFm phase④ but a basic calcium carbonate. Such phase have been reported as synthetic products and as a natural mineral, defernite.

Permeability of the Interfacial Transition Zone

Winslow and Liu concluded from an investigation using MIP⑤ that the cement phase in mortars or concretes was more porous than that in a neat paste hydrated to the same extent. The increase was mainly in the larger pore entry sizes detectable by this technique. In further work, a series of mortars of differing sand contents was studied. The results confirmed a suspicion that the extra porosity resided in the ITZ. For mortars made using plain Portland cement, the porosity increased sharply at a volume fraction of sand between 45% and 49%. This was attributed to the onset of percolation of the interfacial transition zone. Computer modelling indicated that an ITZ thickness of 15～20μm would account for this result. This thickness agrees well with the SEM evidence on the thickness of the highly porous part of the ITZ closest to the aggregate surfaces. The authors concluded that percolation of the ITZ would occur in most constructional concretes, a result that agreed with the generally high permeabilities of concretes compared with those of cement pastes.

Composite Cements and Other Topics

Partial replacemant of cement by silica fume increases the strength in concrete, but not in pastes. This supports the view that the effect is due to a strenthening of the paste-aggregate bond. Studies of concretes by backscattered electron imaging showed that the increase in porosity in the ITZ is much less marked if silica fume is present. Scrivener and Gartner found some increase in porosity, but attributed it almost entirely to the presence of hollow-shell grains. With pastes vibrated against a single piece of aggregate, in contrast, the replacement had no significant effect on the distribution of porosity within the ITZ, and some clumping of the silica fume was observed. Clumping was found to occur in pastes even when a superplasticizer was used, suggesting that the coarse aggregate breaks up the clumps by crushing or shearing during mixing.

Computer modelling of the ITZ confirmed that silica fume would be expected to decrease the gradient of capillary porosity in the ITZ but indicated that it would not eliminate it completely. The model also predicted that the effectiveness of mineral additions in increasing the integrity of the ITZ would depend on both their particle size and their reactivity. Inert additions would, with some reservations, have little effect, and flyash would be less effective than silica fume, because of its larger particle size and lower reactivity. The porosity in the ITZ may also be increased by dissolution of CH. An experimental study showed that partial replacement of cement by flyash can either increase or decrease the width of the ITZ, depending on the characteristics of the flyash, but that slag had relatively little effect.

Interfaces of calcium aluminate cements with aggregates are discussed in Chapter 10. The ITZ between Portland cement and steel has been studied by SEM, using various techniques of specimen preparation. The major features observed have been substantial deposits of CH and, further away from the interface, a relatively weak, porous zone. Bentur *et al*. also reported the occurrence of a duplex film. Interfaces of cement or C_3S pastes with zinc or copper have been studied.

Selected from "Cement Chemistry." H. F. W. Taylor, 2nd Edition. Thomas Telford Publ. 1997

Words and Expressions

1. interfacial transition zone 界面过渡带
2. aggregate-free 无骨（料）的
3. duplex film 双层膜
4. ion-thinned 离子减薄的
5. back-scattered electron imaging 背散射电子影像
6. superficial [ˌsjuːpəˈfiʃəl] *a*. 表面的
8. defernite [diˈfənait] 碱式碳酸钙
9. percolation [ˌpəːkəˈleiʃən] *n*. 渗滤，渗透
11. clumping [klʌmpiŋ] *n*. 凝聚，团集
12. integrity [inˈtegriti] *n*. 整体，实体

Notes

① 本句中有一让步从句，另外使用了 either… or 表示 a duplex film 与 CH 的并列关系。翻译时可根据上下文与中文特点意译，较直译更中文化。参考译文：尽管在浆体与管料的界面有时存在 CH，但是透射电子显微镜研究离子减薄的沙浆薄片并未证实存在与骨料接触的双层膜或者 CH。

② 本句为并列句，用 but 连接的两部分在结构上完全对称，前半句谓语为 could strengthen，后半句谓语为 could weaken，并都用 by＋现在分词表示原因和过程。这里 could 是科技文章中用虚拟语气表示比较婉转，不绝对的。参考译文：原则上，灰浆与骨料之间的反应侵蚀了骨料的表面，从而增加了接触面积，能增强二者的键合，但是由于二者之间产生了间隙或者产生了太强的膨胀力，使键无法承受，这些化学反应也能削弱材料。

③ 两个 that 引导的同位语从句，说明 evidence 的内容。参考译文：另一方面，有充分的证据证明存在着灰浆与方解石骨料的表面反应，并证明反应增强了它与灰浆的结合。

④ AFmphase—AFm (Al_2O_3-Fe_2O_3-mono) phases have the general formula $[Ca_2(Al,Fe)(OH)_6]\cdot X\cdot YH_2O$, where X denotes one formula unit of a singly charged anion, or half a formula unit of a doubly charged anion.

⑤ MIP—Mercury intrusion porosimeter.

Exercises

1. Translate the following expressions into Chinese or English.

identical with	durability	poorly crystalline
superficial pozzolanic reaction	carbonate-containing	MIP
account for	silica fume	inert addition
界面过渡区	水泥与骨料的界面	高取向层
硅质骨料	归结于	强化
弱化	天然矿物	证实了猜疑

2. Translate the following into Chinese.

① In use，Portland cement is mixed with aggregate and water which sets to form concrete. The role of the aggregate is twofold. It reduces the cost of concrete production and it increases the fracture strength. In the absence of aggregate，set cement crumbles easily. Other additives，such as pozzolans，fuel ash from power stations and blast furnace slag may be mixed in with Portland cement to reduce costs. Some of these additives are beneficial in that they mop up $Ca(OH)_2$ liberated during hydration of cement，and thereby increase the resistance of the set cement to chemical attack.

② Leaching of concrete by percolating or flowing water has sometimes caused severe damage，e. g. in dams，pipes or conduits，and is potentially important for the long-term storage of nuclear wastes. Pure water may be expected to remove alkali hydroxides，dissolve CH and decompose the hydrated silicate and aluminate phases.

3. Answer the following question in full sentences.

① Many scientists pay attention to the study on the cement—aggregate interface，why?

② How could chemical reactions between paste and aggregate affect the mechanical strength of concretes?

③ Why do concretes show in general higher permeability than corresponding meat cement paste?

④ Which factors would influence the effectiveness of mineral additions in increasing the integrity of the ITZ?

Reading Material 21

Fibre Reinforced Concrete-myth and Reality

Fibre reinforced concrete (FRC) may be defined as a composite material made with portland cement，aggregate，and incorporating discrete，discontinuous fibres. Asbestos fibre cement was developed in about 1900；since then，a number of other types of fibres have been used in FRC，including：steel，glass，polypropylene，carbon，nylon，cellulose，acrylic，polyethylene，wood fibres，sisal，and so on. Some of these fibres have higher elastic moduli than plain concrete, while others have lower elastic moduli.

Plain, unreinforced concrete is a brittle material, with a low tensile strength and a low strain capacity. The role of the randomly distributed discontinuous fibres is to bridge across the cracks that develop in concrete either as it is loaded or as it is subjected to environmental changes. This provides some post-cracking "ductility." If the fibres are sufficiently strong, sufficiently bonded to the material, and are there in a sufficient quantity, they will help to keep the crack widths small, and permit the FRC to carry significant stresses over a relatively large strain capacity in the post-cracking (or strain softening) stage.

In the brief review which follows, some of the myths surrounding the use of fibres in concrete will be contrasted with modern FRC practice.

MYTH1 #: FIBRES INCREASE THE STRENGTH OF CONCRETE

In fact, particularly at the fibre volumes currently used, fibres have little effect on the static mechanical properties *per se*. Compressive strengths, even with high volumes (~2%) of steel fibres, are unlikely to increase by more than 25%. Polypropylene fibres at higher volumes, and carbon fibres, may actually lead to small reductions in strength because they tend to increase the amount of entrapped air. Similarly, tensile strengths are not much affected, though at high fibre volumes perhaps a 6% increase in tensile strength may be achieved. However, fibres do have a large effect on flexural strength, with increases of more than 100% having been reported at high fibre volumes.

When added to plain concrete, fibres have little effect on torsional strength or shear strength. They have also little effect on abrasion resistance.

Fibres are, however, quite effective in improving the dynamic mechanical properties of concrete. Fibres improve the fatigue strength of concrete. They also lead to much better properties under impact loading.

There are, of course, other (and probably cheaper) ways of increasing the strength of concrete. The real contribution of the fibres is to increase the toughness of the concrete, under any type of loading. That is, the fibres tend to increase the strain at peak load, and provide a great deal of energy absorption in the post-peak portion of the load vs. deflection curve.

MYTH2 #: FIBRES CAN ELIMINATE CRACKING OF THE CONCRETE

In fact, it is virtually impossible to eliminate cracking of concrete, particularly that due to shrinkage. Such cracking is an inherent property of a matrix which is weak in tension and which has a low strain capacity. The role of the fibres is to reduce the crack widths, by bridging the cracks and typing the two sides of the crack together. It is not so much the total amount of cracking, but the crack widths that are reduced, though there is at least some evidence that the total amount of cracking may be reduced somewhat.

Polypropyene fibres, at the usual addition rate of 0.1% by volume, are marketed as a means of reducing the amount of plastic shrinkage (i. e., the shrinkage that occurs in about the first 12 hours, before the concrete has developed much strength). They are quite effective in this application, though proper attention to placing, compaction and curing of concrete would probably be equally effective.

Because of the low fibre volumes in practice, fibres are unlikely to do much to prevent cracking due to structural loading, though again crack widths will generally be reduced.

MYTH3# : FIBRES GREATLY REDUCE THE PERMEABILITY OF CONCRETE

In principle, since fibres help to control both microcracking and macrocracking in concrete, they would be expected to reduce permeability as well. This is indeed the case, with reduction of permeability of up to 80% having been reported in the literature. Unfortunately, this is not as impressive an improvement as it appears to be. For a decrease in permeability to be considered significant in practice, it should be in the vicinity of an order of magnitude, and not merely a factor of about two.

MYTH4# : FIBRES CAN BE USED TO REPLACE THE CONVENTIONAL REINFORCING STEEL IN CONCRETE

This myth, which can be a dangerous one if taken too literally, is due to a lack of understanding of the very different roles that fibres and conventional steel reinforcement play in concrete.

Steel reinforcement (bars and stirrups) is placed at specific locations in structural members, in order to carry the design tensile, shear, and occasionally compressive stresses. Fibres, being both discontinuous and randomly dispersed in the concrete matrix, are not very efficient in this regard. Though fibres might be used to replace some of the shear reinforcement (stirrups) in reinforced concrete members, their primary function is to control matrix cracking.

Fibres are effective in controlling cracks because there are so many of them, and because they are therefore very closely spaced. The differences between any of the fibre types and conventional steel reinforcement are enormous.

Rather than seeing fibres as a replacement for steel reinforcement, they should be seen as a complementary material, for use with steel reinforcement; from the literature, it is clear that the properties of virtually all types of reinforced concrete elements are enhanced by the presence of a sufficient volume of steel or other fibres, for both static and dynamic loading. For concrete members containing both fibres and reinforcing bars, the fibres act in two ways:

1. They permit the tensile and/or shear strengths of the FEC to be used in design, since the matrix will no longer lose its load-carrying capacity at first crack.
2. They improve the bond between the matrix and the reinforcing bars once cracking has begun, by suppressing the growth of cracks emanating from the bar deformations.

Selected from "Advances in Cement and Concrete." Ed. By M. W. Gutzeck&S. L. Sarhar. American Society of Civil Engineers. 1994

Words and Expressions

1. polypropylene [pɔli'prəupili:n] *n*. 聚丙烯
2. acrylic [ə'krilik] *a*. 丙烯酸的 *n*. 丙烯酸类树脂
3. polyethyllene [pɔli'eθili:n] *n*. 聚乙烯
4. sisal ['saisəl] *n*. 剑麻
5. *per se* 本质上（拉丁文）
6. entrap [in'træp] *vt*. 诱捕，使入陷阱
7. torsional ['tɔ:ʃənəl] *a*. 扭转的
8. abrasion resistance [ə'breiʒən] 耐磨性

PART Ⅴ REFRACTORIES

Unit 22 Materials Development in Refractories during the 20th Century

Refractories are enabling materials in that their primary function is to facilitate the production of other materials, such as metals, glasses, petrochemicals, and cements; they have enabled the utilization of heat to make materials since the Bronze Age. Without refractories, most of the scientific and technological developments of the past 100 years would not have taken place. The refractories industry, by necessity, has developed in response to advances in the materials—producing industries, in particular, to those of the iron and steel industry, which currently utilizes >60% of all refractories used.

Fireclay was probably the first fired refractory used and, being plastic when mixed with water, was shaped into crucibles for small batch melting of metal or glass①. Increased alumina contents were needed to improve refractoriness. The 1920s and 1930s-with the development of X-ray diffraction (XRD) techniques for elucidating the crystal structures of clays and oxide-silicate systems, and the determination of the important binary and ternary phase diagrams-was a rich period for refractories research. The Phase Diagrams for Ceramists Series published by The American Ceramic Society since 1933 remains an invaluable resource. The crystal structures and microstructures of the various clays and, in general, the mechanisms of thermal decomposition to mullite, glass, and cristobalite are now well understood. The application, often in combination, of modern characterization techniques-such as magic angle spinning nuclear magnetic resonance (MAS-NMR) and transmission electron microscopy (TEM) -to examine the microstructures of these traditional materials is further improving our understanding of their formation mechanisms.

These clay-derived aluminosilicate refractories were acidic in chemical nature and, therefore, able to contain reasonably well acidic metals, slags, and fluxes, and they were adequate during the early industrial revolution. Crushed Dinas rock from Wales was utilized in England from 1822 to form silica brick made of nearly pure silica, cemented together by the least possible amount of some binding flux, like lime②. They were the most suitable refractory for lining acid open hearth (OH) furnace, where temperatures were much higher than in Bessemer converters. The development of the basic OH process for steel production in the 1990s led to the need for basic refractories. Greek magnesite was one early raw material, but this did not sinter at the temperatures available, and an Austrian source of breunnerite became the predominant source by 1900. Breunnerite formed periclase crystals containing fine intragranular iron oxide precipitates on firing, making it much easier to sinter and more resistant to hydration, always a problem in lime-or periclase—containing refractories[3].

The use of dolomite as a refractory appears to have started in 1878, when an experimental Bessemer converter was first lined with tar-bonded, burned dolomite to provide the basic conditions needed to remove phosphorus from the molten iron. Dolomite is, apart from limestone, which has even more serious hydration tendencies, the most ubiquitous of basic raw materials. The use of dolomite remained unchanged until about 1930, when it was discovered that the refractoriness under load of chrome-magnesite brick made by firing graded mixtures of chrome ore and dead-burned magnesite was much higher than that of either material separately[4]. This led to the concept of an all-basic OH furnace with a chrome-magnesite roof, operating at high temperatures and, therefore, faster and more economically than previous furnaces that had silica roofs[5].

Chrome refractories, which were chemically neutral, were introduced as a buffer between basic lower and acidic upper brick courses in basic OH furnaces in the latter part of the 19th century, but their use did not become widespread until the development of direct bonding. The advantages of direct bonding included much improved hot strength, reduced slag attack, and greater dimensional stability.

With the introduction of the basic oxygen furnace (BOF) after WWII, standard basic brick that contained magnesia, dolomite, and chromite aggregates and matrix powders were developed containing tars and pitches for use in steel melting, which resulted in the terms "tar-bonded" and "pitch-bonded" basic brick[6]. The original function of the tar in refractories was as a binder and prophylactic coating to protect the easily hydrated basic grain. However, it was realized that, under the conditions of rapid working and minimum standby of BOF steelmaking, the life of magnesia and dolomite linings was longer if they contained carbon. This eventually led to the universal use of unfired pitch-and tar-bonded magnesia containing additions of graphite. The Japanese introduced, in the late 1970s, a revolutionary product containing phenolic resin as a cold bond for a mixture of periclase, graphite, and metallic antioxidants. Resin-bonded basic brick have replaced the tar-bonded variety during recent years because of their superior properties and the less carcinogenic nature of the fumes produced on their decomposition. These oxide-carbon brick are true composite materials, with the oxide conferring oxidation resistance while the graphite provides increased thermal conductivity and work-of-fracture, nonwetting behavior, and slag resistance. These brick contain 4～30 wt% natural graphite as well as carbon from the pitch bond or additional carbon black and produce beautiful colors when observed under crossed polar in a reflected-light microscope.

Natural graphite has been used as a refractory material since the 15th century and became more widespread in the 19th century with the discovery of widespread deposits in Sri Lanka. Significant deposits have been found in only a few other countries, including Madagascar, Brazil and China, so that the use of graphite in oxide-carbon refractories, which has accelerated rapidly during the past 30 years, has been governed by exportation of the raw material. An important trend in the refractory industry has been of countries with extensive sources of raw materials initially exporting to others to manufacture the final product but now more often they are performing the fabrication themselves, often with the assistance of established manufacturers[7]. The prime example of this is China, which has rich sources of many minerals, including bauxite, magnesite and graphite.

The 1990s have witnessed the culmination of a trend in the conduct of refractories research and development that has led to the use of refractories generated in situ, either within the refractory brick or monolithic itself or within the furnace, tank, or kiln. This research and development trend will continue. More recently, other factors have become significant, such as the need to protect the environment and, therefore, people, from unhealthy waste and emissions. This need, for example, has led to replacement of chromium-containing linings, particularly in cement rotary kilns, with chromium-free refractories because of the generation of carcinogenic Cr^{6+} during the kiln campaign, and to a change from pitch and tar to resin-bonded brick in primary steel furnace linings because of the excessive poisonous fume produced from the former[8].

Selected from "Evolution of in situ refractories in the 20th century" William E Lee etal, J. Am. Ceram. Soc., 1998, Vol 81 (6): 1385-1410

Words and Expressions

1. refractory [riˈfræktəri] *n.* 耐火材料；*a.* 耐熔的，难熔的
2. facilitate [fəˈsiliteit] *v.* 使容易，使便利
3. petrochemical [ˌpetrəuˈkemikəl] *a.*，*n.* 石油化工的，石油化工产品
4. utilization [ˌjuːtilaiˈzeiʃen] *n.* 利用
5. fireclay [ˈfaiklei] *n.* 耐火粘土，耐火泥
6. elucidate [iˈluːsideit] *n.* 阐明，说明
7. Phase Diagrams 相图
8. decomposition [ˌdiːkɔmpəˈziʃən] *n.* 分解
9. characterization [ˌkæriktəraiˈzeitʃən] *n.* 表征
10. magic angle spinning nuclear magnetic resonance (MAS-NMR) 幻角自旋核磁共振
11. dinas [ˈdinəs] *n.* 硅石
12. open hearth furnace (OH) 平炉
13. Bessemer [ˈbesimə] *n.* 酸性转炉钢
    Bessemer converter 酸性转炉
14. dead-burned 死烧，烧僵
15. magnesite [ˈmægnisait] *n.* 菱镁矿
16. breunnerite [brənəˈrait] *n.* 铁菱镁矿
17. chromite [ˈkrəumait] *n.* 铬铁矿，亚铬酸盐
18. basic oxygen furnace (BOF) 碱性氧气转炉
19. WWII World War II 第二次世界大战
20. tar [taː] *n.* 焦油

21. pitch [pitʃ] *n*. 沥青
22. prophylactic [ˌprəufiˈlæktik] *a*.，*n*. 预防疾病性的，预防药
23. phenolic [fiˈnɔlik] *a*. 酚的，石炭酸的，酚醛树脂的
24. antioxidant [ˌæntiˈɔksidənt] *n*. 抗氧化剂，抗老化剂
25. carcinogenic [kɑːˈsinədʒənik] *a*. 致癌的，发生癌的
26. in situ (拉丁语)原地，就地，现场(制作)

Notes

① 本句为具有同一主语 Fireclay 的并列句，其中，being plastic when mixed with water 为带有时间状语从句（省略了 fireclay was）的现在分词短语，做第二谓语的条件状语。

② 本句中 cemented together by the least possible amount of some binding flux，like lime 为省略了 being 的独立分词结构，其逻辑主语与句子主语相同，做伴随状态状语。

③ 本句带有两个现在分词短语，containing fine intragranular iron oxide precipitates on firing 为名词 periclase crystals 的后置定语，making it much easier to sinter and more resistant to hydration 为结果状语，修饰全句。always a problem in lime-or periclase-containing refractories 为独立结构。

④ 本句中以 when 引导的从句为定语，修饰 1931，从句中的 it 为形式主语，由 that 引导的从句做真实主语，主语从句中的过去分词短语 made by firing graded mixtures of chrome ore and dead-burned magnesite 做 brick 的后置定语。

⑤ 本句中的现在分词短语 operating at high temperatures and，therefore，faster and more economically than previous furnaces that had silica roofs 为名词 OH furnace 的后置定语，其中带有一个定语从句 that had silica roofs，修饰名词 furnaces。

⑥ 本句中 that contained magnesia，dolomite，and chromite aggregates and matrix powders 为名词 brick 的后置定语从句，现在分词短语 containing tars and pitches for use in steel melting 为方式状语从句，which resulted in the terms "tar-bonded" and "pitch-bonded" basic brick 为非限定性定语从句，修饰全句。

⑦ 本句为并列句，由 but 连接，前一句中的现在分词短语 exporting to others to manufacture the final product 为名词 countries 的后置定语，后一句中的主语 they 代表 countries。

⑧ 本句为简单句，由 and 连接的两个介词（to）短语做谓语动词 has led 的并列宾语，第一个 to 介词短语所带的 with 介词短语是 replacement 的搭配关系。

Exercises

1. Translate last but one paragraph into Chinese.
2. Translate the following phrases into English or Chinese：
   ① 二元、三元相图的确定
   ② 粘土类硅铝酸盐耐火材料
   ③ 焦油粘接的煅烧白云石
   ④ 方镁石、石墨与金属抗氧化剂的混合体
   ⑤ 导热性，断裂功，不湿润性和抗熔渣性
   ⑥ being plastic when mixed with water

⑦ periclase crystals containing fine intragranular iron oxide precipitates on firing
⑧ unfired pitch-and tar-bonded magnesia containing additions of graphite
⑨ the less carcinogenic nature of the fumes produced on their decomposition
⑩ under crossed polar in a reflected-light microscope

Reading Material 22

Refractories Manufacturing Techniques

Nineteenth century brick manufacture was performed manually, was labor intensive, and was primitive, utilizing aluminosilicate systems based on local, clay-derived firebrick. Brick were produced by the soft-mud process (using clays with 35% water), in which the clay was fed into sanded molds that were shaken until the clay filled the mold. This process could be done by hand or in hand-operated presses. Because of its thixotropy, the clay stiffened after the shaking stopped, allowing the brick to maintain their shape. They then were fired in small batches, so that production runs might be 5000 brick/day for a typical firm. During the 20th century, many of these small firms merged or were incorporated into larger companies that could be more competitive, a process continuing to this day! Between 1900 and 1920, the greatest technological change in brickmaking was the change from hand molding to machine pressing. During this time, two new processes, dry pressing (using clays with 5%～10% water) and the stiff mud (United States) or wire cut (United Kingdom) procedure (using clays with 12%～15% water), were introduced, although initially producers resisted the capital investment needed to convert to these new techniques. In the latter process, a column of clay is extruded through a die and cut with taut wires into bricks. The increased automation possible with the new forming techniques meant that 5000 brick/h could be made. These brick are denser, with a more uniform shape than hand molded brick; therefore, bricklaying is easier, and the machine-made brick were adopted rapidly by the industry. Although clay-based brick can continue to be produced by these routes, basic and carbon-bonded brick are made by pressing techniques. Over the years, brick production has become fully automated, with the tendency toward increased pressures and vacuum pressing to confer isotropic properties via an isomorphous microstructure.

Continuous tunnel kilns were introduced before WWI, and the first refractories tunnel kiln was built for Norton Company in Pittsburgh in 1915. Such kilns enabled continuous, more-rapid firing with lower firing times and temperature variations, and greater fuel economy, leading to a higher-quality product. The development, in the 1970s, of carbon-bonded brick, which are fired in situ, was a bonus for the manufacturers, because the users had to pay for the firing process. Although this also was true of metal cased, chemically bonded brick developed earlier, their use was not as generally adopted. It would be remiss not to mention another significant development in mechanization for brickmakers after WWII, i.

e., the use of the forklift truck and palletization for handling and transportation.

However, the most fundamental change associated with manufacturing technology has been the installation procedures evolved for monolithics over the past 25 years. Because the installer often has to add water or other liquids to the mix, great care must be taken. Variables, such as the water quality (it must be potable), ambient temperature and humidity, and mixing techniques vary significantly from one country to another, and they may have a critical effect on the setting behavior of the monolithic. Casting has been used for installation of Portland-cement-type concretes for many years, and this technology was applied to refractory systems in the 1920s. Important variables in this process are the flow and setting behavior of the castable. The cement mix is pumped via a hose into the ladle, which has a form arrangement to provide the shape, and is vibrated to remove trapped air. The vibration casting process uses the thixotropic properties of low-moisture, refractory particle mixes that become fluid when mechanically vibrated and return to the hardened state when left standing. Low-cement castables (LCCs) are thixotropic, with high fines (i. e., small particle) content. Low water content is desirable, because it makes drying easier and increases strength. Anisometric grains can align perpendicular to the direction of vibration, leading to anisotropic properties. However, self-flow systems may be used in the future in many applications presently using vibratables. One disadvantage of these installation techniques is the formwork needed to establish the hot face. Complex-shaped components currently are made by casting (so-called precast shapes) and sold in this form, similar to brick. Monolithics often have a few percent of steel fibers incorporated into them to improve spalling resistance and limit crack propagation, because the fibers act as crack arresters. In the 1960s, castable manufacturers developed systems with minimum rebound so that they could be gunned in place. This obviates the need for formwork; a great advantage of this technique over casting.

In the dry gunning process, the water is mixed with the powder batch at the nozzle. The wet gunning or shotcreting process has been known since 1960s but only recently has it been widely applied to refractories, in part because of the environmental need to reduce dust emissions in the work place and the high levels of rebound in dry gunning. In this process, the raw material and water are premixed and, under pressure, projected into place through a nozzle. In both cases, these mixes are useful for repair work, because they can be sprayed directly onto the required area - either walls or floors. Currently, up to 30 metric tons of material can be gunned in an 8 h shift, and this process can be automated and computer controlled. Rheology control is important, because the mix must flow under pressure when pumped along the hose from the mixer to the nozzle. High-pressure air is injected at the nozzle, and the concrete is sprayed from the gun nozzle. Once on the wall, the mix must stay in place and not flow away or rebound. Typical rebounds range from 15% to 30% for dry gunning but can be 0% for shotcreting. Various setting agents, accelerators, retarders, and other additives can be used in both procedures. Deflocculants in shotcreting usually are added during wet mixing in the mixer, and coagulants or accelerators are added at the nozzle to stiffen the material so that a continuous slurry is placed. Shotcreting appears likely to become the prime procedure in the future because of low rebound, and it even can be used to install roofs by shotcreting slurry from below! In plastic gunning, moistened materials are supplied in slabs that are shredded and fed into the gunning machine. The product then used for in-service repair of worn refractory linings in, e. g., coke ovens, BOF converters, degassing vessels, and teeming ladles. In this technique, material is (partially) melted, using various heat sources, and projected in place via a lance. In many cases, the Japanese have led the way in steel quality improvements, secondary steelmaking developments, and continuous casting. The Japanese also have introduced carbon-based systems, flame gunning, and many novel monolithic systems, and they continue to make significant contributions.

The current emphasis on refractories product development and the increasing focus on modeling of processes has resulted because refractories are, in general, so complex in their chemistry, texture, and response to use conditions that simple chemical and physical models are difficult to apply. Furthermore, the internationalization of ownership of refractories producers has resulted in centralization of research and heightened concern for standards. This, with the impact of increased regulation, especially in the areas of toxicity and recycling requirements, will govern the nature of refractoreis research, at least at the beginning of the next millennium.

Selected from "Evolution of in situ refractories in the 20th century" William E Lee etal, J. Am. Ceram. Soc., 1998, Vol. 81 (6): 1385-1410

Words and Expressions

1. thixotropy [θik'sɔtrəpi] n. (凝胶等所具有的)触变性
2. extrude [ek'stru:d] v. 挤压
3. bricklaying ['brikleiiŋ] n. 砌砖(工作)
4. forklift ['fɔ:kˌlift] n. 铲车,叉式升降机
5. palletization [ˌpælitai'zeiʃən] n. 造球,球粒化作用
6. hose [həuz] n. 软管
7. ladle ['leidl] n. 勺,长柄勺,盛钢桶,钢(铁)水包
8. anisometric [ˌænai'sɔmətrik] a. (结晶等)不等轴的
9. align [ə'lain] v. 排齐
10. anisotropic [ˌænaisə'trɔpik] a. 各向异性的
11. vibratable [vai'breitəbl] a. 可振动的
12. formwork [fɔ:m'wə:k] n. 模板,(模子用)材料
13. spall [spɔ:l] v., n. 碎片,弄碎,剥落,散裂
14. arrester [ə'restə] n. 制动器,避雷器
15. rebound [ri'baund] n., v. 回弹,脱落
16. gunning process 喷射成型法
17. obviate ['ɔbvieit] v. 消除,排除

18. shotcreting [ʃɔtkreitiŋ] *n*. 喷射混凝土
19. shotcreting process 喷涂法
20. emission [iˈmiʃən] *n*. 发射
21. rheology [riːˈɔlədʒi] *n*. 流变学
22. deflocculant [diːflɔkjulənt] *n*. 抗絮凝剂
23. coagulant [kauˈægjulənt] *n*. 凝结剂，凝血剂
24. slab [slæb] *n*. 厚平板，厚片
25. shred [ʃred] *v*.，*n*. 撕碎，碎片
26. toxicity [tɔkˈsisiti] *n*. 毒性
27. millennium [miˈleniəm] *n*. 千禧年，一千年

Unit 23 Refractory Bonds and Binders

The importance of bond phase in refractories, in holding the aggregate/grain phases together and enabling large components to be fabricated, is indicated by use of the type of bond in the refractory name. The fired integrity of refractories relied on natural bonding or the silicate or aluminosilicate bonds derived from vitrification reactions. Bonds initially were synthesized through the use of fine additions, termed "mineralizers," later followed by the introduction of separate cementitious and glassy bond systems.

One of the most significant developments in bond systems has been of those used for monolithic or unshaped refractories that can be formed and shaped in situ. Monolithic refractory materials are mixtures that contain aggregates and binders prepared ready-for-use either directly in the condition in which they are supplied or after the addition of suitable liquids①. Monolithic refractories have been known for many years, but it is only since the 1960s that their use has gained general acceptance in the refractory community. The types of monolithics now commonplace, such as castables (a dry mix, which, when mixed with water, can be shaped by casting or vibrating), gunning mixes (free-flowing mixtures specially made for placing by pneumatic or mechanical projection), and moldables or plastics (a plastic "clay" form, which can be rammed into position), all have evolved from bond systems largely different from those used in brick②. Unshaped refractories, in general, use similar aggregate materials as shaped brick. However, the binders used to form the bonding phase are very different, and it has been developments in aluminate-, silicate-, and phosphate-bond systems or combinations of these systems that has led to the widespread use of monolithics. Initially, monolithics were used for repair or in less-severe positions, but they now account for 60% of refractory production and are used in almost all areas of furnace linings.

The bonds formed in monolithics during processing or service may be of several types:

A ceramic (physical) bond, which is present at room temperature but develops on firing and may be a glass and/or ceramic bond. These typically are formed from clays on firing.

A hydraulic (chemical) cementlike, silicate, or aluminate bond, which involves setting and hardening at room temperature when water is added to the system. When it is heated, the bond strength may decrease as the hydraulic bond is destroyed but increase again as a high-temperature ceramic bond forms. These are the most common bonds in modern castables, and they usually are based on calcium aluminate (CA) cements.

A mineral (chemical) bond which involves hardening at room temperature or above but below the sintering temperature. The most common of these utilize phosphoric acid or sodium silicate. This bonding produces high strengths when heated to temperatures of 150 ℃. Phosphate bonds can be developed by simply adding phosphoric acid or less-acidic media, such as $Al(H_2PO_4)_3$ or $NH_4H_2PO_4$, to a mixture containing Al_2O_3, or MgO fines. $AlPO_4$ is formed on reaction with Al_2O_3, and it is a highly refractory bond phase. There are serious problems of aging of stored products, and reactions during storage must be inhibited. The bonding mechanism was first reviewed by Kingery, and Gonzalez and Halloran thoroughly studied the basic chemistry of the aluminum phosphate bond and correlated high-temperature mechanical behavior to the texture and chemistry of various phosphate-bonded refractories.

The first plastic monolithics were made as semibaked, puttylike, firebrick that were installed in chunks with a hammer. Initially, these plastic refractories were used in boilers, but, by 1930, they were being used successfully in forge furnaces, gas generators, coke ovens, and heat-treatment furnaces. Plastics and ramming mixes are now available as heat- or air-setting versions with phosphate or organic resin as well as clay-based bonds. Installation can be via ramming, vibration, or gunning, the latter techniques being developed in the 1970s and 1980s.

The hydraulic properties of calcium aluminate castable cements (CACs) were discovered in France before 1856. CACs first were manufactured by sintering or fusing bauxite and/or alumina plus limestone in rotary or shaft kilns. In 1902, however, CACs had been produced by heating low-grade aluminous materials with limestone, but this material was marketed as a rapid-hardening additive to Portland cement and plaster, not as a refractory cement by itself. By WWII, refractory concrete was well established in many industries for furnaces or ovens and as linings in boilers and stacks, although early cements were impure, so that use temperatures were limited to < 1500℃ up. Development of dry cement-aggregate mixes from improvements in binders, in particular, the use of submicrometer particles, led to better slip rheology and product sinterability (because of greater surface area). The dry mix for the castable contains a carefully graded range of aggregates, the required amount of cement, and additives to improve workability, flow, and setting behavior. The water content in a typical dry-pressed refractory brick is 0.5%~3%, but it is 8%~15% in a castable mix to allow the hydration products to form and give suitable rheology for casting.

Conventional concretes contain 15%~20% calcium aluminate cement. Reduction of cement content to 5%~8% without loss in strength was achieved by addition of fine particulate refractory bond material, which promoted homogeneous distribution of cement; therefore, made the hydraulic bond fully utilized③. More careful control of the size of grain fractions and bond-matrix components led to the improved particle-packing efficiency. Cement contents were reduced to <1% by adding deflocculant and two very fine particle sizes consisting of 1~100μm powder that was nonhydrating and 0.01~0.1μm powder that did not form gels with water. Mixing these in a 1 : 100 ratio, respectively, so that the finer can fill the space between the coarser particles reduces water consumption and porosity of the concrete, giving greater strength④. Some low-cement monolithics cannot be cast because of the low water content, and, therefore, are vibration compacted; others flow without vibration (self-flowing castables, SFCs). These are self-leveling, with high flowability, and have comparable properties to conventional casting-vibration castables because of the auto-degasification that occurs without external forces, conferring higher density⑤. The SFC composition and interparticle surface chemistry are carefully controlled to give self-flowing ability. Although conventional castables may require 3 d to cure and dry, SFCs can be installed in 8-24 h. The grading (granulometry) is critical to achieving self-flowing behavior, and the larger the critical particles in the basic formula, the poorer the flowability and the poorer the segregation. The difference of the ratio of each particle size in the superfine (colloidal) particles has a strong influence on the flowability.

Selected from "Evolution of in situ refractories in the 20th century" William E Lee etal, J. Am. Ceram. Soc., 1998, Vol. 81 (6): 1385-1410

Words and Expressions

1. vitrification [ˌvitrifiˈkeiʃən] *n*. 玻璃化
2. mineralizer [ˈminərəlaizə] *n*. 矿化剂
3. monolithic. [ˌmənəuˈliθik] *n*. 整体的，单块
4. castable [ˈkɑːstəbl] *n*. 浇注料
5. unshaped refractory 不定形耐火材料
6. commonplace [ˈkəmənpleis] *a*., *n*. 平凡的事，平常话，平凡的
7. gunning mixes 喷补料
8. pneumatic [njuːˈmætik] *a*. 风力的，气动的
9. projection [prəˈdʒkʃən] *n*. 喷射
10. moldable [ˈməuldəbl] *a*. 可塑的，可模制的
11. ram [ræm] *v*. 捣圆，捣打
12. puttylike [pʌtlaik] *a*. 油灰似的
13. heat-setting 热硬性的
14. air-setting 气硬的
15. shaft kiln 竖窑
16. submicrometer [subˌmaikrouˈmeitə] *n*. 亚微米
17. sinterability [sintəˈbiliti] 烧结性
18. workability [ˌwəkəːˈbiliti] *n*. 成型性
19. degasification [ˌdigəsifiˈkeiʃən] *n*. 脱气，除气，去气作用
20. self-leveling 自水平的
21. flowability [fləuˈəbiliti] *n*. 流动性
22. confer [kənˈfəː] *v*. 授予，赠予，协商
23. interparticle [intəˈpɑːtikl] *a*. 粒子间的
24. granulometry [grænjuːˈləmitri] *n*. 颗粒分析，粒度分析
25. segregation [ˌsegriˈgeiʃən] *n*. 分层
26. superfine [ˈsjuːpəˈfain] *a*. 超细的

Notes

① 本句为主从复合句，由 that 引导的从句做定语，修饰名词 mixtures，定语从句中的过去

分词短语 prepared ready-for-use 做 aggregates and binders 的后置定语，其后的 either directly in the condition in which they are supplied or after the addition of suitable liquids 为 ready-for-use 的搭配关系，其中 in which they are supplied 为定语从句，修饰 condition。

② 本句中的 now commonplace 为主语 The types of monolithics 的后置定语，由 such as 引导出的三个并列名词，以及谓语动词 have evolved 前的 all 均为主语的同位语。

③ 本句为主从复合句，从句子的含义分析，由 which 引导的从句为限定性定语从句，修饰 addition of fine particulate refractory bond material，该定语从句为并列句，由分号并列两个谓语。

④ 本句为主从复合句，主句的主语为动名词短语 Mixing these in a 1∶100 ratio，respectively，随后的从句 so that the finer can fill the space between the coarser particles 为 mixing 的搭配关系，即动名词短语所带的结果状语从句，主句的谓语动词为 reduces，现在分词短语 giving greater strength 为结果状语，修饰全句。

⑤ 本句为主从复合句，主句为并列句，由连词 and 并列两个谓语，第二个谓语中的 that occurs without external forces，conferring higher density 从句为名词 auto-degasification 的定语。注意，现在分词短语 conferring higher density 是修饰该定语从句（而非主句）的结果状语。

Exercises

1. Translate underlined sentences in the text into Chinese.
2. Translate the following phrases into English or Chinese：

   ① 耐火材料中结合相的重要性

   ② 含有骨料和粘结剂的混合物

   ③ 在室温下的固化和硬化

   ④ 降低水泥用量而不失去强度

   ⑤ 颗粒尺寸和结合相-基体相组成的严格控制

   ⑥ natural bonding or the silicate or aluminosilicate bonds derived from vitrification reactions

   ⑦ the binders used to form the bonding phase

   ⑧ hardening at room temperature or above but below the sintering temperature

   ⑨ as a rapid-hardening additive to Portland cement and plaster，not as a refractory cement by itself

   ⑩ a carefully graded range of aggregates，the required amount of cement，and additives to improve workability，flow，and setting behavior

Reading Material 23

Mullite and Its Use as a Bonding Phase

Mullite is the only stable crystalline phase in the aluminosilicate system at room through elevated temperatures and under normal atmospheric pressure. Its chemical composition ranges from 3 $Al_2O_3 \cdot 2SiO_2$ to approximately $2Al_2O_3 \cdot SiO_2$, and it crystallizes in the orthorhombic system. Mullite is one of the most widely encountered and important compounds found in many industrial ceramic products.

As early as 1847, researchers told of fine needles in porcelains fired at high temperatures. These were suspected to be essentially alumina and silica in combination, and at the time they were assumed to be the mineral silimanite. Not until 1924 in the classic study by Bowen and Greig was it shown that mullite was the only intermediate stable phase at high temperatures in the Al_2O_3-SiO_2 system. This work, in the form of the Al_2O_3-SiO_2 phase diagram was generally accepted for 30 yr. In the past 40 yr., however, many investigators have questioned the data on the melting behavior and composition of mullite.

Why is mullite use in refractories, advanced ceramics, structural ceramics, and electronics so ubiquitous? Mostly because cheap raw materials can be used to produce high-purity mullite, and the properties obtainable through ceramic processing and firing are outstanding. Mullite as a bonding phase exhibits high refractoriness, low creep rate, low thermal expansion and thermal conductivity, good chemical and thermal stability, and good toughness and strength.

The Al_2O_3-SiO_2 system seemed straightforward, especially with regard to mullite thermochemistry. Mullite were placed at a specific composition of 3 $Al_2O_3 \cdot 2SiO_2$ (71.8 wt% Al_2O_3) and indicated melting to be incongruent at 1810℃. It is well accepted today that mullite has no fixed composition but exhibits a solid-solution range. The solid-solution range is still under intensive discussion because of conflicting results obtained by various workers. Processing of the starting materials and firing conditions seem to affect the solid-solution range.

The structure of mullite is better understood by comparing it to that of silimanite. The sillimanite structure as described in the work of Davis and Pask and the mullite structure possess many similarities. Sadanaga et al compared a $2Al_2O_3 \cdot SiO_2$ mullite and sillimanite to find that the unit cell of the mullite contained 6/5 of the formula unit, being $Al_{4.8}Si_{1.2}O_{9.6}$, and is very similar to the sillimanite unit cell except for the c-axis dimension which is one-half that of sillimanite.

The orthorhombic symmetry and atomic structure underlie one of mullite's frequent characteristics: needle-like habit. This habit seems to be compositionally unrelated but instead appears to be function of the way it is produced. Lohre and Urban reported a chunky morphology formed while preparing mullite by sintering in the absence of a liquid phase, whereas the needle-like habit apparently requires a liquid phase and a fairly raid cooling rate. All studies show the needle shape growth to be along the c-axis. This observed habit can be loosely used as a tool to interpret the mechanism active in forming mullite in a bonding phase. Chunky habit is observed in the case of most sintered refractrories and is deemed advantageous in reducing the amount and effects of the residual glassy phase. This glass occurring more with needle-shaped crystals is the weak link in high-temperature properties and corrosive environments.

The formation of mullite as a bonding phase requires extensive experimentation to determine the silica content needed to form an appropriate amount of mullite. A continuing study at the University of Missouri-Rolla focuses on just this point. A fully dense mullite bonding phase would be ideal, giving optimal properties. Many attempts have been made to form fully dense mullite, and most have been successful only when firing specimens to > 1700℃. Boch *et al*, using reaction sintering, produced a fully dense mullite at 1620℃. They stated that there are three discrete stages in the process of mullite reaction sintering: I. Densification begins at <1250℃ to 1300℃ in amorphous silica and quartz-alumina mixes. II. From 1300℃ to 1400℃, the silica converts to beta cristobalite, and shrinkage rates decrease. Conversation occurs from a lower-density silica phase to denser cristobalite. III. At > 1400℃ mullite develops, and densification continues. However, the shrinkage rate decreases, and an overall expansion due to the formation of a less-dense, 3.16-g/cm^3 mullite compared to a calculated theoretical density of 3.31 g/cm^3 may be seen. Contrary to opinions of earlier researchers that sintering took place only after mullite had formed, Boch *et al* and others showed that finer particles and fast heating rates provide densification before mullitization. Early mullitization results in a rigid structure which inhibits the full densification of the mullitic phase. Reports on mullitization dependent on variations in composition, temperature, and processing techniques are inconsistent to say the least. Principal factors reported to affect mullite formation are: character of the starting materials, nature and concentration of impurities, firing temperature-time program, and atmosphere and pressure during firing.

Mullite used as bonding phase in most refractory and structural ceramic applications are produced by sintering in situ. The density and formula weight are noted to be 3.16 to 3.22 g/cm^3 and 425.94 g/mol, respectively. From chemical properties of mullite, the high refractoriness and excellent corrosion resistance to acid slags at high temperatures can be appreciated. The mechanical and thermal properties of mullite underscore the high levels of hot-load resistance, abrasion resistance, and spalling resistance.

Expanded knowledge of mullite will improve engineering properties through efforts by developers of refractories designed for progressively more-rigorous service. Not only refractories developers but structural and advanced ceramic producers should also pay close attention to the current high level of activity in mullite research for benefits which can be employed in their respective fields. Industries that reallize this potential use of mullite as a bonding phase include: steel, aluminum, copper, glass, cement, chemical, and ceramic producers. Other industries will follow their lead as the full potential of mullite bonding phases is tapped.

Selected from "Refractory of the past for the future: Mullite and its use as a binding phase" Andrew J Skoog *et al*, J. Am. Ceram. Soc., 1988, Vol 71 (7): 1180-1184

Words and Expressions

1. thermochemistry [ˌθəːməuˈkemistri] *n*. 热化学

2. mullitization [ˌmʌlaitəˈzeiʃən] *n*. 莫来石化
3. refractoriness [riˈfræktənis] *n*. 耐火度
4. incongruent [inˈkəngruənt] *a*. 不一致的
5. underlie [ˌʌndəˈlai] *v*. 位于，在……之下
6. chunky [ˈtʃʌŋki] *a*. 矮矮胖胖的
7. reaction sintering 反应烧结
8. densification [ˌdensifiˈkeiʃən] *n*. 密实化
9. formula weight *n*. 分子量
10. underscore [ˌʌndəˈskɔː] *v*., *n*. 划线于……之下，强调，底线
11. hot-load resistance 抗热载性
12. spalling resistance 抗剥落性
13. rigorous [ˈrigərəs] *a*. 严厉的，严酷的

Unit 24 Thermomechanical Properties of Refractories

Thermal Properties

Thermal conductivity (λ) remains a critical property in all furnace designs, appearing in many indexes of refractories performance, such as thermal shock resistance parameters. Refractories often contain gases that can significantly alter the transfer of heat through them, and numerous failures have occurred through neglect of this consequence. Wygant and Crowley measured λ values of insulating refractories saturated with hydrogen- and helium-rich gas mixtures and found the conductivities of brick containing gases followed the mixture rules reasonably well. In-depth studies of gas composition and concentration effects were reported by Litovsky *et al.*, who applied their modeling to measured values of λ for chrome-magnesite, yttria, alumina, and fireclay thermal insulators.

The coefficient of thermal expansion (CTE, α) is the controlling property in temperature induced growth of furnace structures and is important in thermal shock. The thermal expansion of a polycrystalline and polyphasic refractory is affected by many aspects of the microstructure. Houldsworth and Cobb investigated the effects of texture and constitution on the reversible thermal expansion of fireclays, and they found a strong effect of induced porosity (by the incorporation and burn-out of 0.176 mm diameter rape seeds). Typical data for traditional refractory brick reveal the phenomenon of bloating of certain fireclay refractories. An interferometer method was used in CTE measurements for relatively pure refractory oxides. It was noted that both CTE and λ play a major role in thermal shock behavior. It was also noted that the expansion of porous aggregates is lower than that of denser ones and that phase purity correlates to higher expansion①. Marked differences in CTE between the outer and core regions of silica brick were measured after 10 years in a coke oven because of the differential conversion of cristobalite to tridymite. Consistent CTE data for β-Al_2O_3 using a quartz dilatometer for the measurements could not be obtained because of alkali attack of the SiO_2 components. The complex expansion behavior contributed by the calcium aluminate cement phase of monolithic refractory concretes has been studied extensively. The curing temperature of a calcium aluminate cement has a pronounced effect on expansion behavior. The study, over the range ambient to 550℃, showed that shrinkage increased greately as the curing temperature increased from 22℃ to 60℃. Peretz and Bradt used Turner equations for estimating the CTE of mixtures from component CTE values and concentrations of constituents, and they compared these to results of the regression of CTE on phase concentration. When mullite served as the matrix component among all of the systems studied, correlation was excellent for three aggregate types: andalusite, tabular alumina, and calcined kaolin. The higher the mullite content in the combination of matrix and aggregate, the better was the correlation.

Strength and Toughness

Strength of refractories can be sensitive to temperature, and a brittle-to-ductile transition often is observed once any glassy phase starts to soften. The relaxation of internal stresses leads to a strength increase in the temperature range of elastic behavior. The amount and viscosity of the glassy phase formed at temperature is controlling in aluminosilicate refractories and silicate-containing basic refractories. Brezny and Shulz correlated decreased modulus of rupture (MOR) with the amount of liquid phase in magnesia-chromite refractories with differing C : S ratios[②]. The C : S ratios and the extent of reducing conditions in periclase refractories determine, at high firing temperatures, whether the CaO goes into solution in the MgO or remains available to form low-melting phases with a pronounced effect on the high-temperature strength[③]. Despite the complexity of the chemistry and texture of most refractories, it is possible to note the effects of loading rate on fracture strength. Darroudi and Landy have demonstrated a pronounced effect of loading rate and a strong dependency of slow crack growth rate with amorphous content of various brick as well as a correlation to modulus of elasticity (E)[④]. A major problem with the high-temperature flexure strength data for refractories has to do with whether creep is present. If loading rates are slow, creep is possible in the outer volumes. In applications where strength is important (when impact-erosion or crack initiation resistance need to be high), it is critical to achieve high density in the matrix phase of a refractory and to bond that phase to the usually much denser aggregates. Recent attention has focused on the testing of the strength of the aggregates, using Weibull statistics to characterize the stochastic nature of aggregate strength data.

Toughness of refractories was not measured properly until the 1960s. When aluminosilicate brick were formulated from coarse grains and underfired, they were more likely to survive thermal shock. The loose texture of these brick and the presence of numerous cracks made it difficult for cracks to extend. Refractory crack propagation or growth resistance needs to be substantial in areas where impact loading or thermal shock is high. Resistance to crack initiation or nucleation is closely related to fracture strength as measured by the MOR test. However, the MOR and crushing tests reveal nothing about the fracture process itself, because fracture is the propagation of a crack through a specimen, and these tests do not monitor that process. Nakayama devised a specimen configuration with a specially introduced crack geometry (a saw notch, now often a V notch), and he built a stiff testing machine so that he could monitor the growth of a controlled single crack in a bend-test configuration. Integrating the area under the load-displacement curve gives an energy term that can be divided by fracture surface area A to yield a fracture surface energy, which is defined as the work of fracture (WOF)[⑤]. The curve can be divided into two regions, 1 and 2, on either side of the maximum load, where region 1 is the work done before crack initiation and region 2 the work done after crack initiation. For good refractory thermal shock resistance, the area of region 2 should be larger than that of region 1. R-curve behavior in refractories where there is increased crack growth resistance as the crack grows is an area worthy of greater study⑥.

Selected from "Evolution of in situ refractories in the 20th century" William E lee *et al*, J. Am. Ceram. Soc., 1998, Vol 81 (6): 1385—1410

Words and Expressions

1. in-depth [in'depθ] *a*. 深入的
2. chrome-magnesite 铬镁质
3. yttria ['itriə] *n*. 氧化钇
4. polycrystalline [poli'kristəlain] *a*. 多晶的
5. polyphasic [poli'feisik] *a*. 多相的
6. rape seeds 菜籽
7. bloat [bləut] *v*. *a*. 发胀
8. interferometer [ˌintəfə'rɔmitə] *n*. 干涉仪
9. dilatometer [dilə'tɔmitə] *n*. 膨胀计
10. regression [ri'greʃən] *n*. 回归
11. modulus of rupture 断裂模量
12. magnesia-chromium 镁铬质
13. crack initiation resistance 抗裂缝发生性
14. impact-erosion 冲击腐蚀
15. underfired [ʌndə'faiəd] *a*. 欠火的
16. propagation [ˌprɔpə'geiʃən] *n*. 宣传，扩展
17. notch [nɔtʃ] *n*. 凹口，槽口

Notes

① 本句为复合句，It 为形式主语，由 that 引导出二个主语从句。

② 本句为简单句，第一个介词短语 with the amount of liquid phase in magnesia-chromite refractories 为名词 MOR 的前置定语 decreased 所带的搭配关系，第二个介词短语 with differing C∶S ratios 则与谓语动词 correlates 有关。

③ 本句为复合句，由 whether …or 引导出两个从句，做谓语动词 determine 的宾语。

④ 本句为简单句，由 and 和 as well as 连接三个短语，做 have demonstrated 的并列宾语。

⑤ 本句为复合句，分词短语 integrating the area under the load-displacement curve 做主语，that can be divided by fracture surface A to yield a fracture surface energy 为定语从句，修饰前置名词 energy term，此定语从句还带有一个定语从句 which is defined as the work of fracture (WOF)，修饰前置名词 surface energy.

⑥ 本句为复合句，由 where 引导的从句为定语从句，修饰主语 R-curve behavior，此定语从句还带有一个由 as 引导的从句，做时间状语。形容词短语 worthy of greater study 为后置定语，修饰名词 area。

Exercises

1. Translate underlined sentences in the text into Chinese.

2. Translate the following phrases into English or Chinese：
   ① 耐火材料性能指标
   ② 热传导系数的测量值
   ③ 在热冲击性能中起主要作用
   ④ 内应力的弛豫
   ⑤ 耐火材料化学与织构的复杂性
   ⑥ effects of texture and constitution on the reversible thermal expansion of fireclays
   ⑦ a pronounced effect on expansion behavior
   ⑧ a strong dependency of slow crack growth rate with amorphous content of various brick
   ⑨ the loose texture of these brick and the presence of numerous cracks
   ⑩ monitor the growth of a controlled single crack

Reading Material 24

Corrosion Behavior of Refractories

Attack of refractories is a complex phenomenon involving chemical wear (corrosion) and physical/mechanical wear (such as erosion and abrasion) processes as well as thermal shock and spalling. Postmortem analysis of failed refractories has been used throughout this century in attempts to determine the cause of failure. At the start of the century, optical microscopy was the only available technique for microstructural characterization. The discovery of techniques, such as X-ray diffraction, X-ray fluorescence, cathodoluminescence, electron probe microanalysis, and electron microscopy means that, at the end of the century, failure analysis is far more detailed.

Most research has examined effects of contact of refractories with glasses, slags, and other liquids although interaction between refractories and various dusts and vapors also is significant. The various tests used to measure the corrosion of refractories by slags and glasses have evolved little from the original tests. The modern rotary slag test with slag sloshing around the inside of a cylindrical furnace with an oxyacetylene flame impinging on the refractory lining was developed in the mid 1960s. As in any chemical reaction between a solid body and a liquid, corrosion of refractories by molten liquids involves reactant contact, enabling the reaction to take place, and product transport, to allow it to proceed. For reaction contact, the refractories composition, physical texture (including porosity), and, especially, nature of the bond phase (which is the first to be penetrated by liquid), play the dominant role, whereas, for product transport, the characteristics of melt and reaction products determine the rate of the reaction. Consequently, to understand the corrosion mechanisms, refractory microstructures (in particular, composition and texture of grain and bond phases), melt properties (especially composition and viscosity as a function of temperature), and wetting and interaction at high temperatures should be examined together.

Many phase diagrams have been developed specifically to help explain the occurrence of reaction products, and early texts contained extensive collections of diagrams.

Practically all liquid metals do not wet ceramics, whereas almost all slags, glasses, and fluxes do attack at the slag line where the less dense (typical silicate) liquids floating on the denser metal liquid is frequently a problem. Carbon-based ceramics are not wetted by silicate liquids, a characteristic which has led to their extensive use in ironmaking and steelmaking refractories. Wetting behavior gives an indication of penetration (simple permeation via open porosity without chemical reaction) but not attack (penetration and chemical reaction). Wetting is expected to be affected by chemistry and temperature, but surface roughness and time of exposure are significant variables for refractories. Comeforo and Hursh have measured contact angles between liquid glass and aluminosilicate refractories and found that the effect of time on wetting angle of many refractories important in glass tank construction is dramatic. High-purity refractories, alumina, silica, and mullite apparently are wet much more readily than complex fireclay-based refractories.

Corrosion rate is a function of many variables, including temperature; refractory-liquid interface composition; and liquid density, viscosity, diffusivity and degree of agitation. Post-mortem analyses have shown that, if the reaction product is soluble or dissociates directly in the liquid slag, then active corrosion may continue to the destruction of the refractory. If, however, the reaction product is not completely soluble in the liquid slag, it may form an impenetrable barrier so that, after its formation, further attack is prevented (passive corrosion). In the latter case, possible corrosion-rate-determining steps are the chemical reaction forming the layer, diffusion through the layer, or diffusion through the slag. Examples of passive corrosion include the formation of a $MgAl_2O_4$ spinel layer in the corrosion of alumina refractories by magnesia-containing slags and of a C_2S layer on magnesia-dolomite refractories attacked by silica-containing slags. It is this type of corrosion that the refractories engineer now attempts to design into the solid-liquid system of interest: to develop an in situ refractory. It is this type of corrosion that has become the theme in recent efforts to reduce corrosion of refractories by corrosive liquids.

Early studies of alkali attack were mostly relevant to the glass industry and involved observation of the effect on the refractory as a powder or in bulk exposed to selected alkali sources. Alkali attack was the scourge of early aluminosilicate blast furnace linings, resulting in a peeling of the lining in the lower regions. The peeling was interpreted to be the result of a reaction between K_2O and the fine matrix component of aluminosilicate brick, with the formation of the high-specific-volume reaction products leucite ($K_2O \cdot Al_2O_3 \cdot 4SiO_2$) and kaliophilite ($K_2O \cdot Al_2O_3 \cdot 2SiO_2$).

Because most refractories are not wetted by metals, in general, no corrosion occurs. However, there are notable exceptions, e. g., in aluminum processing. One type of reaction that can lead to refractory attack related to the reduction of SiO_2 in the aluminosilicate refractory by aluminum. Consequently, CeO_2 was used as additive to improve alloy attack resistance. The beneficial effect of CeO_2 added to bauxite was attributed to enhanced corundum grain growth, greater matrix crystallinity, and a weblike morphology of the cerium-rich regions, constituting an impediment to aluminum transport.

The disintegration of refractories by CO had been reported since before the turn of the century. After use, aluminosilicate brick exposed to gases in retorts, blast furnaces, and other equipment with a gas train containing CO displayed "iron spots," which were filled with a fine sooty deposit. Disintegration could occur in any brick or concrete containing iron or iron oxide in the appropriate form. The carbon was derived from the reaction $2CO = CO_2 + C$, the Boudouard reaction being catalyzed by a suitable state of iron. O'Harra and Darby described a test arrangement for exposing crushed brick to pure CO. They found that metallic iron was a highly effective catalyst and that the disintegration of the brick by reaction of the CO with reducible iron oxide in the brick occurred at or below 550℃.

The other form of chemical attack of refractories that persists but cannot be as effectively eliminated is the hydration of CaO- and MgO-containing refractories. Consequently, it must be countered by chemical and/or thermal processing. Magnesite is usually dead-burned, meaning calcined to temperatures as high as 2100℃, to cause densification and grain growth, which decreases the available surface area and minimizes hydration tendencies. Dolomite also is calcined and can be further stabilized with glass-forming additives and often protected with tars or pitches to preclude hydration, because lime-containing refractories are even more vulnerable to hydration than periclase. Malarria and Tinivella recently examined degradation of magnesite-chrome brick by this mechanism, using all the modern characterization techniques available.

Selected from "Evolution of in situ refractories in the 20th century" William E Lee etal, J. Am. Ceram. Soc., 1998, Vol 81 (6): 1385-1410

Words and Expressions

1. wear [wɛə] *v*. 磨损
2. cathodoluminescence [ˌkæθədəˈluːmiˈnesəns] *n*. 阴极激发光
3. probe [prəub] *v*., *n*. 探针，探测器，(以探针等) 探察，查明
4. microanalysis [ˌmaikrəuəˈnæləsis] *n*. 微量分析
5. slosh [slɔʃ] *v*., *n*. 溅，泼，泥泞
6. oxyacetylene [ˌɔksiəˈsetiliːn] *a*. 氧乙炔的
7. impinge [imˈpindʒ] *v*. 撞击
8. permeation [pəːmiˈeiʃən] *n*. 渗入，透过
9. slag line 渣线
10. agitation [ˌædʒiˈteiʃən] *n*. 搅动
11. destruction [diˈstrʌkʃən] *n*. 破坏，毁灭
12. impenetrable [imˈpenitreibl] *a*. 难以渗透的
13. magnesia-dolomite 镁质白云石
14. scourge [skəːdʒ] *n*., *v*. 侵 (磨、烧) 蚀

15. specific-volume 比容
16. leucite [ˈljuːsait] *n*. 白榴石
17. kaliophilite [ˌkæliɔfə，lait] *n*. 钾霞石
18. weblike [webˈlaik] *a*. 网状
19. morphology [mɔːfˈɔlədʒi] *n*. 形貌
20. cerium-rich 富铈的
21. impediment [imˈpedimənt] *n*. 妨碍，阻碍，障碍物
22. disintegration [disinˈtigreiʃən] *n*. 瓦解
23. sooty [ˈsuti] *a*. 煤烟熏黑的，乌黑的
24. vulnerable [ˈvʌlnərəbl] *a*. 易受攻击的

Unit 25 Glassmaking Refractories

Early glassmakers relied upon sandstones and siliceous clay for the manufacture of pots for glassmaking. The clays used with wood-fired furnaces were adequate for low-temperature melting (1100℃), but, with the introduction of coal in the 1600s by English glassmakers, furnace temperatures increased, making clay selection more critical. A major advancement came in the mid-18th century with the development of producer gas-fired regenerative furnaces where the firebrick traditionally used for the crown were replaced by Welsh Dinas silica brick because of higher operating temperatures (1400～1450℃). The fireclay brick in other areas also performed poorly at these higher temperature and were improved after the recommendation of Bontemps to use clays with minimum impurities and a high alumina, silica ratio and by adding three parts prefired grog to one part clay①. The use of grog dramatically increased the brick strength.

The outstanding development was of fused cast refractories in 1921 when irregular chunk of fused sillimanite were ground into blocks and tested in a glass furnace. Further testing indicated that fused alumina and mullite refractories had superior corrosion resistance. Patents were awarded to Corning in 1926 for fused mullite and for addition of 10%～60% zirconia, i. e., AZS, although this was not manufactured commercially until the 1940s. A manufacturing facility was set up in 1928 to manufacture the fused blocks jointly by Corning and Hartford-Emprie, giving the company name, Corhart Refractories. St. Gobain in France began to manufacture the fused refractories, under license and in conjunction with Corning, which continues in operation, now known as SERP②.

By 1940, however, fused alumina was more common, and a fused 13% chrome block was introduced. After 1947, the increasing use of fused AZS saw campaign lives increase from 11～13 months to 3～5 years and melting temperatures increase from 1400℃ in the mid-1930s to 1550 ℃ by 1970. By the mid-to late-1950s, AZS was replacing silica in the superstructure and sidewalls, and the first AZS crown was installed in a borosilicate furnace in 1959. However, the AZS at this time was a non-oxidized product and, on heating, exuded large quantities of glassy phase from the block surface with a consequent effect on product glass quality③. It was not until the late 1960s that oxidation during production of AZS by bubbling oxygen through the melt became common, dramatically reducing the levels of exudation.

The development of fused AZS refractories was a critical advance for the glass industry, enabling glass-tank campaigns to be extended to their current length of more than a decade. Originally, zirconia was added to the alumina compositions in an attempt to alleviate some of the problems associated with cracking on cooling the cast blocks. This currently is known to be an error, because it is more difficult to produce crack-free blocks with higher zirconia contents because of the tetragonal-to-monoclinic phase transformation. However, zirconia does increase corrosion resistance to soda-lime-silica glass. The mechanism by which AZS refractories resist corrosion is now well understood and results from the morphology of the microstructure, low permeability of the dense fusion cast blocks, and solution of alumina in the tank glass, which creates a viscous boundary layer next to the refractory enriched in alumina. Zirconia has a low solubility and, thus, a low rate of dissolution in this alumina-saturated interface. The microstructure of fusion-cast AZS consists of alumina-zirconia laths of near-eutectic structure, corundum laths, zirconia dendrites and 10～20 vol % zirconia-containing aluminosilicate glass. Most of the zirconia is in a skeletal (eutectic) form, which is difficult to dislodge by corrosion, and it acts to hold the corrosion products in place. The glass in the microstructure is viscous enough at temperature to deform and accommodate the large stress associated with the tetragonal-to-monoclinic phase transition in zirconia, which occurs at 1000～1200℃ on heating and 1000～800℃ on cooling. Zircon is used in glass contact refractories for borosilicate glasses and glass fibers, and high-aluminas and mullites are used in the superstructures. Chromic oxide, with its high melting temperature is extremely resistant to molten glass and is used in the manufacture of corrosive glasses, where the coloring effect of the chrome is not important④. A range of pressed AZS products also have been developed. Recently, the major change has been the increased use of oxy-fuel firing for smaller furnaces, driven largely by the need to reduce levels of nitrous oxides (NO_x). However, increased concentration of soda in the furnace atmosphere has meant that it was necessary to find suitable alternatives to silica for the crowns and superstructure based on fused AZS and aluminas.

In regenerative furnaces exhaust gases are passed through a massive open stack of refractory brick, called checkers (or packings), which absorb heat. After 20 min, the flow is reversed and incoming air to the fuel burners is drawn through the checkers, extracting heat and saving energy. The refractories used in this application must resist the corrosive action of batch dust, vapors, and condensates; have high thermal conductivity and heat capacity to maximize heat exchange efficiency; and resist thermal shock resulting from the reverse flow of hot/cold air⑤. The top third of the checkerwork is at the highest temperature and is most affected by alkali vapor and lime and silica batch carryover. The lower courses are most affected by thermal shock, and surfates deposit about a third of the way up the checkers, so that different refractory grades are needed for the various courses. The major advances came in the 1950s, with the use of magnesia-chrome in walls and lower checkers and magnesia in upper checkers. Early checkers were constructed in a variety of designs, using standard brick shapes. However, because of minor variations in size, these often would rotate in-service, leading to early blockage. This led to the increased use, since the 1970s, of various interlocking brick shapes, such as cruciforms and chimney blocks. Major improvements in raw-material quality and bonding systems in the 1970s led to use of high-fired C_2S-bonded magnesia brick in the upper courses and M_2S and spinel-bonded magnesia brick for the surfate zone.

Selected from "Evolution of in situ refractories in the 20th century" William E Lee *et al*, J. Am. Ceram. Soc., 1998, Vol 81 (6): 1385-1410

Words and Expressions

1. siliceous [siˈliʃəs] *a*. 硅酸的，硅土的
2. regenerative [riˈdʒenəreitiv] *a*. 再生的，更生的
3. crown [kraun] *n*. 炉顶
4. prefired [priˈfaiəd] *a*. 预烧的
5. grog [grɔg] *n*. 熟料
6. campaign [kæmˈpein] *n*. 炉龄（期）
7. superstructure [ˈsjuːpəstrʌktʃə] *n*. 上部结构
8. sidewall [saidˈwɔːl] *n*. 侧墙
9. exude [igˈzjuːd] *v*.（使）渗出，（使）慢慢流出，发散
10. alleviate [əˈliːvieit] *v*. 减轻，缓和
11. permeability [ˌpəːmiəˈbiliti] *n*. 渗透性
12. fusion-cast 熔铸
13. lath [læθ] *n*. 板条状
14. near-eutectic 接近共晶的
15. dendrite [ˈdendrait] *n*. 树枝状晶体
16. skeletal [ˈskelətəl] *a*. 骨架状的
17. dislodge [disˈlɔdʒ] *v*. 移动，除去
18. oxy-fuel 含氧燃料
19. checker [ˈtʃekə] *n*. 格子砖
20. checkerwork [tʃekəˈwək] *n*. 格子砖结构
21. carryover [kæriˈouvə] *n*. 飞料
22. blockage [ˈblɔkidʒ] *n*. 堵塞，封锁
23. cruciform [ˈkruːsifɔːm] *a*., *n*. 十字形（的）
24. chimney [ˈtʃimni] *a*. 烟囱状的

Notes

① 本句中的不定式 to use clays with minimum impurities and a high alumina: silica ratio 和介词短语 by adding three parts prefired grog to one part clay 是用于修饰前置名词 recommendation 的并列结构。

② 本句中由 which 引导的从句是非限定性定语从句，which 代表全句，本句最后的 now known as SERP 为定语从句中 which 的同位语。St. Gobain（圣哥班）是世界上最大的玻璃集团之一，SERP（西普）则是世界上著名的耐火材料制造公司。

③ 本句为并列句，由 and 连接，主语共用。on heating 短语为状语，修饰第二并列句。

④ 本句中由 where 引导的从句为定语，修饰 the manufacture of corrosive glasses。

⑤ 本句由三个并列句组成，由分号连接，主语共用。不定式短语 to maximize heat exchange efficiency 为目的状语，修饰第二并列句，现在分词短语 resulting from the reverse flow of hot/cold air 为定语，修饰第三并列句中的 thermal shock。

Exercises

1. Translate underlined sentences in the text into Chinese.
2. Translate the following phrases into English or Chinese:

① 含杂质最少的粘土
② 一份粘土加三份预烧熟料
③ 玻璃池炉的炉龄
④ 含氧化锆的硅铝酸盐玻璃
⑤ 各种连通形砖，如十字形砖、烟囱形砖
⑥ irregular chunk of fused sillimanite
⑦ some of the problems associated with cracking on cooling the cast blocks
⑧ corrosion resistance to soda-lime-silica glass
⑨ the large stress associated with the tetragonal-to-monoclinic phase transition in zirconia
⑩ thermal shock resulting from the reverse flow of hot/cold air

Reading Material 25

Development of Refractories in Specific Applications

Ironmaking and Blast Furnace Refractories

Iron in malleable form was made historically by direct reduction of its ores with charcoal in deep-hearth furnaces built originally against a bank to induce sufficient draught. Early furnaces were lined with natural sandstones or were carved directly into stone ledges. The higher temperatures achieved by 17th century blast furnaces led to development of manufactured firebrick from kaolinite-rich clays. Such linings were used until the increased iron demands of the industrial revolution of the 19th century in the United Kingdom made further improvements necessary. Until WWII, the hearth walls were a simple chimneylike structure built of fireclay brick and water cooled either through cast-iron staves with cooling channels or by external water sprays. Unfortunately, this arrangement did not prevent breakouts of molten metal. The use of high-thermal-conductivity, metallurgical, coke-based carbon brick combined with efficient water cooling of the hearth walls of the furnace overcame this problem. Most hearths until 1960s were composed of carbon wall and ceramic pads, which were substantial masonry blocks that could be 4 m thick. Following the introduction of effective underneath cooling systems, carbon hearth pads could be used in addition to carbon hearth walls. The thermal approach was based on high-thermal-conductivity carbon and water cooling, and, from this, the ceramic approach was developed, using a combination of low-conductivity ceramic in contact with the metal but cooled by a carbon backing. The goal of the thermal approach is to reduce chemical attack and thermal stressing of the lining and lead to freezing of a skull on the surface as protection. The ceramic approach, which relies on the refractory properties of the hot-face materials, initially used a low-cost firebrick but switched to high-alumina brick when it was realized that this kept the iron freeze line closer to the hot face. Both approaches need efficient cooling systems to remove heat from the pad, using air, water, or graphite.

Primary Steelmaking Refractories

The problem of converting iron from the blast furnace into steel was solved by the invention of the acid Bessemer process in the 1850s and the acid OH process a few years later. Although these processes initiated the era of bulk steel production, it was soon appreciated that world demand was unlikely to be met unless a method of making steel from phosphorous-containing irons could be found. The success of the basic Bessemer process led to the introduction of the basic OH process in which dephosphorization was achieved under a CaO-rich slag on a basic hearth. Bessemer and open hearth processes were superseded by the production of primary steel from blast furnace iron in the basic oxygen furnace (BOF) and from scrap in the electric arc furnace (EAF). EAF now is the fastest growing steelmaking process worldwide and the least consumer of refractories. In the 1950s, the refractories used in the EAF were typically doloma lower sidewalls with chemically bonded MgO-Cr_2O_3 brick for hot spots and the slag line. Roofs were made of silica brick. From 1960 to 1970 the sidewall linings were direct-bonded magnesite-chrome or chemically bonded, metal-cased, steel-reinforced brick, and the roof was a high-alumina bauxite-based brick. In the late 1970s, the slag line was fused magnesia-chrome and high-purity magnesia brick with pitch-impregnated magnesia sidewalls and a direct-bonded magnesia-chrome roof in high-output furnace. The introduction of water-cooled steel panels for the EAF roof and upper sidewalls rapidly reduced the demand for sidewall and roof refractories in EAFs by 75%. The concept of the water-cooled paneling is to freeze some of the viscous furnace slag onto the panels to generate an in situ refractory. The center part, where the graphite electrodes are inserted, continued to be a high-alumina refractory castable, and the hearth was a high-density magnesia monolith with pitch-impregnated magnesia-carbon at the slag line. Resin-bonded magnesia-graphite brick at the slag line was introduced in the 1980s. Adoption of the BOF process worldwide was not rapid. Currently, BOF is used to produce 60% of world steel, with the remainder being via EAF. Unitl 1970, BOF vessel linings were based primarily on tempered doloma, because it was an attack-resistant, basic, cheap refractory. The tap hole, where wear is more sever, was pitch-impregnated, fired magnesia. In the late 1970s, fired, pitch-impregnated magnesia linings were introduced because of the reduced hydration of magnesia and beneficial effects of carbon with respect to wetting by slag and thermal shock. These modifications increased lining lives to 800～900 heats. The development of carbon-bonded, graphite-reinforced magnesia brick provided a refractory with excellent slag resistance because of the nonwetting carbon/graphite and improved thermal shock resistance because of its high thermal conductivity and crack-propagation-resistant microstructure.

Refractories for Cement Production

Portland cement clinker has been produced from rotary kilns that are long (60～200 m), up to 6 m in diameter, rotating (1～3.5 rpm) cylindrical tubes. Such kilns also are used to make lime and calclined magnesia, bauxite, and dolomite. The kiln has a fuel burner flame at one end, and the raw material is fed in at the other end with a slight downward slope from inlet to outlet. Because the temperature gradient varies with the process from ambient to 1600℃ in a wet process kiln along its length, different refractories are used. From the input end of the kiln, the zones are termed drying, calcination, preheat, upper transition or security, burning or sintering, lower transition, and discharge. Zone lengths vary in modern kilns with the process. Throughout most of the 20th century, various grades of aluminosilicate brick have been used to line the different zones. For the feed or preheat end, dense fireclay brick are used for good abrasion resistance. For higher refractoriness in the transition zones, superduty fireclays are used. For the burning zone, high-alumina (70%～80%) brick are used. It also has been realized that basic (sintered, dead-burned magnesia-chrome or doloma) brick offer good chemical resistance to basic cement and also gain additional resistance to attack by their ability to hold protective in situ coatings of partially melted cement clinker in the upper transition and burning zones. This coating also adds additional thermal insulation and may adhere strongly to the refractory brick because of the formation of a $C_{12}A_7$ reaction bond. In general, the refractories used in the low-temperature zones of rotary kilns in the 1990s remain aluminosilicates, such as firebrick or alumina brick, although there may be a trend to castables and other dense monolithics in these zones. The most dramatic changes, however, have occurred in the high-temperature, transition, and burning zones. Direct-bonded magnesia-chrome bricks were popular in these areas in the 1960s and 1970s, but the carcinogenic nature of Cr^{6+} generated from Cr^{3+} in cement kilns during service and concern about disposal after use has led, in the 1990s, to its total replacement in this application in Europe and North America by magnesia-spinel, magnesia-zirconia, and doloma-zirconia brick.

Selected from "Evolution of in situ refractories in the 20th century" William E Lee etal, J. Am. Ceram. Soc., 1998, Vol 81 (6): 1385-1410

Words and Expressions

1. malleable [ˈmæliəbl] *a.* 有延展性的，可锻的
2. ledge [ledʒ] *n.* 壁架，架状突出物，矿层
3. stave [steiv] *n.* 狭板，棍棒，芯盒；*v.* 击穿，凿孔
4. breakout [breikˈaut] *n.* 烧穿炉衬，金属冲出
5. metallurgical [ˌmetəˈləːdʒikəl] *a.* 冶金学的
6. pad [pæd] *n.* 底座

7. masonry [mæsənri] *n*. 砌筑，炉墙
8. skull [skʌl] *n*. 结渣，渣壳
9. dephosp horization *n*. 除磷，去磷
10. supersede [ˈsjupəsid] *n*. 代替，取代
11. tap hole 出钢口
12. pitch-impregnated 沥青浸渍的
13. heat [hit] *n*. 次（包龄），焙炼
14. crack-propagation-resistant 抗裂纹扩展的
15. doloma [dələmə] *n*. 煅烧白云石
16. superduty [sjupəˈdjuːti] *a*. 超级耐高温的，超耐用的
17. magnesia-spinel 镁尖晶石
18. magnesia-zirconia 镁锆质
19. doloma-zirconia 煅烧白云石锆质，锆白云石质

PART Ⅵ GEMMOLOGY

Unit 26 An Introduction to the Geology of Gem Materials

The division of the sciences into various subjects, such as biology, chemistry, geology and physics, is convenient for their study, and for teaching purposes. To study any of these subjects effectively, the student should have, at least, some knowledge and understanding of the related sciences. Gemology is no exception to this and a basic understanding of the geology and mineralogy of gemstones will be helpful.

The Crust

The solid crust of the continents on which we live varies from about 25km (15 miles) to about 70km (45 miles) in thickness. Under the oceans it averages about 6km (4 miles).

Much of the crust has a thin covering composed chiefly of sedimentary material. This is material, which has been deposited by wind, rain, and seawater or by chemical precipitation, and then cemented or compressed to form rocks. These sedimentary rocks are chiefly limestone, clay, shale and sandstone.

Granites, basalt and metamorphic rocks form the major part of the crust (the middle and lower layers). The first two have been formed by the solidification of molten rock and are termed "igneous" rocks. Metamorphic rocks are any rocks that have undergone change (metamorphism), principally by heat or pressure in the depths of the earth.

The middle layer of the crust varies between 16 and 24km (10~15 miles) in thickness, beneath the continental landmasses. It is sometimes referred to as "granitic layer", as granite is its main constituent. Similarly the lower layer is known as the "basaltic layer", as basalt and other basic rocks predominate.

In the Atlantic, the Pacific and other major oceans, the crust is very thin, and its major component is the basaltic layer.

The Intermediate Zone or Mantle

Beneath the crust lies the mantle with a thickness of about 2900km (1800 miles). It is hot and plastic, in contrast to the cooler and more rigid crust.

The Core

The core extends about 3500km (2150 miles), from the mantle to the center of the Earth. Scientists are uncertain as to its temperature and its composition.

One theory is that it is chiefly composed of molten nickel and iron (partly solid, partly molten). (Using the chemical symbols for these two elements, Ni and Fe respectively, geologists sometimes call this portion of the Earth, "NIFE".)

The core, mantle and crust each have different physical characteristics. The core is under the highest pressure, and its temperature is higher than those of the mantle and crust. Because of these differences there are discontinuities and relative movement between these regions.

It is these factors, together with the effects of gravity and the forces exerted by the other members of our solar system, that are considered to be responsible for such natural phenomena as volcanic eruptions, earthquakes, the slow drift of the continents and the buckling of the surface of the Earth to form mountain ranges and valleys.

The surface features of the Earth are produced by two sets of opposing forces - destructive and constructive.

The destructive forces① , such as those due to wind, rain, rivers, glaciers, the action of the sea and some earthquakes, continuously break down the rocks, and minerals, which form the features of the Earth's crust. This is a slow never-ending process.

The constructive forces②, due to such Earth movements as the drift of the landmasses (plate tectonics) and volcanic activities, are continually forming new features. Some of these changes may be relatively rapid, as in the case of volcanoes, whilst others may take millions of years, as with the gradual movement of the continents. Nevertheless, the formation is continuous.

The Composition of the Earth

There are 92 naturally occurring elements in the Earth's crust and, of those, eight account for approximately 98% of the crust. They are oxygen (46.6%), silicon (27.2%), aluminum (8.1%), iron (5.0%), calcium (3.6%), sodium (2.8%), potassium (2.6%) and magnesium (2.1%).

It should be realized, however, that the elements forming the Earth are not evenly distributed through the crust, for example basalt has a composition different from granite, and both these differ from limestone.

These natural elements combine together chemically to form compounds and some of these chemical compounds are minerals.

A mineral, in most cases, is a naturally formed inorganic substance, which possesses a definite chemical composition and a definite atomic structure.

A mineral may consist of just one element (e. g. diamond is composed of just one element - carbon) or of several elements, chemically combined to form a compound (e. g. quartz is a compound made up of silicon and oxygen atoms).

Rocks, however, consist of mineral particles which have grown together, or which have become cemented together by chemical processes or by heat and pressure, and have formed aggregates.

Some rocks, which possess desirable form and color (such as lapis lazuli), are used as gemstones or for decorative purposes.

Most gem materials are minerals, but some owe their origins to plants and animals, such as pearl, coral and ivory. These are not minerals, although many organic substances are partially composed of minerals such as calcite and aragonite.

Selected from "Gem Diamond Course", The Gemmological Association and Gem Testing Laboratory of Great Britain, 1991.

Words and Expressions

1. gemmology [dʒeˈmɔlədʒi] *n.* 宝石学
2. gem [dʒem] *n.* 宝石
3. gemstone [dʒemˈstəun] *n.* 宝石
4. sedimentary [sediˈmentəri] *a.* 沉积的，由沉积物形成的，～ rock 沉积岩
5. shale [sheil] *n.* 页岩
6. granite [ˈgrænit] *n.* 花岗岩，/grantic [græˈnitik] *adj.* 花岗质的
7. basalt [ˈbæsɔːlt] *n.* 玄武岩～ic *a.* 玄武岩的
8. metamorphic [metəˈmɔːfik] *a.* 变质的，变形的，改变结构的，～rock 变质岩
   metamorphism [metəˈmɔːfizm] *n.* 变质作用
9. igneous [ˈigniəs] *a.* 岩浆的，火的，似火的，～rock 火成岩；～magma 岩浆
10. landmass [ˈlændmæs] *n.* 陆块、地块，大片陆地，尤指大陆
11. mantle [ˈmæntl] *n.* 地幔
12. eruption [iˈrʌpʃən] *n.* 爆发，喷发，喷发物
13. buckle [ˈbʌkl] *v.* 弯折，纵向弯曲，挤弯作用，(纵向) 压曲，隆起
14. glacier [ˈglæʃəː] *n.* 冰川，冰河
15. lapis lazuli [læpisˈlæzjulai] *n.* 青金石，青金岩
16. coral [ˈkɔrɔl] *n.* 珊瑚；*a.* 珊瑚的，珊瑚色的
17. ivory [ˈaivəri] *n.* 象牙，(海象等的) 长牙；*a.* 象牙制成的，似象牙的
18. aragonite [ˈəræɡənait] *n.* 文石，霰石

Notes

① destructive force 外力地质作用，主要是指对地球表面进行破坏、侵蚀等作用，如风化作用、沉积作用等。

② constructive force 内力地质作用，由于地球内部的能量引起的地质作用，如岩浆作用、变质作用、火山活动和地震等。

Exercises

1. Answer the following questions according to the text.
   ① Where do gemstones occur?
   ② What is the relationship between gems and minerals?
   ③ What is the composition of the Earth?

2. Translate underlined sentence in the text into Chinese;
3. Translate the following phrases into English or Chinese.
   igneous rock　volcanic eruption　a definite atomic structure
   a definite chemical composition　inorganic substance
   花岗质层　玄武岩质层
4. Write a short essay to describe simply the structure of the Earth.

Reading Material 26

Red Tourmaline

Judging the various qualities of tourmaline is one of the most difficult challenges facing gem professionals today. Why? Because tourmaline is the look-a-like stone. For centuries tourmaline has been evaluated mainly on how closely it resembled other gemstones. Historically, green tourmaline was compared to emerald, blue tourmaline to sapphire and red tourmaline to ruby. The discovery of Paraiba tourmaline in 1989 signaled the beginning of the end to this approach to grading. Thanks to Paraiba, tourmaline has shed its second class status, established its own aristocracy and has begun to be taken seriously as a gemstone in its own right. Consider red or what is called rubellite tourmaline.

Red tourmaline is found in every conceivable variation along a continuum from pink through red. Despite the misleading appellation "rubellite," red tourmaline looks like red tourmaline -that is to say, not at all like ruby. Red tourmaline exhibits a unique combination of primary and secondary hue and a more distinct visible dichroism than ruby. Finally, the two gems behave quite differently in incandescent light.

Hue

Using the ruby standard, stones with a visually pure red hue with the absolute minimum of secondary hue should be the most valued in the marketplace. However, red tourmaline is never a visually pure red. Tourmaline always shows a distinct secondary hue, usually 20 percent or more of pink, violet or purple. Vividly pinkish, violetish and purplish secondary hues lend to tourmaline a distinctive appearance that can be quite beautiful though not particularly "ruby-like."

Dichroic effect, the tendency of a stone to show two or more distinct hues or tonal variations of the same hue in different parts of the stone, is very pronounced in tourmaline. Considered a defect in ruby, dichroic effect partly defines the beauty of red tourmaline.

Incandescent lighting further muddies the issue - red tourmaline can be a real Jekyll and Hyde! When observed under a light bulb one of two things will happen: Red tourmaline will either pick up a distinct brownish mask or more rarely the violet/pink component (sometimes with the addition of a bit of gray) will strengthen. Thai ruby behaves exactly the opposite. A strongly violetish or purplish red tourmaline is much more attractive than a muddy brownish "rubylike" stone.

Crystal

Diaphaneity, transparency or more commonly "crystal" is the true fourth "C" of colored gemstone evaluation. Tourmaline is a day stone. That is, it look sits best in natural lighting. Incandescent lighting normally produces a negative effect. The brownish mask that shows up under the lightbulb, if it is strong, causes the stone to lose its transparency too literally "close up" under the light bulb. Thus, it is important when considering a purchase to carefully observe the stone in incandescent light. This is the crucial test. A stone that is a limpid pinkish red in daylight but becomes a muddy brownish red in incandescent is less than desirable.

Tone

Color scientists tell us that the ideal tone for red is 80 percent, which is also the ideal tone in ruby. However, in red tourmaline, lighter tones when combined with a higher percentage of secondary hue will often result in a marvelously beautiful gemstone. Gems with tonal values between 40 and 50 percent will appear rosy, while pinkish stones in the 50 to 60 percent ranges ape the color of Maraschino cherries. The best of the darker toned purplish reds resemble the bing cherry.

Clarity

Tourmaline is a type III gemstone. Eye-visible inclusions are the norm. Stones with inclusions that are visible but affect neither the durability nor beauty of the gemstone are acceptable. Visibly flawless gemstones are rare and therefore should, and do, command a substantial premium.

When evaluating the red variety of tourmaline the emphasis should be placed on the beauty of the tourmaline and not on theoretical comparisons to ruby. In fact, the term rubellite should be consigned to the dustbin. Unlike ruby, this variety of tourmaline will normally exhibit a distinct secondary hue and strong dichroic effect. A key issue is the stone's behavior when it is shifted from a natural to an incandescent lighting environment. All other factors being equal, red tourmaline with little or no brown mask that exhibits good crystal in all lighting environments is the *creme de la creme* of this tourmaline variety.

Selected from "Gemkey magazine", Richard W. Wise, Gemkey Co., Ltd., May-June 1999.

Words and Expressions

1. tourmaline [ˈtuəməlin] *n.* 碧玺，电气石；电气石色
2. look-a-like [luːkəˈlaik] *a.* 与（其它宝石）相似的，看起来象
3. emerald [ˈemərəld] *n.* 祖母绿，绿宝石，翠绿色；*adj.* 翠绿色的

4. sapphire [ˈsæfaiə] *n*. 一种刚玉，蓝宝石，蓝宝石色；*adj*. 深蓝色的
5. Paraiba [pɑːrɑːˈibɑː] *n*. 帕拉伊巴（巴西东北部的州，首府若昂佩索阿）
6. aristocracy [ærisˈtɔkrəsi] *n*. 贵族统治；寡头统治；最优等的人
7. appellation [æpeˈleiʃən] *n*. 称呼，名称，称号
8. rubellite [ruːˈbelait] *n*. 红色碧玺，红电气石
9. dichroism [ˈdaikrəuizəm] *n*. 二色性（宝石因方向性不同而表现出不同的颜色的性质）
10. incandescent [inkænˈdesnt] *a*. 白热的，白炽的；极亮的，灿烂的；闪闪发光的；炽热的
11. Jekyll and Hyde [dʒekəlˈhaid] 好坏两面兼而有之，双重人格的人
12. hue [hjuː] *n*.（色彩）的浓淡，色相，色调
13. diaphaneity [daiəfəˈniːiti] *n*. 透明性，透明度
14. limpid [ˈlimpid] *a*. 明显的，清澈的，清晰的，平静的
15. ape [eip] *vt*. 模仿，学……的样；*n*. 类人猿，无尾猿；学样的人
16. premium [ˈpriːmjəm] *n*. 奖赏，奖金；[喻] 非常珍贵
17. *creme de la creme* [ˈkremdəlɑːˈkrem] [法语] 精华，最优秀的分子，最好的部分

Unit 27 Mechanical Properties of Gemstones

Gemstones may show mechanical characteristics as a result of the application of force, for example gemstones may be damaged, broken and, in some cases, be divided into two or more pieces, etc. Mechanical properties involved in gemology are cleavage, parting and fracture, hardness, density.

Cleavage, Parting and Fracture

Cleavage is the ability, possessed by some gemstones, to split along certain well-defined directions leaving more or less flat faces (possibly showing pearly luster), lying parallel to crystal faces, even though crystal faces may not be present in particular specimen.

In certain minerals, this difference in strength is sufficient to allow the crystal to split, parallel to the densely packed planes, when appropriate force is applied. This particular type of splitting is called cleavage, is always parallel to an ideal crystal face, and can only occur in a single crystal.

Because cleavage is a directional characteristic of weak atomic bonding, any direction in a crystal lying parallel to layers of atoms is a potential cleavage direction, although most minerals resist splitting along these various planes. It is for this reason that cleavage is a highly diagnostic feature, possessed to a marked degree by only a few gemstones.

When we refer to a gemstone with noticeable cleavage, we need to discuss not only its direction, but also the cleavage quality. Citing the examples already given, diamond has perfect octahedral cleavage, and graphite has perfect cleavage parallel to the basal plane (of the hexagonal crystal), called basal cleavage. Other possible directions of cleavage include rhombohedral, prismatic, pinacoidal. Cleavage faces may often be recognized by a series of very shallow steps, where the break has occurred along several layers of atoms at the same time.

The gemmologist obtains benefit from cleavage because it is an aid to identification, and the cutter obtains some benefit because poor quality areas can be removed easily from rough materials. While this feature is of particular importance to the diamond cutter, there are probably more disadvantages than advantages associated with cleavage. It is virtually impossible to polish a gemstone parallel to a cleavage direction.

Parting is the breaking or splitting along lamellar twinning planes. Sometimes the internal structure of a gemstone causes a physical effect similar in appearance to cleavage. However, the gemstone breaks or splits along twinning planes. For example ruby exists splits at rhombohedral and basal directions.

Fracture is the random, non-directional breakage, which occurs in most gemstones as a result of sharp impact, and is often considered to be a typical and identifying feature of glass. Up to a point this is true, but it is also quite typical of amorphous substances in general, and of those crystalline materials that have no pronounced planes of weakness, for example, quartz or beryl.

Several types of fracture are recognized, those normally seen by the gemologist being conchoidal or shell-like. When a mineral breaks with curved concavities, then the break is called conchoidal fracture, from the resemblance of the concavity to the valve of a shell.

The fibrous, tough structure of nephrite jade produces another kind of fracture - hackly. This refers to the uneven, and often jagged, break that occurs when this material is broken.

Other terms are used as earthy, splintery significance for the in mineralogy to describe fractures such and uneven, but these has little significance for the gemologist.

Hardness

Hardness is the ability of gem to withstand abrasion, and is one of the prime qualities of a gem material. The scale of hardness, which is used universally for gemology and mineralogy, is comparative one.

The German mineralogist, Friedrich Mohs produced practical scheme for hardness assessment in 1822. After a number of selection trails, he brought together ten easily obtained minerals, which could be obtained in a high degree purity, and listed them in order of ability to withstand scratching by other members of the group. This resulted in which is now known as Mohs'Scale of Hardness①.

The scale in increasing order of resistance to abrasion is:

Talc	1	gypsum	2	calcite	3	fluorite	4	appetite	5
orthoclase	6	quartz	7	topaz	8	corundum	9	diamond	10

It is important to note that this is only an order of hardness and that the difference in hardness between any two adjacent members of the scale is not an indication that a uniform difference of hardness exists between other pairs of members②. But the comparable hardness of some other common substances would be noted, for example finger nail (2. 5), window glass (5～5. 5), steel knife blade (5. 5～6) and steel file (6. 5～7).

Density and Specific Gravity③

The carbon atoms that unite to form either graphite or diamond, do so in different ways, not only producing difference in hardness and cleavage, as described in the earlier section, but also differences in their weight/volume ratios, which are termed as "density"④.

The density of every substance, including all gemstones, is determined by the arrangement of its constituent atoms. Density is measured by the number of units of mass contained in 1 unit volume.

Density=Mass /Volume

It is always expressed in terms of units of weight and volume, e. g. pounds/cubic feet (lbs/cu. ft.), grams/cubic centimeters (g/cm^3), kilograms/cubic meters (kg/m^3), There are other units used, particularly for liquids and gases, as such as pounds/gallons or grams/ litres.

The density of a substance is difficult to test directly, so the term, specific gravity, is often used in gemology. Specific gravity is the ratio between the weight of a substance and the weight of an equal volume of water, at a temperature of 4℃ and at standard atmospheric pressure.

Selected from "Gem Diamond Course", The Gemmological Association and Gem Testing Laboratory of Great Britain, 1991.

Words and Expressions

1. cleavage [ˈkliːvidʒ] *n*. 解理；劈开，分裂；劈开处
2. parting [ˈpɑːtiŋ] *n*. 裂理，裂开；分裂，分离
3. diagnostic [daiəgˈnɔstik] *a*. 诊断的，特征的；表示特性的
4. pinacoidal [pinəˈkɔidəl] *a*. 底面的，轴面的，板面的
5. conchoidal [kɔŋˈkɔidl] *a*. 贝壳状的
6. nephrite [ˈnefrait] *n*. 软玉，闪石
7. hackly [ˈhækli] *a*. 粗糙的，参差不齐的，锯齿形的
8. splintery [ˈsplintəri] *a*. 裂片（似）的，易碎裂的，锯齿状的，粗糙的
9. topaz [ˈtəupæz] *n*. 托帕石，黄玉
10. file [fail] *n*. 锉刀，资料，文件

Notes

① Mohs'Scale of Hardness 摩氏硬度计（或表），1822年由德国矿物学家Friedrich Mohs选用自然界中常见的易得到高纯度的十种矿物，按其相互之间刻划能力从小到大排列构成。

② It is important to note that … other pairs of members. it 是形式主语，指的是 to note that this is … and that …。

③ Specific gravity 相对密度（S. G.），宝石的相对密度等于宝石在空气中的质量与同体积的水在4℃及标准大气压条件下的质量之间的比值，是一个没有单位的物理量，与宝石的密度值相等。

④ The carbon atoms that … which are termed as 'density'. 碳原子按不同的排列方式可形成石墨和金刚石，这种不同的排列方式不仅产生了如前面所提到的不同的硬度和解理，同时使得他们的质量与体积之比也不相同，质量与体积之比就称为"密度"。

Exercises

1. Translate the underlined sentences in text into Chinese.
2. Answer the following questions:
   ① What is the Mohs hardness scale?
   ② What is the cleavage?
   ③ How to measure the specific gravity of a gemstone?
   ④ How to distinguish the definitions of cleavage and parting?

3. Translate the following expressions into Chinese or English.

   mechanical properties　lamellar twinning planes　conchoidal fracture　specific gravity

   解理面　底面解理　八面体解理　参差状断口　相对硬度

4. According to the text, complete the following sentences:

   ① Fracture includes ______, ______, ______, ______, and give a typical example respectively ______, ______, ______, ______.

   ② The cleavage directions vary from different gemstones, and the usual ones are ______, ______, ______, ______ etc.

   ③ Mechanical properties of gemstones include ______, ______, ______, ______, ______ etc.

5. Write a short essay to introduce the use or importance of mechanical properties in gemmology.

Reading Material 27

Heat Treatment

The Beginnings of Heat Treatments

It can only be guessed when the enhancement of gemstones by heat treatment first evolved.

There were a number of early technological studies on the effect on gems and minerals of heating in various atmospheres and at various temperatures, often with the aim of understanding the cause of the colors.

Since the 1970s there has been a tremendous increases in the use of heat treatments, particularly as applied the corundum family although, in retrospect, it is clear that this technique has been steadily developed over the years. The almost total absence for some time of the brownish or purplish Thai rubies indicate that almost all such stones had been heat treated to remove the brownish or purplish shade, without any note being taken of this activity.

Heat Treatments and Furnaces

There are a number of names both for the process of heating as well as for the apparatus in which it is performed. One can speak of annealing, baking, browning, combusting, cooking, firing, frying, heating, incinerating, pyrolizing, roasting, scorching, searing, soaking, tempering, toasting, and so on. These operations occur in a brazier, cooker, furnace, heater, kiln, lehr, muffle, oven, pot, retort, roster, and the like, a list that also includes terms usually found only in crossword puzzles, such as calcar, oast, and salamander. Some of these may be combined with a variety of qualifiers. There are subtle differences involved in some of these terms, but they are unimportant in the present context; for simplicity, 'heating' in a 'furnace' is used herein. There are also many different heat-generating agents, including various gases, oil, charcoal, wood, coal, coke, a variety of applications of electricity, as well as optical-image systems that use the sun or other intense light sources.

Most gemstone materials require heating at a rather gentle rate so as to avoid fractures. This is usually achieved by burying the material in some inter powder or placing it in a series of nested crucibles (usually of high-purity alumina for use up to 1900℃), so that the heat penetrates slowly to and into the gemstone. The whole arrangement is then placed into the cold furnace which is not opened again until the heating is completed and the stone has cooled to room temperature.

One way in which gemstone materials may self-destruct during heating is by the enlargement of existing cracks; it may therefore be advisable in some instances to trim away all damaged regions. Since this trimming process is part of the gemstone-shaping process, heating is frequently performed on the preformed or the finished gem; repolishing may then be required.

Another cause of fractures, either local or overall, is the presence of inclusions of various types. If an inclusion has a higher thermal expansion than the surroundings, a large stress will result if the material is heated above the original formation temperature. Below the formation temperature the inclusion will have shrunk into a smaller space. Chemical decompositions or reactions that yield gases or bulkier products can also produce damage. In some instances this type of damage can reveal that a heat treatment has been used.

Heat-treatment Conditions

The important factors in specifying the conditions for the heat treatment of a gemstone material are the following:

(1) The maximum temperature reached.

(2) The time for which the maximum temperature is sustained.

(3) The rate of heating to temperature.

(4) The rate of cooling down from temperature and any holding stages while cooling.

(5) The chemical nature of the atmosphere.

(6) The pressure of the atmosphere.

(7) The nature of the material in contact with the gemstone.

These seven factors may even vary during the course of a specific heat treatment. In any given treatment several of these factors may not be important.

Exact conditions for heat treatments cannot usually be specified for two reasons: first, because most heat-treatment processes are held as closely guarded secrets and have never been fully revealed; and second, and most importantly, because of the wide variability of natural materials.

To given one specific example, the blue color of sapphire as it is found in nature is derived from a subtle interaction between two impurities, iron and titanium. This color can be further modified by the presence of other impurities, such as the red-causing chromium, or even by white silk- and asterism-producing titanium itself; this last factor is controlled in part by heating and cooling conditions to which the material was last exposed in its geological history. The exact shade of blue also depends not only on the relative amounts of iron and titanium present, but also on the valence states involved, namely ferrous, Fe^{2+}, and ferric, Fe^{3+}, as well as titanous Ti^{3+}, and titanic, Ti^{4+}, states; this is controlled by the oxidizing-reducing conditions during formation and subsequent heating and cooling in nature. The exact appearance of any specific, as mined, Fe-Ti-colored blue sapphire, which can range from almost colorless via yellow, green, and blue to almost black with red, purple, brown, or milky overtones, either clear or combines with silk or asterism, is not indicative of an exact composition, but could be derived from a broad range of different compositions and past environment histories. In attempting to produce a specific color enhancement in such a gemstone by a heat treatment, it is obvious that a wide range of conditions might have to be tried to find the correct process, which could be quite different for a similarly appearing stone from a different locality containing different impurity concentrations or having had a different history.

In some instances, no enhancement may appear possible at first glance, as in a ruby, where the color is caused by chromium and where a heat treatment cannot change the valence state or the color of the Al_2O_3-Cr^{3+} combination. Yet here, too, the color may contain a brown, purple, or milky component derived from iron and titanium impurities, which could be enhanced by a heat treatment, with the same complexities present as discussed above.

The Effects of Heat

Heat can have many different effects; the nine that are most important in gemstone materials are summarized in table 6. 1.

Table 6. 1 The effects of heat on gemstone materials

Effect	Mechanism	Examples
Darkening	Gentle charring and/or oxidation	"Aged" amber and ivory
Color change	Destruction of color center	Blue or brown topaz and zircon to colorless; 'pinked' topaz; amethyst to pale yellow or green; smoky quartz to greenish yellow or colorless
Color change	Change in hydration, aggregation	Carnelian to orange, red, or brown; sapphire to deep yellow or orange
Structural change	Reverse the irradiation induced metamict state	'Low' zircon to 'high' zircon
Color change	Oxidation state change, usually with oxygen diffusion	Green aquamarine to blue; amethyst to deep citrine; colorless/yellow/green/blue sapphire; brown or purple ruby to red
Structural change	Precipitation or solution of a second phase	Development or removal of silk or asterism in corundum
Color addition	Impurity diffusion	Diffused color and asterism in sapphire
Cracking	Rapid change of temperature	Fingerprints in sapphire; 'cracked' quartz
'Reconstruction' and clarification	Flow under heat and pressure	Reconstructed and clarified amber, reconstructed tortoise shell

Omitted from the above table are those effects of heat that are completely reversible, one example being the turning green of a ruby when heated to red heat, where the original color returns when the ruby is cooled back to room temperature.

Selected from "Gemstone Enhancement", Great Britain by Butler & Tanner Ltd., 1991.

Words and Expressions

1. enhancement [in'hɑːnsmənt] *n.* 优化，提高，增强
2. incinerate [in'sinəreit] *vt.* 烧尽，焚化
3. pyrolize [pai'rɔlaiz] *vt.* 热解，高温分解
4. scorch [skɔːtʃ] *vi.* 烧焦，烤焦，使枯萎
5. sear [siə] *vt.* 烙，烧灼
6. nest [nest] *n.* 巢，窝，穴；*v.* 筑巢；相互套入；使套入；～ed crucible 套坩埚
7. trim away [trim'əwei] 去掉，修剪，刨平，整理
8. bulky ['bʌlki] *a.* 庞大的，笨大的
9. carnelian [kəniːljən] *n.* 肉红玉髓
10. metamict ['metəmikt] *n.* 混胶状，蜕晶质，晶体因辐照而造成的无定形状态
11. aquamarine [ækwəmə'riːn] *n.* 海蓝宝石，蓝绿色

Unit 28 Optical Properties of Cut Gemstones

Light and Gemstones

Truly, without light there could be no beauty of the precious minerals, which are, termed gems. Light, however, to the student of gemology has a more vital interest even than that of beauty the value it possesses as a means for gem identification. Light is the physical cause of our sensation of sight, and it is simply an effect interpreted by our brain through the medium of the eye and has no real existence.

Scientists recognize two different theories to explain the way in which light is transmitted: (1) the electromagnetic wave theory and (2) the quantum theory.

The electromagnetic wave theory states that light energy is travelling through space at approximately 300000km per second as wave motion. The whole range of wavelengths from the extremely long to extremely short (cosmic rays), form what is known as the electromagnetic spectrum: radio waves→infra-red→visible light→ultra violet→X-rays→gamma→cosmic rays.

When energy has a shorter wavelength than the violet rays or has a longer wavelength than infra-red, it is therefore invisible, and the energy of wavelength between them is visible light, which is composed red, orange, yellow, green, blue and violet. When these visible lights are mixed, it is white light, or it is often termed mixed light. When light is produced which has one wavelength only it is then termed monochromatic light. Each of visible lights has a different wavelength, as shown as follows:

red	770～620nm	orange	620～592nm	yellow	592～578nm
green	578～500nm	blue	500～446nm	violet	446～390nm

The unit of measurement used for short wavelengths is the nanometer, which is 10^{-9}m (or 10^{-6}mm). Nanometers are indicated by nm.

The electromagnetic wave theory can explain such optical effects as reflection, refraction, interference and polarization.

The quantum theory, put forward by Plank and Einstein, states that light energy can be emitted and absorbed only in small discrete amounts, called quanta. This theory is used to explain certain causes of color in gemstones and the phenomenon of fluorescence.

All the qualities, which go to make up the beauty of precious stones, are directly due to the powerful influences, which they exert upon reflected and transmitted light. These qualities are color, luster, transparency, brilliance, dispersion, refractive index, and special effects, such as labradorescence, adularescence, chatoyancy, asterism, and iridescence or play of color①.

Color

In most of transparent gemstones color is an important quality. But color is not a property of a gemstone, it is only a sensation in the brain produced by the action of light on the eye.

The (body) color of a gemstone is the mixed residual color, which is left after selective absorption by the gemstone.

Gemstone color may be caused when light is reflected from, or transmitted through a gemstone, which contains some coloring agents, called pigments, or chromophore. Additionally, dispersion, interference, and fluorescence can also cause color.

Most gemstones contain elements, either as traces or as part of their essential chemical composition, which cause the selective absorption of light in gemstones, and according to this, gemstones can classify allochromatic and idiochromtic gemstones. They are mainly transition elements as follows: titanium, vanadium, chromium, manganese, iron, cobalt, nickel, copper and some rare earth elements.

Luster②

The luster of a gemstone is the optical effect created by the reflectivity of the stone's surface. It is mainly a function of the gemstone's refractive index (RI), structure and transparency. There are different kinds of luster for various gem materials, as below: metallic luster, adamantine luster, vitreous luster, resinous luster, waxy luster, greasy luster, pearly luster and silky luster.

Transparency

The transparency of a gemstone is the ability of a substance to transmit light. It is roughly divided into different degrees as follows: transparent, semi-transparent, translucent and opaque. The color and thick of a gemstone and internal flows or inclusions have an effect on its transparency.

Refractive Index and Double Refraction

The constant, i. e. the ratio of sine of the angle of incidence to the sine of the angle of refraction, when a ray of light travels from air to another medium, is termed the refractive index (usually termed RI) of that medium and is a measure of its refractive power. Different gemstones have different RI.

The materials, such as glasses, resins and all liquids, and all crystals of cubic system, are isotropic. The materials in which light does travel as one ray are said to be singly refractive. But in the other crystal systems, i. e. tetragonal, hexagonal, trigonal, orthorhombic, monoclinic and triclinic systems, the incident ray is split into two rays, which are polarized at right angles to each other. The two rays have different RI, and the value of subtracting the RI of the lowest ray from that of the highest ray is double refraction (DR) of a gem.

Dispersion

Dispersion or fire may be defined as the splitting of white light into its component colors (wavelengths). It is normally expressed as the difference of RI's measured using light corresponding to the B and G lines of the Frauhofer spectrum, which have wavelengths of 686.7 nm and 430.8 nm, respectively.

Pleochroism

The pleochroism is a general term used to describe the different directional colors which may be seen in certain doubly refractive colored gemstones, and covers both dichroism and trichroism. These gemstones are ruby, iolite, andaluzite, green tourmaline, etc.

Luminescence③

Luminescence may be expressed as the emission of energy in the form of light, and includes fluorescence and phosphorescence. Only in effect of external energy (i. e. visible light, ultraviolet light or X-rays) luminescence can be observed.

Special Optical Effects④

Special optical effects are the effects generally created by light rays reflected back, interfered and diffracted from beneath the surface of the gemstones. There are several descriptive names which are used to describe the various types of special optical effects exhibited by gemstones. These names are as follows: chatoyancy or cat's-eye effect, asterism, iridescence, labradorescence, adularescence, color change or alexandrite effect.

Selected from "Gem Diamond Course", The Gemmological Association and Gem Testing Laboratory of Great Britain, 1991.

Words and Expressions

1. labradorescence [ˈlæbrədɔːˈsiːns] *n*. 拉长石晕彩
2. adularescence [ˈædjulɛəˈsiːns] *n*. 泛蓝光，青白光彩，冰长石晕彩：由光的干涉作用产生，多见于月光石，其含义同 blue schiller 和瑞利散射（Raleigh scattering）
3. chatoyancy [tʃəˈtɔiənsi] *n*. 猫眼效应
4. asterism [ˈæstərizəm] *n*. 星光效应；星座
5. iridescence [ˌiridˈsiːns] *n*. 晕彩，虹彩
6. pigment [ˈpigmənt] *n*. 色素，颜料
7. chromophore [ˈkrəuməfɔː] *n*. 发色团，生色团
8. allochromatic [ˈæləukrəuˈmætik] *a*. 他色的，他色性的
9. idiochromtic [ˈidiːəukrəumˈtik] *a*. 自色的，自色性的
10. adamantine [ædəˈmæntain] *a*. 金刚石似的，坚硬的；*n*. 金刚合金
10. pleochroism [pliːˈɔkrəuizəm] *n*. 多色性

11. trichroism ['traikrɔizm] *n*. 三色性，三向色性
12. iolite ['aiəlait] *n*. 堇青石

Notes

① play of color 变彩效应，是某些宝石对光的干涉和衍射等作用的结果，表现为宝石表面呈现多种颜色；
② luster 宝石表面对光的反射能力，有金属光泽、金刚光泽、玻璃光泽、树脂、蜡状、珍珠光泽、丝绢光泽等；
③ luminescence 发光性，是指一些宝石在外来能量的激发下，能发出可见光的性质，包括荧光和磷光。当激发源撤除后发光立即停止，称为荧光；如果激发源撤除后，仍能在较短的一定时间内继续发光，称为磷光；
④ Special optical effects 特殊光学效应，宝石内部的包裹体或结构对光的折射、反射、干涉、衍射、散射等综合作用所引起的一些特殊的光学现象，主要有猫眼效应、星光效应、变彩效应、晕彩效应、变色效应、月光效应和砂金效应等。

Exercises

1. Translate the underlined sentences in text into Chinese.
2. Answer the following questions.
   ① What does the electromagnetic spectrum include?
   ② How to define the term of "nm"?
   ③ Which luster is a diamond with? And a pearl is?
3. Translate the following expressions into Chinese or English.
   the electromagnetic wave theory   the quantum theory   optical properties
   the electromagnetic spectrum   折射率和双折射率   变色效应
   砂金效应   月光效应
4. Read the following paragraph and answer the questions.

   Garnet is really the name for a group of minerals all of what have a common crystal habit and some similarity of chemical composition. In fact there are six members of the family. These six end members can be classified into two isomorphous series, i. e. pyralspite series and ugrandite series. These species have the general formula $A_3B_2(SiO_4)_3$. In the pyralspite series A may be Mg, Fe or Mn, and B is always Al. This series includes pyrope, almandrite and spessartine. In the ugrandite series, A is Ca, and B may be Cr, Al or Fe. This series consists of uvarovite, grossular and andradite.

   Substitution is most extensive within each isomorphous series, but may occur to a lesser degree between them. Therefore , the compositions of garnets rarely correspond with those of the pure end members given above, and their physical properties may vary.

   ① Which can not occur in nature in the following?
   A. $Mg_3Al_2Si_3O_{12}$ B. $Ca_3Al_2Si_3O_{12}$ C. $Mn_3Fe_2Si_3O_{12}$ D. $Ca_3Fe_2Si_3O_{12}$
   ② Which is not pyralspite series?
   A. $Mg_3Al_2Si_3O_{12}$ B. $Ca_3Al_2Si_3O_{12}$ C. $Mn_3Al_2Si_3O_{12}$ D. $Fe_3Al_2Si_3O_{12}$

③ Please give a correct title to this paragraph.

Reading Material 28

The Identification of Treated Gems

Detection is, or ought to be, an exact science and
should be treated in the same cold and unemotional manner.
Sir Arthur Conan Doyle

The brief outline of gem-testing techniques is not intended to enable the inexperienced reader to perform his or her own treatment identifications. What is required is that ultimate of gemmological instruments, the experienced eye, with the informed mind to direct the investigation. Such experience is best gained through one of the hands-on gemstone-identification courses, such as those given by the GIA, the Gemmological Association of Great Britain, London, etc.

Only by knowing the full range of possible enhancing treatments can all the tell-tale signs be interpreted to lead to the best answer. At the same time it must be recognized that this best answer is not necessarily the correct one in the sense that there are certain treatments which leave no evidence of their use or which would require unacceptable destructive tests for their certain identification.

Gemstone Testing

One of the serious limitations on gemmological identification is the inability to perform destructive tests- one can hardly blame the owner of a valuable gemstone for wishing it to retain its full worth. The research gemmologist who is involved in developing the required non-destructive tests has no such constraints and frequently does destroy, intentionally or even unintentionally, the specimens. Nevertheless, certain 'slightly' destructive tests are occasionally performed when the situation requires it.

The problem of the detailed examination of a gemstone in a totally enclosed setting is more tractable, in that careful removal and resetting of a gemstone does not normally produce damage. Certain tests, with the color grading of a diamond being a prime example, just cannot be carried out with a stone in its setting. In the field of enhancement, it is the use of color behind a stone and the presence of difficult composite stones that is most troublesome in this respect.

In approaching an unknown gemstone, the obvious first question is the nature of the material, making due allowance for the possibility of composite, coated, and dyed stones. With the nature established, the next step concerns the possibility that one of many treatments may have been used. Both of these determinations may require the use of the full range of gemmological tests.

Over the years a number of instruments have been developed to assist the visual and tactile senses in gemstone testing; a number of these are indispensable to the gemmologist.

Visual inspection can reveal many of a gemstone's secrets under favorable conditions. A thorough but gentle cleaning is an essential first step in any examination. The color, as seen by the naked eye, gives surprisingly little information since so many gemstones occur in a wide variety of colors (such as sapphire, spinel, tourmaline, quartz), or colorants may have been used. The luster, indicative of the refractive index, fire caused by the dispersion, birefringence (double refraction), and dichroism all can be evaluated approximately by the trained eye. Special optical effects such as asterism are also noted.

Evidence of surface coatings, external junctions, of cement layers in doublets, characteristic fracture (cleavage, conchoidal, and so forth), any filling in cracks, and the presence of characteristic inclusions and other growth features, all can provide diagnostic data.

Magnification is most important for this, either in the form of a simple 10× loupe, or as one of the sophisticated microscopes, possibly equipped with provisions for binocular viewing and dark-field illumination. The type and distribution of imperfections and growth irregularities are the most important characteristics examined. By the ability to focus down through a stone, it is possible to detect boundaries such as those in doublets or triplets, as well as surface coating. A photography attachment can help with documenting the observations, although the information is rarely as detailed as that observed by the eye. The use of a refractive-index matching fluid permits the observation of color localization. Immersion in any fluid is helpful; water frequently serves as does a saturated salt solution. Olive oil or glycerin with an RI of 1.47 often gives much better results. Methylene iodide at 1.74 is very useful, but should not be used on porous or easily stained materials.

The refractometer, together with a polariscope and a dichroscope permit the determination of the refractive indices, the optical character, the presence of double refraction or anomalous strain, and the pleochroism. If the RI is higher than the limit of the refractometer scale, a reflectometer may give useful information. A thermal probe can readily distinguish diamond from other gemstones except synthetic and may also help in other identifications. It should be recognized, however, that these instruments usually only probe the surface layer, so that their output must be treated with care if a coated, overgrown, or a composite doublet or triplet stone may be at hand.

The spectroscope, usually equipped with a source of bright light is most useful, both for identifying the material and showing the presence of dyes and coatings from their characteristic spectra. The fluorescence under ultraviolet light, both under short-wave (254nm) and long-wave (365nm) radiation, and the transparency and fluorescence under X-rays can be helpful, but allowance must be made for the wide variability in fluorescence for different localities, possibly derived from the presence of small amounts of unusual impurities.

Specialized instruments include a conductometer, which measures the electrical conductivity and helps establish the origin of the blue color of a diamond (conducting if natural), and a hot point, an electrically heated needle, carefully applied to the back of a cabochon or an inconspicuous carving, which can sometimes reveal the wax or plastic impregnation of turquoise; the color can even identify the impregnating compound. Similarly, amber, more recent resins, and plastic imitations may be distinguished. The careful use of acids can distinguish calcite, coral, and other carbonates from other materials.

The question of 'slightly destructive' testing, particularly for fading colors in those instances where there is no indirect test, is not clear. Certainly a number of tests in common gemological use are not, in fact, totally non-destructive.

Selected from "Gemstone Enhancement", Kurt Nassau, Butler & Tanner Ltd., 1991.

Words and Expresses

1. GIA Gemological Institute of America 的缩写，美国宝石学院
2. tell-tale [ˈtelteil] *a*. 搬弄是非的，泄露秘密的，说明问题的
3. tactile [ˈtæktail] *a*. 触角的，能触知的
4. indispensable [indisˈpensəbl] *a*. 必不可少的，必需的，责无旁贷的
5. loupe [luːp] *n*. 放大镜
6. binocular [baiˈnɔkjulə] *a*. 双目的，双筒的；*n*. 双目镜
7. doublet [ˈdʌblit] *n*. 二层拼合石，二层石；双合透镜，（光谱）双重线；成对物，对偶物
8. triplet [ˈtriplit] *n*. 三层拼合石，三层石；三个一组，三件一套
9. glycerin [ˈglisərin] *n*. 甘油基，丙三基
10. methylene iodide [ˈmeθiliːnˈaiədaid] *n*. 二碘甲烷
11. refractometer [riːfrækˈtɔmitə] *n*. 反射仪
12. polariscope [pəuˈlæriskəup] *n*. 偏光镜
13. dichroscope [daikrəuˈskəup] *n*. 二色镜
14. cabochon [kæbəˈtʃən] *a*. 弧面的，凸面的，素面的
15. turquoise [ˈtəːkwɑːz] *n*. 绿松石，绿松石色；*a*. 青绿色的

Unit 29 Diamond

Introduction

Diamond is carbon, for many years it was thought to be pure carbon, but modern methods of analysis have shown that it contains minute quantities of other elements, such as nitrogen, aluminium, boron, etc., some of which are responsible for the color in diamond. And diamond and graphite are known as polymorphs of carbon.

During growth, diamond may incorporate impurities as single atoms or as ready-made minerals. When the impurities are distinguishable by microscopy they are called inclusions, which are relevant to more than 20 mineral species, e. g. olivine, enstitute, garnet.

Within the Earth, diamond has formed in two distinct environments, one associated with peridotite and the other with eclogite. Inclusions in peridotitic diamonds indicate that they formed between 900 and 1300℃ (average 1050℃) at pressures of 45～60kbar. While results obtained from inclusions of eclogitic type suggest temperatures of formation of about 1250℃, but the pressure data from some of these diamonds suggest they may have come from depths considerably in excess of 180km.

The ages of diamonds are estimated by inference from the ages of their inclusions. These indicate that diamonds are of different ages and are all very old. For example, in South Africa the peridotitic diamonds are about 3300 million years old, whilst the elogitic diamonds from Argyle and Orapa (Botswana) are 1580 and 990 million years old respectively.

There are nearly 30 countries in the world, which produced diamonds commercially. In alphabetical order the producing countries in the word are as follows: Angola, Australia, Botswana, Brazil, Central Africa Republic, China, India, Liberia, Namibia, South Africa, Tanzania, Russian, Zaire and other countries.

The Structure, Crystallography of Diamond

Pure diamond consists of carbon atoms, which are linked in a regularly repeating or crystalline pattern. They are linked together in such a way that all the equidistant from one another (0. 154nm). This regular and compact crystal structure is the basis of most of its properties. These include its extreme hardness, extremely high thermal conductivity, extremely low electrical conductivity, great resistance to attack by acids, and high transparency.

Diamond is the cubic or isometric system, and its crystals occur in a variety of shapes, of which the above are a small selection. The main crystal shapes of diamond include octahedron, cube, rhombic dodecahedron, but diamonds may also occur in more complicated shapes which are combinations of two or more forms. Sometimes a diamond will form as a twin crystal, besides there are two different types basically: contact twin and interpentrant twin①. An important crystal form of diamond that is a contact twin is known as a macle (maccle)[②], which is typically flat and triangular with a distinct herring-bone pattern around the stone, where the two plane surfaces of the twins join together. The one recognizable characteristic of a macle or twinned diamond is the herringbone line, and it is known as the naat in the diamond trade.

The Properties of Diamond

Diamond possesses certain physical and optical properties that give rise to its extremely high brilliance and fire[③].

1. The physical properties

The structure of diamond makes it a dense and relatively heavy material, and its density is 3.52 g/cm^3. Diamond is the hardest substance known, at the top of Mohs′ Scale (see unit 2). Diamond can be cleaved along the octahedral planes with comparative ease, that is to say, diamond is with octahedral cleavage. Diamond is very tough if squeezed in a vice and will withstand extreme confining pressures. In other words, it is quite brittle - much more so than nephrite jade, but not so brittle as glass or paste used in jewelry.

2. The optical properties

A large percentage of all diamonds mined are colored. The colors range from yellow, brown, and black to the more exotic red, pink, mauve, blue and green. When the hue of color becomes clear and attractive enough to bestow extra value on the diamond, these deeply colored diamonds are called "fancies". But the vast bulk of gem diamonds are near-colorless because they reveal a slight trace of yellow (sometimes brown), which belongs to the Cape Series[④].

Diamond is isotropic body, and has singly refractive index that is 2.417, and dispersion of diamond is 0.044, higher than that of all other natural colorless gemstones. The type of luster displayed by diamond is typical adamantine.

Some diamonds are inert under long-wave ultraviolet, but the others fluoresce, besides behave different kinds of color, for example, some diamonds of the cape series (colorless to yellow tint) have blue fluorescence, and brown diamonds show yellow-green fluorescence usually.

The absorption of blue light by Cape Series diamonds will be seen as dark lines in the blue end of the spectrum. These dark lines occur at definite wavelengths and can be measured. The 415.5nm absorption is the strongest but the others may be difficult to observe. And each different color of diamond tends to have a particular spectrum, such as all natural pink and mauve diamonds show a broad band at 563nm.

3. Other properties

The thermal expansion is very low in a diamond, one result of which is that sudden changes of temperature have a minimal affect. But diamond is an extremely good conductor of heat, especial to type IIa diamond[⑤]. The blue type IIb diamond, extremely rare, is a semi-conductor, which is known to be caused by a boron impurity.

Selected from "Gem Diamond Course", The Gemmological Association and Gem Testing Laboratory of Great Britain, 1991.

Words and Expressions

1. peridotite [peri'dəutait] *n*. 橄榄岩
2. eclogite ['eklɔdʒait] *n*. 榴辉岩
3. Argyle ['ɑːgail] *n*. 阿盖尔，澳大利亚著名的钻石产区
4. dodecahedron ['dəudikə'hedrən] *n*. 菱形十二面体，十二面体
5. macle ['mɑːkl] *n*. 钻石的三角薄片双晶
6. naat [nɑːt] *n*. 钻石中的结节，扁平的钻石双晶，钻石双晶的接合缝，晶结
7. tough [tʌf] *a*. 韧性的
8. mauve [məuv] *a*. 紫色的，淡紫色的；*n*. 淡紫色
9. fancy ['fænsi] *a*. 花式的，奇特的，fancy diamond 花色钻石，彩色钻石

Notes

① contact twin and interpentrant twin 接触双晶和穿插双晶，是指两个或两个以上的晶体按一定的规律生长在一起。
② macle (maccle) 薄片状，文中是指钻石中一种常见的三角形薄片双晶。
③ brilliance and fire 亮度和火焰。
④ Cape Series 开普系列，是指无色至黄（褐）色系列的钻石。
⑤ type IIa diamond IIa 型金刚石，根据金刚石中的杂质元素的种类（主要是 N、B 等）和含量把金刚石分为四种类型：Ia 型、Ib 型、IIa 型和 IIb 型。

Exercises

1. Answer the following questions according to the text.
   ① What is the chemical composition of diamond?
   ② In what conditions does diamond form?
   ③ What are the main crystal shapes of diamond?
   ④ What colors do usually diamonds take on?
2. Translate the underlined sentences in the text.
3. Translate the following expressions into Chinese or English.
   the cubic or isometric system　　thermal expansion
   蓝色彩钻　　橄榄岩型金刚石　　榴辉岩型金刚石
4. Write a short story about "Diamond and me".

Reading Material 29

Amethyst

If you appreciate fine wine, you'll love this stone.

Quartz is one of the earth's most plentiful minerals. It is the primary component of dust, making up 12 percent of the earth's crust. It is surprising, therefore, that the finest examples of amethyst, the purple variety of quartz, are so difficult to find.

By definition, amethyst occurs in a continuum of primary hues from a lighttoned slightly reddish violet through a deep Concord grape purple. Amethyst is expected to be eyeclean and given its relatively low cost.

Hue/Tone

Amethyst will normally exhibit one of two secondary hues, red and blue. A light rosy red, what we think of as pink, is usually a secondary hue found in lighter toned stones. The ideal tone for amethyst is between 75 to 85 percent on a tonal scale where window glass is 0 percent and coal is 100 percent tone. Commercial grade amethyst occurs in tonal variations of violet to rosy violet from 10 to 60 percent tones.

Like the Concord grape, which has a blue skin but produces purple juice, color in amethyst sometimes occurs in alternating zones of purple and blue. When the stone is viewed face-up the color will be a slightly, 10 to15 percent bluish violet. The blue adds a velvety richness to the purple hue. As shown on the color wheel, mixing red and blue make purple. When the stone is faceted, the relatively yellowish light of the incandescent bulb breaks the red out, drawing deep red flashes of brilliance from the depths of the stone.

The red flash defines the finest color in amethyst and those that have it are called deep Siberian. The difference between deep Siberian and No. 2 color, which is called simply Siberian, is the red flashes.

Deep Siberian color is exceptionally rare. This writer has spent weeks searching for the quality in Brazil and Africa and has often returned home empty-handed.

Saturation

The usual saturation modifier or mask in amethyst is gray, although brown sometimes occurs. In darkertoned stones the gray may be very hard to see. The effect, dullness, will be apparent. The more gray, the duller the stone. Once the gray has been detected, it is possible to use the mind's eye to peel away the mask in order to judge the amount of gray overlaying the hue. The finest stones will show little or no gray mask.

Close your eyes and savor the tart sweet taste of the grape. The deep red flashes of the gem are like a visible astringency - a sharp bite on the end of the tongue that augments the flavor of the fruit.

Lighter-toned stones can be quite attractive if they are completely free of gray. Stones of this type that exhibit exceptional diaphaneity, what experts term "crystal", are quite desirable and inexpensive. A light, bright violet/pink of a bright but delicate hue of 30 percent tone is often referred to as a *rose de France*.

Beware of Synthetics

Brazil, the largest exporter of amethyst, is also the world's largest importer of synthetic quartz. Synthetic amethyst, like most synthetics, is made to imitate the finest grades of the natural gemstone. A simple test will separate most synthetics. Natural amethyst will exhibit what is called Brazil law twinning, a zebra stripe pattern, when viewed immersed in baby oil under the crossed lenses of a polariscope.

Although it is possible to produce twin-crystal synthetics, to date most manufacturers have not bothered to produce a twinned product. Ken Scarrat, director of the AGTA lab in New York, has seen fewer than one twinned synthetic in over ten thousand samples. In natural amethyst, color zones grow parallel to the "C" axis and the crystal faces. In synthetics, the zones normally grow perpendicular to the C axis and across the crystal face.

Production

Amethyst has a number of sources. Brazil, traditionally the largest supplier, boasts several major mining areas: Pau Darco, Maraba and Rio Grande do Sul. Pau Darco is about played out. A trickle still comes out of Maraba and Rio Grande doSul. A new find has been reported in the state of Espirto Santos. Amethyst is also found in Bahia at Carnaiba and Brejino.

Zambia, justly famous for its highly saturated bluishpurple stones, was a big producer in the late 1980s but very little has been heard from the African nation since the early 1990s. Uruguay has taken up some of the slack, particularly in the commercial grades. Recently a new find in the US, at Twin Peaks, Arizona, has begun to produce some finer quality amethyst.

Selected from "Gemkey Magazine", Richard W. Wise, Gemkey Co., Ltd., July-August 1999.

Words & expressions

1. amethyst [æmi'θist] *n.* 紫晶，紫石英；紫色，紫罗兰色
2. velvety ['velviti] *a.* 天鹅绒般的，柔软光滑的；（酒）温和的，可口的
3. facet ['fæsit] *n.*（多面体的）面，（宝石等的）刻面，小面；*vt.* 在……上刻面
4. dull [dʌl] *a.* 麻木的，（色彩、光线等）不鲜艳的，暗淡的
5. darkertoned ['dɑːkə'təund] *a.* 色调暗淡的，颜色较深的
6. lighter-toned ['laitə-'təun] *a.* 淡色调的
7. imitate [imi'teit] *vt.* 仿制，模仿，仿造
8. AGTA Lab 美国宝石贸易协会实验室（American Gem Trade Association Lab）
9. take up the slack （企业）使用闲置人员和设备重新发挥作用，抓紧松弛环节；拉紧绳的松弛部分，拉直松弛的绳索

PART Ⅶ INORGANIC MATERIALS ENGINEERING

Unit 30 Furnaces

Glass melting is an art that is confronted with two major problems. These are the development of high temperatures and the development of suitable containers for molten glass. The problem of containers has been only partially solved. It will be discussed in Chapter 24 on refractories. Temperatures up to the limits that containers and furnace refractories will endure are easily obtained with modern fuels and methods of firing. The further efforts of furnace designers and combustion engineers are directed toward the economical generation and application of heat.

The melting of glass is carried out at temperatures ranging from 1300℃ to 1600℃. The heat must be sufficiently intense not only to bring about the reactions between the ingredients of the batch and to dissolve the silica, but also to reduce the viscosity of the liquid glass so that the bubbles of gases may readily escape. The temperatures selected for specific melting operations are determined by the type of furnace used, the time available for securing clear glass, and the character of the glass melted.

Two general types of furnaces are in use. In one the glass is contained in separate pots and each furnace may contain a single pot or as many as twenty. In the second type, called the tank furnace, the glass forms a pool in the hearth of the furnace, across which the flames play directly upon the raw batch and the molten material.

Pot Furnaces

A few of the simpler and smaller pot furnaces for glassmaking are direct fired. i. e., without provision for preheating air or fuel gas. For open pots, these take a form similar to the pot arch. One or two pots are placed in a rectangular furnace. The fire, usually natural gas or oil enters near the bottom at the back. Behind a "bag wall" which directs the flames upward to the crown, whence they pass down and around the pots and out at the flue openings in the sides or bottom, near the front. Access to the pots is gained by openings in the doors at the front.

Updraft furnaces for closed pots are usually circular in plan, fired by a single burner in the center of the bench. The flame rises directly to the crown, and spreads outward, passing down between the pots to flues built beside each pot in the outer wall. A large conical stack extending over the entire crown carries away the products of combustion, and also serves as a ventilator for the factory.

Furnaces of this sort were fired with coal on a grate placed centrally below the bench in early American factories. This type is now obsolete, having been replaced by regenerative, or in a few instances, by recuperative designs.

The Tank Furnaces

The idea of melting glass in a furnace whose walls serve as the container was first developed in modern times by the Siemens brothers of Germany about 1850. The glass and steel industries owe to these enterprising industrialists and engineers the development of the regenerative furnace. Many sites and styles, of tanks have since been made. The principles of construction and operation common to tanks are: the direct contact of the flame with the charge of batch and the molten glass and walls of refractory blocks closely fitted together without mortar or cement, exposed to the atmosphere on their outer faces. No attempts will be made to mention all the forms of tanks, but a few of the types in common use will be described in some detail. Such writers as Devillers and Vaerewyck and Lamort may be consulted for more complete information.

Continuous Tanks

In the continuous tank, the glass is a constant level, the raw materials being fed at a rate equal to that at which the melted glass is worked out or withdraw. It is thus especially adapted to mechanical production, or any continuous method of working requiring large quantities of glass delivered at a constant rate level. To insure that clear glass is presented for working, means must be provided to retain the partially melted batch and unrefined glass in the "melting end," separate from the clear glass in the "working end." This is accomplished either by the bridge-wall type of construction, or by the longer, window glass style of tank.

Day tanks

The day tank is a small melting unit, in which a charge of a few tons may be melted and refined in one day, to be worked out by hand shops during the following day. It consists of a single rectangular compartment, with side walls not over two feet height. The depth is limited by the requirement that glass-workers be able to reach the glass with their gathering irons as it is worked out. The length and breadth vary according to the capacity desired: 4×8 is a common and convenient size. This area of 32 sq. ft. With a 2-ft. depth gives a content of 64 cu. ft. With ordinary lime glass weighing 150 lbs. per cu. ft., the capacity of such a unit becomes nearly tons. The walls and bottoms are commonly12 inches thick.

Jamb walls of silica brick, of 12-in , thickness, may be built directly upon the block walls, to a height of 18 in, or thereabouts. Better practice is to support the superstructure on steel angles so that the refractory blocks in contact with the glass can be replaced without tearing down the whole furnace. The jamb walls provide sprung across the narrow dimension of the tank with a radius equal to its span. Opening through the jamb walls, 8×10 in., on one or both sides serve for charging batch, and for removing the melted glass for working. These "ring holes" are closed by fire-clay stoppers during the melting process. Usually a ring of fire clay is floated on the molten glass in front of the ring hole to separate the surface from which glass is taken for work from the rest of the surface and to skim scum and other defects floating on the surface of the melt .

Day tanks offer flexibility and relative economy of construction and operation for the melting of small quantities of glass, particularly where frequent changes of color or composition are required. The quality of glass produced is inferior to that made in either pots or continuous tanks, for reasons that will appear. The day tank is usually limited to hand-working although at times it may be used to melt glass which is ladled into a reheater to feed a continuous machine.

Tanks For Flat Glass

Window glass and plate glass require a higher quality —— freedom from bubbles and other defects——than that needed for bottles. Therefore, the tanks are made much longer and deeper for flat glass production. A depth of five feet is common, but some manufacturers are successful with a four foot depth. The tanks have no bridge walls. Jack arches cut down the radiation from the combustion chamber to the flowing or drawing chambers. The jack arch, spanning a constricted width of the tank, is a solid wall of arch construction, sprung from the side walls. A suspended wall, hung from above the crown, and adjustable in height, serves the same purpose.

Flat glass tanks range from 100 to 200 ft. in length. More area must be used per ton of glass drawn than is required in bottle tanks because better glass is called for. Widths run from 30 to 35 ft.

Selected from "Modern Glass Practice, Samuel R. Scholes, Cahners Publishing Company, 1975"

Words and Expressions

1. pot furnace 坩埚窑
2. bag wall 挡火墙
3. tank furnace 池窑
4. day tank 日池窑
5. dog house 投料口，加料室
6. jamb wall 侧墙
7. jack arch 平拱

Exercises

1. put the underlined in the text into Chinese.
2. put the following into English:

   横火焰　纵火焰　马蹄焰
3. Answer the following questions:

   (1) What kinds of furnaces are in use? please descript them in your own words.

(2) What differences are between the continuous tanks and day tanks?

Reading Material 30

Stack Dimensions

The internal diameter of a stack should be a great enough so that the flue gas at the maximum temperature does not need to have a velocity greater than 12 ft per second. A tank furnace, consuming 20000cu. ft. of natural gas per hour and supplied with 25% excess air, will produce 276000 cu. ft. of flue gas per hour, or approximately 77 cu. ft. per second, measured at N. T. P. At the stack temperature this volume will be approximately 2. 5 time as great, or 192 cu. ft. per sec. A velocity of ft. per sec. requires, therefore, a cross-sectional area of 16 sq. ft. Hence the standard practice of giving the stacks for large tanks an internal diameter of at least 5 ft.

Furnaces of either regenerative or downdraft recuperative type require higher stacks than direct-fired furnaces in order to overcome the chimney effect of the regenerators or recuperators. If , for example, the height of a regenerator chamber and uptake, measured from the level of the stack flue to the level of the port, is 15 ft. , and the mean temperature of the gases passing down through the regenerator is 1100℃ , the draft vacuum, created by this column of hot gas, calculated from the formula given above, will be 0. 2 in. of water. This number represents the very minimum of stack draft required to keep the furnace atmosphere at rest with no gases moving in either direction. In practice, a furnace of this type requires a draft vacuum at the base of the stack, where it is regulated by adjustment of the damper, amounting to approximately 0. 6 in. water. This overcomes the resistance of the various flues and reversing valves, and of the checker orifices themselves , and maintains a suitable velocity of combustion gases and flue gases through the system,. This draft must be increased as the furnace ages, and the narrow passages through the checkers become obstructed with dust or slag.

Meanwhile, the air, entering the furnace through the hot regenerator on the ingoing side, is given a pressure by the chimney effect of the regenerator. This is also true of the producer gas, when it is the fuel being used, which is similarly entering through a hot regenerator. This chimney effect of the regenerators on the ingoing side delivers combustion air to the furnace, making the use of a fan for this purpose unnecessary until the checkers are badly obstructed by dust or slag deposits.

A positive pressure is maintain in the furnace chamber and adjusted to value of about 0. 01 in. of water by suitable adjustment of the stack damper. It is visually evident by what is called the "sting-out," or the jet of flame or hot gas that appears at every orifice of the furnace. These stingouts-which may be smoky jets, incandescent flames, or almost invisible hot gas-serve as guide to the experienced furnace man in the control of his firing conditions.

Some degree of internal pressure is essential to a properly heated furnaces. When there is no internal pressure, and ever so little negative pressure exists at any point in the superstructure of the furnace, the outside air will enter at any orifice and thus the uniform distribution of heat in the furnace will be impossible. Good firing practice requires that a positive internal pressure, made evident by visible sting-outs, be maintained at all times, It must be kept in mind that, because of the buoyancy of hot gases in the furnace atmosphere, the internal pressure increases by almost 0.01 in. of water for each foot of height above the glass surface, so that the pressure at a measuring point above the glass line must be kept at an appropriate positive value to insure that it does not become negative at the glass level.

In modern installations, furnace pressure is regulated automatically by means of a sensitive gauge which operates electrical contacts so that any variation in internal pressure may be made to bring about a correcting change in the stack chamber. That is, the damper is raised slightly as the pressure rises beyond an established limit, and is lowered slightly when the pressure falls. In this way a constant internal pressure may be maintained.

If the stack draft is insufficient, it is quite possible to carry excessive pressure in a furnace, causing a partial smoothering of the flame. The products of combustion are not removed rapidly enough to permit the necessary volumes of fresh combustion mixture to enter . Furnace are kept at high temperatures by maintaining a high rate of combustion. This demands sufficient draft to remove the large volumes of flue gases created and to permit the entrance of fresh fuel. Although there is such a thing as excessive draft when it is carried to the point of creating negative pressure in the furnace, it is futile to attempt to conserve heat by throttling the stack flue. A further disadvantage of excessive furnace pressure is that the furnace gases which escape through leaks in the superstructure carry dust and flux vapors which attack the refractories and which may occur at cracks in the superstructure carry dust and flux vapors and destroy the furnaces structure, for this reason it is most important that any leaks. Which may occur at cracks in the superstructure be promptly sealed with an appropriate cement. It is particularly unfortunate when excessive sting-out, due to high furnace pressure, impinges on steel work bracing the tank structure and softens or corrodes it.

Selected from "Modern Glass Practice, Samuel R. Scholes, Cahners Publishing Company, 1975"

Words and Expressions

1. stack [stæk] *n*. 烟囱
2. flue gas 烟道气
3. recuperative [riˈkjupəretiv] *a*. 换热的
4. regenerator chamber 蓄热室
5. draft [drɑːft] *n*. 抽力，通风
6. damper [dæmpə] *n*. 烟道，隔板
7. combustion gas 燃烧（发生的）气体
8. buoyancy [ˈbɔiənsi] *n*. 浮力

Unit 31 Storage (Silo)

General Characteristics of Silos

General characteristics of silos used for storing powders and granular materials are as follows:

1. General materials can be collected, distributed, and stored in bulk efficiently.

2. Transportation costs, which influence the costs of raw materials and products, can be reduced.

3. Compared with storage on a flat surface such as a floor, a silo's storing capacity is several times greater in the same space.

4. Equipment cost per unit of storage capacity is small.

5. Automatic loading, unloading, and control of storage volume are possible.

6. Operations such as pressurization, heat insulation, moisture proofing, and fumigation are easily made.

7. Quality change, decomposition, breaking damage, and damage of stored materials by insects and rats can be prevented.

8. A silo can be incorporated easily as a part of an industrial production system and has labor-saving advantages.

Cassification Of Silos

Shallow Bins and Deep Bins

When studying static powder pressure acting on silo walls, silos are classified into shallow bins and deep bins. The classification is based on the following formulas [Architectural Institute of Japan (1990) and Silo Design Standard of the USSR]:

Deep bins: $h>1.5d$ ($h>1.5a$)

Shallow bins: $h<1.5d$ ($h<1.5a$)

Which h is the height of the silo (meters), d is the inside diameter of a circular silo (meters), and a is the length of a rectangular silo (meters).

Single Bins and Group Bins

For a single bin, a circular cross-section is frequently used because of some advantages in design and construction. In recent year, coal silos 40～50 m in diameter and as high as about 40 m have been constructed, many of which are independent shallow bins. In addition, large single bins such as cement silos and crinker silos have been constructed. Many steel silos are of the single-bin type.

An example of a group bin is the silo for storing grains. Several to several tens of connected bins in a variety of shapes (e. g., circular, rectangular, and hexagonal in cross-section) are used to store various types of powder and granular materials in bulk.

Planning Silos

Calculation of Silo Capacity

In designing a silo, its capacity should be determined from the total storing weight of the materials, the types of the materials to be stored, and the weight of use. Silo capacity has two components: total capacity (geometric capacity) and the capacity of loaded stored materials (effective capacity).

Geometric capacity, also called water capacity, is used as a standard value for calculating the fumigation gas to be employed in treating imported grains. Effective capacity is the base for calculating the storing weight and location for taking in materials whose angle of repose should be taken into consideration.

Load due to Bulk Materials

In designing bulk silos, a proper understanding of the behavior and pressure of bulk materials inside silos is clearly necessary. However, many unsolved unanticipated problems remain. Bulk pressure changes in complexity, depending on various properties of the materials stored and the operating conditions of silos, thus relegating silo design to specialists.

According to the ISO 11697 (1995) (Bases for design of structures -loads due to bulk materials), the bulk pressures inside deep bins are discussed for two specified loading conditions. The filling pressures of bulk materials depend mainly on the material properties and the silo geometry. Discharge pressures are also influenced by the flow patterns which arise during the process of emptying. Therefore, an assessment of material flow behavior shall be made for each silo design.

In the assessment of bulk-material flow, it is necessary to distinguish among three main flow patterns:

(a) Mass flow (Fig. 7.1a): A flow profile in which all the stored particles are mobilized during discharge.

(b) Funnel flow (Figs. 7.1b～7.1f): A flow profile in which a channel of flowing material develops within a confined zone above the outlet and the material adjacent to the wall near the outlet remains stationary①. The flow channel can intersect the wall of the parallel section or extend to the top surface. In the latter case, the pattern is called "internal flow" (Figs. 7.1c～7.1e).

(c) Expanded flow (Fig. 7.1f): A flow profile in which mass flow develops within a steep-bottom hopper, combining with a stationary in an upper, less steep hopper at the bottom of the parallel section. The mass flow zone then extends up the wall of the parallel section. Different pressure distributions are associated with each of the above flow patterns. The conditions necessary for mass flow depend on the inclination of the hopper wall and the wall friction coefficient. under certain conditions the flow pattern can change abruptly between mass and funnel flow, thereby producing unsteady flow with pressure oscillations. If such condition cannot be avoided, the silo shall be designed for both mass flow and funnel flow.

Selected from "Powder Technology Handbook" Reishi Grozoh *et al*, 2nd Edition New York Marcel Dekker, 1997

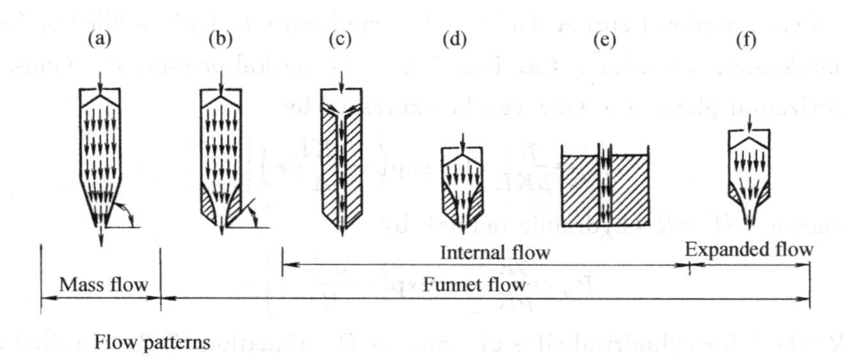

Fig 7.1 Flow

Words and expression

1. silo [siləu] *n*. 料仓
2. fumigation [fjuːmigeiʃən] *n*. 消毒
3. cross-section 横截面
4. angle of repose. 休止角
5. expanded flow 扩展流

Notes

① 在其流动曲线中，出口上方有限区域内形成流动物质通道，而在出口处仓壁附近物料保持静止。

Exercises

1. Put the underlined in the text into Chinese.
2. Put the following into English:
   整体流 漏斗流 隔热 防潮
3. Answer the following questions:
   (1) what should be considered in designing a silo?
   (2) How many flow patterns are there during the process of emptying?

Reading Material 31

Calculation of Static Powder Pressure

In calculating bulk loads, the static powder pressure is the basis to be determined. The

Janssen and Reimbert formulas are employed as silo design standards in various countries. The calculation of the static powder pressure in ISO 11697 is based on Janssent's theory. It is derived from a force balance of the powder stored statically in deep bins, taking into consideration the frictional force generated between the powder and the silo walls.

If a silo of cross-sectional area A (m^2) and circumference L (m) is filled uniformly with a powder of bulk densityγ ($tons/m^3$) (see Fig. 7.2), the vertical pressure P_v ($tons/m^2$) inside the silo on horizontal plane at x (m) can be expressed by

$$P_v=\frac{\gamma A}{\mu KL}\left[1-\exp\left(-\frac{\mu KL}{A}x\right)\right] \tag{7.1}$$

and replacing $A/L=R$ (hydraulic radius) by

$$P_v=\frac{\gamma R}{\mu K}\left[1-\exp\left(-\frac{\mu K}{R}x\right)\right] \tag{7.2}$$

where $R=D/4$ for cylindrical silos of diameter D. Equation (7.2) is called the Janssen formula.

According to the assumption of Janssen's theory, the horizontal pressure P_h ($tons/m^2$) is proportional to the vertical pressure P_v and can be expressed as follows, where the proportional constant is denoted by K:

$$\frac{P_h}{P_v}=K \tag{7.3}$$

$$P_h=KP_v=\frac{\gamma R}{\mu}\left[1-\exp\left(-\frac{\mu K}{R}x\right)\right] \tag{7.4}$$

Assuming that $x\to\infty$ in Eqs. (7.2) and (7.4), the maximum static pressure can be obtained as follows:

$$P_{v\max}=\frac{\gamma R}{\mu K},\ P_{h\max}=\frac{\gamma R}{\mu} \tag{7.5}$$

In calculating the K value, which is called the Janssen coefficient, the Rankine formula, used in silo mechanics, gives the relation to the angle of internal friction δ_i:

$$K=\frac{1-\sin\delta_i}{1+\sin\delta_i} \tag{7.6}$$

To use the foregoing formulas in practice, it is necessary to know certain physical properties of the powder. The bulk density γ ($tons/m^3$) is generally measured in a laboratory. Some powders have increased in bulk density due to accumulated consolidation. The angle of internal friction of powderϕ_i is measured by the shear cell method or triaxial compression test. The most difficult measurement is that of the friction angle (coefficient) of the powder against the wall. At present, it is difficult to obtain a correct understanding of the influence of the smoothness of silo walls on powder friction.

The static pressure of powder in shallow bins is almost negligible with regard to frictional forces between the silo walls and the powder. According to Design Recommendation for Storage Tanks and Their Supports by the Architectural Institute of Japan (1990), the following formula are specified for shallow bins:

$$P_v = \gamma x$$
$$P_h = K\gamma x$$

K, called the Ranking constant, can be determined from Eq. (7.6) for both shallow and deep bins.

Design Pressure

To calculate the design pressure, it is necessary to take into consideration the fact that dynamic pressure can be generated during discharge and impact pressure can be generated during loading. It is clear that powder pressure during discharge are larger than those obtained from the Jassen formula, especially the maximum pressure, which is four to five times higher than the value from Jassen's theory. In the design standards of various countries, the correction factors for dynamic overpressure during discharge and impact pressure during loading are introduced based on practice data. The correction factor for dynamic pressure is usually taken as 2.0 and that for impact pressure is 1.0～2.0. By multiplying the static pressure in the preceding section by the correction factor, the minimum design powder load is determined.

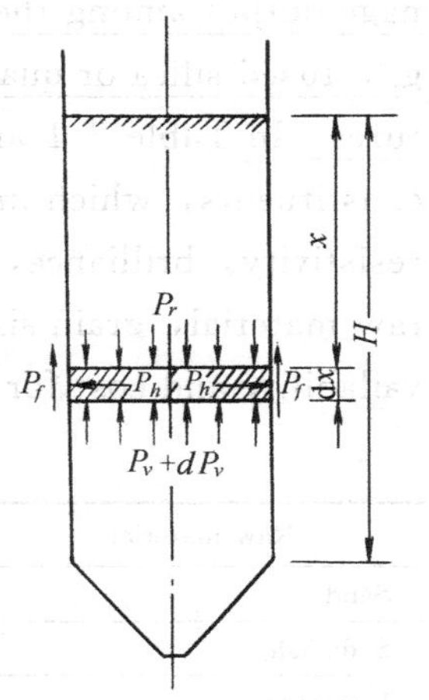

Fig. 7.2 Powder is uniformly filled.

ISO 11697 (1995) shows the design wall (i.e., all flow patters expect internal flow), the design discharge pressure shall be obtained by multiplying the filling loads by the overpressure coefficient C. The value shall be related the silo aspect ratio h/d:

For $h/d < 1.0$, $C = 1.0$

For $1.0 < h/d < 1.5$, $C = 1.35$

For $h/d > 1.5$, $C = 1.35$

These values apply only to materials listed in tables which are indicated in this International Standard.

Selected from "Powder Technology Handbook" Reishi Grozoh *et al*, 2nd Edition New York Marcel Dekker, 1997

Words and Expression

1. frictional forces　　摩擦力
2. triaxial test　　三度试验法

Unit 32 Raw Materials and Mixing

Sand, followed by soda ash and limestone, is the raw material most consumed in glassmaking. These three materials are the major ingredients for soda-lime glass, largest in tonnage output among the various composition fields, which range from the highly viscous (e. g. , fused silica or quartz) to the highly fluid (e. g. sodium silicates) at melting temperatures. In Table 7. 1 are listed some glass raw materials, together with their glassmaking constituents, which impart such properties as chemical and/or thermal durability, electrical resistivity, brilliance, or opacity, among others, to specific compositions. In selecting any raw material, grain size and purity are the technical counterparts to the strategic ones of availability and cost for the glassmaking constituents.

Table7. 1 Glassmaking Materials

Raw material	Chemical composition	Glassmaking oxide	Percent of oxide
Sand	SiO_2	SiO_2	99. 8
Soda ash	Na_2CO_3	Na_2O	58. 5
Limestone	$CaCO_3$	CaO	56. 0
Dolomite	$CaCO_3$-$MgCO_3$	CaO MgO	30. 5 21. 5
Feldspar	$K_2(Na_2)O$-Al_2O_3-$6SiO_2$	Al_2O_3 $K_2(Na_2)O$ SiO_2	18. 5 12. 8 68. 0
Nelpheline	$NaAlSiO_4$	SiO_2	60. 6
Syenite		Al_2O_3 $Na_2(K_2)O$	23. 3 14. 8
Borax, 5-mol	$Na_2B_4O_7$-$5H_2O$	Na_2O B_2O_3	21. 8 48. 8
Boric acid	H_3BO_3	B_2O_3	56. 3
Litharge	PbO	PbO	99. 9
Potash, anhydrous	K_2CO_3	K_2O	68. 0
Fluorspar	CaF_2	CaO F^-	69. 9 47. 1
Zinc oxide		ZnO	100. 0
Barium carbonate	$BaCO_3$	BaO	76. 9

Grain size distribution is very important for the refractory materials (e. g. , sand, feldspar, petalite), as too coarse a fraction results in residual stones and or knots after the melting process while too fine a product allows dusting during handling and/or too rapid a solution reaction. In fossil-fueled tanks the latter effect can result in an insulating foam upon the glass bath which decreases energy passage through the surface and thus inhibits melting rates①. Segregation during handling is theoretically lessened as the different materials move toward a common grain size distribution and density; however, in practice, melting considerations generally result in sand grains one to two screen sizes finer than the commercial grades of fluxes available.

Purity is the other major technical consideration in the selection of a batch material. The primary contaminant, in particular with mineral raw materials, is iron, which can add objectionable color to the product and difficulties to the melting-conditioning process. Dependent upon the product, acceptable limits, can be 0.005 to 0.03% Fe_2O_3 for sand and up to 0.1% Fe_2O_3 for the limestones and feldspars. Aside from iron, sand can have Al_2O_3, ZrO_2, and Cr_2O_3 as contaminants, with the chrome causing a visual color problem. Other coloring oxides (e.g., NiO, Co_3O_4, CuO) cause contamination problems if present in sufficient amounts in the glass fill.

Aside from coloring oxides, sulfates and chlorides, as batch material contaminants, can cause melting and/or forming difficulties. Sulfate is present as salt cake (sodium sulfate) in soda-lime glass batches to remove seeds and blisters (i.e., precipitated gases), but its presence in certain glasses can result in precipitation of SO_2 seeds[2]. In similar fashion salt (sodium chloride) is a common fining agent for borosilicate glasses, but its anion component, Cl^-, can enter into attack upon forming equipment surfaces when present in the hot glass in excess. Soda ash has been the largest source of chloride contamination on account of the 0.25% or so Cl^- level from Solvay-process material. Increasing proportions of soda ash are now available from the natural trona deposits in WyOming, $<0.02\%$ Cl^-. Often overlooked, organics can be potent contaminants, particularly as they affect iron oxidation-reduction colors in nonoxidized glass batches.

Waste glass, or cullet, is an almost universal addition to the batch melted in glass furnaces. The purity of this cullet is as important as that of the raw materials. Unless care is taken, the cullet may have a considerably higher iron content than the original batch. Some contamination from refractories in previous meltings is invariably present. Glass in contact with metals of glass-forming machinery can acquire some scale, while piles of cullet usually act as a magnet for scrap materials unless properly policed. Magnetic contamination (including that from the crushers usually employed to produce cullet of a manageable size) is mainly removed by magnetic head pulleys, plates, grids, etc. Once metallic contamination enters the melting unit, it can exit as a color addition to the glass, as bubbles (from reaction) in the glass, or as a spontaneously drilled hole in the melting unit's bottom.

Accuracy in weighing out the various constituents is important, as well as thorough mixing of all ingredients and prevention of segregation after mixing. In volume production individual component scales or scales with set weight ranges increase accuracy and allow faster cycles as they empty upon a collection belt for the mixer[3]. Whether pan-type, muller-type, horizontal, or otherwise, mixers operate either in the batch house proper or behind the tank upon batch conveyed to them. In many systems liquid is injected during the mixing cycle either as a batch component carrier or as a dusting suppressant for subsequent handling. Generally cullet is added to the mixed batch materials just prior to mixer discharge or proportioned into the batch materials for the tank fill.

Selected from "Glass Engineering Handbook, Third Edition, George W. McLellan and Errol B. Shand, R. R. Donnelley & Sons Company, 1976"

Words and Expressions

1. nepheline [ˈnefəlin] *n*. 霞石
2. syenite [sinit] *n*. 正长岩
3. borax [ˈbɔːræks] *n*. 硼砂
4. litharge [ˈliθɑːdʒ] *n*. 方铅矿
5. residual stone 结石
6. blister [ˈblistə] *n*. 气泡
7. batch material 配合料
8. contaminant [ˈkəntæminənt] *n*. 杂质
9. fining agent 澄清剂
10. pan-type 盘型
11. muller-type 碾盘轮型

Notes

① 在老式窑中，后者可能会在玻璃池窑中产生隔离泡沫，这些泡沫会减少热量通过，并降低熔化速率。

注意：inhabit 在此处意为"抑制、阻止"。

② 在 Na_2O-CaO 玻璃配合料中，硫酸盐以芒硝的形式存在，其目的是除去灰泡及气泡（如产生的气体），但在某些玻璃中，Na_2SO_4 的存在会导致 SO_2 灰泡的产生。

注意：seed 本意为"种子"，此处意为"灰泡"。

③ 在批量生产中，单独称量或预先设定质量范围的方法会提高称量的准确性，而且也会缩短由皮带机运送至混合机的送料时间。

Exercises

1. Put the underlined in the text into Chinese.
2. Put the following into English.

   粒度分布　　结石　　澄清剂　　芒硝　　分离
3. Complete the following paragraph:

   Almost every chemical element can be and is used for the production of glasses, but about 90% of the world-wide glass production contain the three main components ______, ______ and ______. Many physical properties of glass are very sensitive to slight changes in material ______. Even minor ______ in the composition of glass melts cause serious quality problems and affect production operations. For these reasons, a modern glass plant is designed to exercise an exact level of control over its glass plant is designed to entering the glass must have a high level of chemical ______. Silica sand constitutes about 60% of the raw batch composition used by most container and flat glass producers.

Reading Material 32

Weighing and Mixing

When relatively small quantities of batch are to be mixed, ordinary platform scales are often used, and the materials are conveyed in hand barrows from bin to scales, and thence to the mixing box or machine. A variant of this method is the use of a platform scale, flush with the floor, and wheel barrows . Scales which have a floating section of a monorail track to carry the load are convenient. They permit the use of a suspended bucket which can be trundled on a trolley on the monorail to convenient locations-in an open bin of sand, for example, and loaded, weighed, and dumped rapidly. Such devices require the location of the mixing machine on the floor below, or else an elevator with its boot below floor level.

A labor-saving device is a row of overhead bins with a scale hopper attached, from which the materials can be tapped through chutes to a belt conveyor which delivers them to the hopper of the mixer, In connection with this arrangement, a platform scale adjacent to the mixing hopper is provided, and on this the material from barrels, bags, and other containers is weighed out, then shoveled into the hopper.

With modern electrical equipment it is possible to interlock the scales and the valves controlling the filling and emptying of the scale hoppers so that the correct weights of all of the batch ingredients are measured and delivered automatically to the mixer in a fixed cycle. Automatic batch mixing systems of this kind are employed in many large modern factories to avoid human error in formulating batch that unfortunately sometimes occurs in the monotonous and repetitive task of weighing out series of identical batches.

In plants where large tonnages of one batch are made, the missing machine itself may be mounted on scales on a traveling car which runs beneath overhead bins. The machine collects its batch materials, mixes them as it travels, and dumps the batch in a conveyer, cans, or trucks for transportation to the furnace.

By any of these means, it is easily possible to attain an accuracy of weighing of one part in 500, of the major ingredients. Colorants and materials such as arsenic are weighed into pans on small scales or balances, and given a preliminary mixing before being added to the main charge as it enters the mixer. Powerful colorants, such as selenium and cobalt, are diluted to a known strength with some dry batch ingredient, and relatively large quantities of the mixture can be weighed out. Greater convenience and accuracy are thus assured.

Primitive methods of mixing batch consisted of turning it over in piles by means of shovels or holes on a smooth floor or in a box. When power became cheaper and more dependable than hand labor, machines were developed. These are rotary in operation, and depend upon the principle of tumbling the batch over upon itself in a revolving drum or double cone. Blades are also present in the mixer, which act as shovels, and lift and spread the material more effectively. those machines range in capacity from 1000 lbs to a ton or more. They mix a batch effectively in two or three minutes, delivering it in better condition than it appears possible to maintain through subsequent handling.

When batches are made with fine materials which have a tendency to lump such as pulverized sand, it may be desirable to add enough water to moisten the batch and carry out the mixing in a muller type machine where lumps are crushed under heavy wheels and pasty mixtures can be rapidly homogenized. This mixing technique also prevents dusting from the batch and diminishes the tendency for segregation of large from small particles in subsequent handling operations.

In small plants there is little need for the accumulation of batch. It can be run directly into carts from the mixing operation, and shoveled from these into the melting pot or tank. Here the cullet is usually added as the batch is charged. This is sometimes done without crushing the cullet but in general it is better practice to crush cullet to a one-inch size or less before mixing it with the batch. This is particularly important when the cullet is added to the batch before the latter is mixed. Here the possibility exists of sand or other infusible batch raw material being trapped in hollow shapes such as bottles or bits of tubing and thus being introduced into the tank in masses which cannot melt.

When the cullet composition appreciably different from that of the glass produced by melting the batch, it is important that it be finely crushed to avoid inhomogeneity that may be very hard to eliminate by convection or diffusion.

Larger plants, operating continuously, require a supply of batch for each furnace to last through the night. Moreover, hand charging of large units has been supplanted by flowing the batch directly to the furnace from overhead bins. Canisters or portable hoppers, each holding an entire batch or about one ton of material, are in use for the transportation of batch from the mixing room to the furnace . These canisters can be attached directly to mechanical feeding devices in turn, and thus each batch is fed to the tank without having undergone transfer by means of bucket conveyors or conveyor belts and without having been poured into larger storage hoppers, all of which operations are accompanied by some danger of segregation.

Selected from "Modern Glass Practice, Seventh Revised Edition, Samuel R, Scholes, Cahners Publishing Company, 1975"

Words and Expressions

1. monorail [ˈmɔnoureil] *n.* 单轨道
2. trundle [ˈtrʌndl] *v.* (使)滚动,推动
3. elevator [ˈeliveitə] *n.* 提升机
4. hopper [ˈhɔpə] *n.* (料,仓)斗
5. bin [bin] *n.* 料仓
6. arsenic [ˈɑːsnik] *n.* 砷 (As)
7. selenium [siˈliːniəm] *n.* 硒 (Se)
8. canister [ˈkænistə] *n.* 罐,容器

Unit 33 Primary Forming Operations（Ⅰ）

Blowing

A hinged mold is usually used for the blowing operation, and the mold is opened to remove the ware. Paste molds (Fig. 7. 3a), always of circular cross section, are lined with a water-absorbent coating, which develops a steam cushion between the coating and the glass, thus permitting the glass to be rotated in the mold while being blown①. Hot-iron molds may be circular or irregular in cross section (Fig. 7. 3b). The glass contacts the mold directly in a hot-iron mold so that the surface quality of ware blown in hot-iron molds is inferior to that blown in paste molds. With either type of mold, the open end of the ware must be cut off and finished with additional operations.

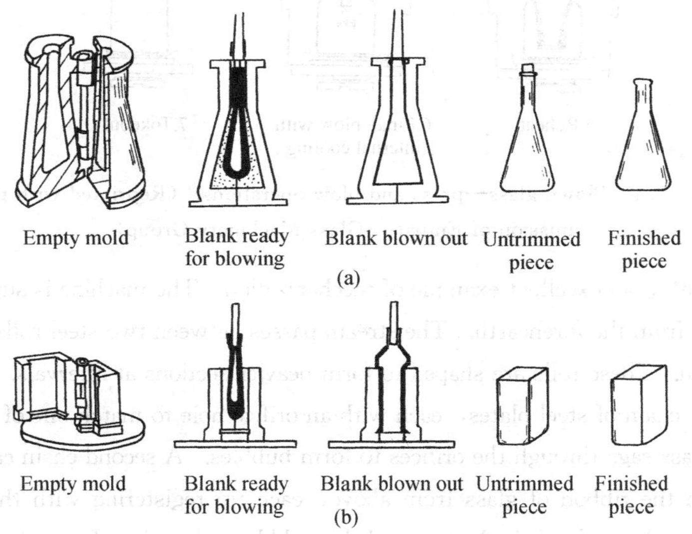

Fig. 7. 3 Blown glass-mold types and blowing operations. (a) Paste mold. (b) Hot. iron mold. (*Courtesy of Corning Glass Works*)

A finished piece of blown ware can be made by combining two fabricating operations, pressing and blowing. The gob is first pressed in a blank mold, after which the blank, or parison, is transferred to a blow mold. The blank is blown to its final shape in this second mold by a blow head that is set over the neck. Fig. 7. 4 outlines this process.

Narrow-mouth containers are made by another two-stage process, the blow-and-blow process. The gob is delivered to a blank mold, where a settle blow and a counter blow form it into a blank. Then this blank is transferred to the blow mold, where it is blown to its final shape.

Ware from either the press-and-blow or blow-and-blow process is ready for use without further fabricating operations.

Bulbs for electric lamps, except for miniature lamps and some large sizes, are made on the Cor-

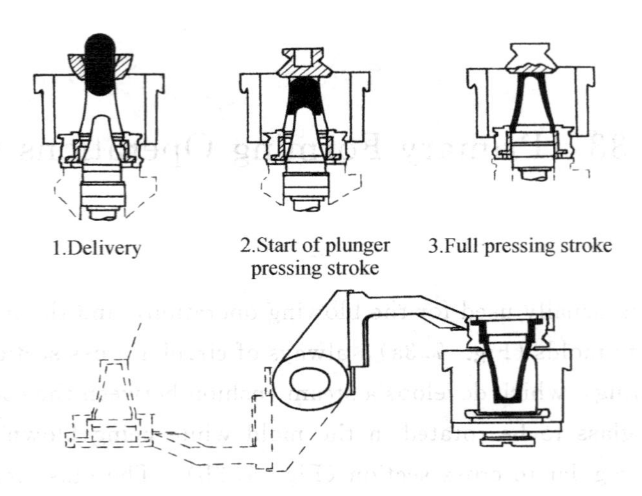

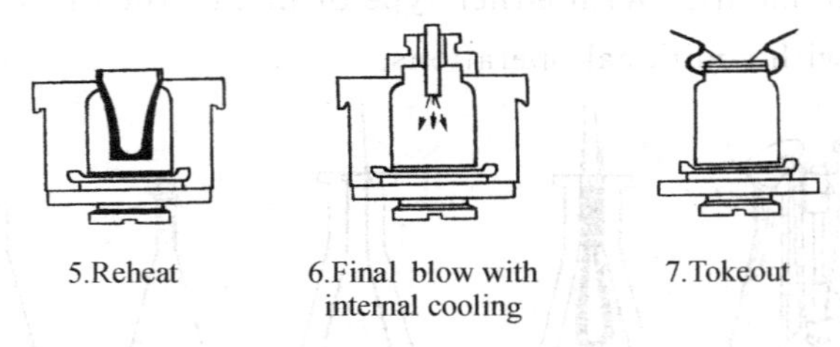

Fig. 7.4 Blown glass—press and blow operations. (Reprinted with per. mission of Embart—Glass Macbinery Group)

ning ribbon machine②, an excellent example of mechanization. The machine is supplied by a continuous stream of glass from the forehearth. The stream passes between two steel rolls, which flatten the stream into a ribbon. These rolls are shaped to form heavier sections at intervals. The ribbon is supported on a moving chain of steel plates, each with an orifice hole to match one of the heavier areas in the ribbon. The glass sags through the orifices to form bubbles. A second chain carrying blowing tips is brought down on the ribbon of glass from above, each tip registering with the hole in an orifice plate. These tips supply puffs of air that expand the bubbles. A series of wet paste molds, traveling under the orifice plates, close around the bubbles of glass and rotate so that each bulb is blown by the final puffs from the blowing tips against a steam cushion. After the bulb is blown, the mold opens and falls away, a tap from a small hammer cracks the bulb from the ribbon into a conveying system that carries it to the annealing lehr. This machine produces small bulbs at rates up to 2200 per minute. Larger bulbs, especially those with heavy wall thickness, are produced at slower rates.

Selected from "Glass Engineering Handbook, Third Edition, George W. McLellan and Errol B. Shand, R. R. Donnelley & Sons Company, 1976"

Words and Expressions

1. paste molds 石膏模

2. blank [blæŋk] *n.* 坯料，半成品，初坯
3. blank mold 初模，雏模
4. blow mold 成型模
5. parison [pærizən] *n.* 型坯
6. settle blow 朴气
7. counter blow 反吹气
8. gob [gɔb] *n.* 料滴
9. sag [sæg] *v.* 下落，下垂
10. orifice ['ɔrifis] *n.* 孔，小洞
11. annealing lehr 退火炉

Notes

① 截面为圆形的石膏模，其内衬一吸水涂层，它会在玻璃和涂层之间产生一气垫，这样玻璃在吹制就可以在模具里旋转。

注：be lined with 意为“加以衬里”

② 康宁履带吹泡机

Exercises

1. Put the underlined in the text into Chinese
2. Put the following into Chinese:

This process is so named because the molten glass flows from the melting tank and floats on a bath of molten tin. The glass surfaces flow and smooth themselves while the glass is on the float bath, and the glass is rigid enough to be handled without damage by the time it leaves the float bath. As a result, surfaces are of high quality and do not require further finishing. Float glass has replaced polished plate, which has replaced polished plate, which required grinding and polishing of both surfaces after forming. Most flat glass is made by the float process.

3. Translate the following Chinese into English:

石膏模　　吹制成型　　压制成型　　气垫　　退火炉

Reading Material 33

Primary Forming Operations (Ⅱ)

Pressing

Figure 7. 5 shows an outline of the pressing operation. The press mold consists of three parts, the mold bottom, the plunger, and the ring which effects the closure between the other two parts. In hand pressing, the molten glass is gathered on a steel rod, or "punty," from which it is allowed to flow or drop into the mold bottom. When the proper volume of glass is in the mold, it is severed from that still on the punty with a pair of hand shears.

The plunger is forced into the mold, which causes the glass to flow into the space enclosed by the mold parts. When this space is filled, the movement of the plunger ceases. When the glass sets up, the plunger is withdrawn and the pressed glass removed from the mold.

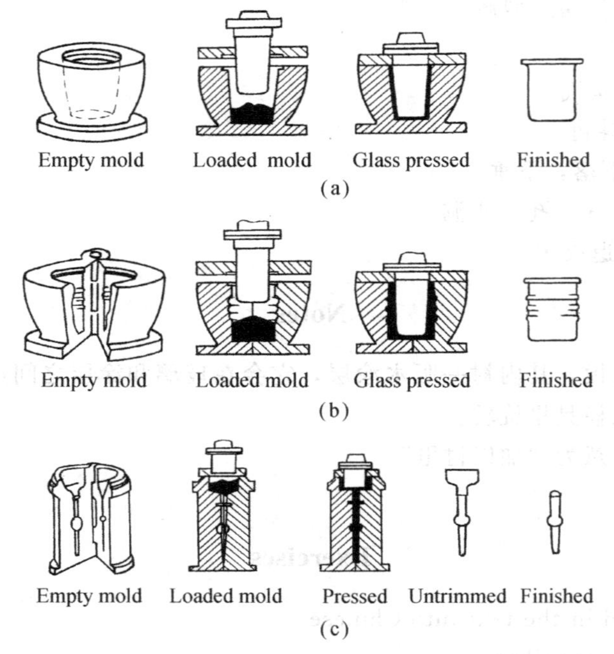

Fig. 7.5 Pressed glass-mold types and pressing operations. (a) Block mold. (b) Split mold. (c) Font mold. (Courtesy of Corning Glass Works)

Machine pressing is similar in principal. A set of molds is mounted on a circular steel table, which is rotated in steps that are usually the angular distance between molds. The glass flows from a forehearth into a refractory bowl, which has a circular orifice in the bottom. A reciprocating plunger of refractory material over this orifice causes the glass to issue downward in pulses, which are seperated into gobs of the proper volume or weight for the articles being pressed by mechanically driven shears immediately under the orifice. The motions of the plunger, shear, and press table are synchronized so that the gobs fall into successive molds as they reach the loading station.

At the following station the plunger descends and presses the gob to the desired shaped, In the remaining stations the glass cools until it can be removed. Air jets usually are employed to cool the mold bottoms and the glass in the molds. The plungers are cooled seperately, often by circulating a cooling medium inside them. Mold temperatures are somewhat critical. If the mold is too hot the glass may stick to it, which can necessitate a shutdown to remove the adhered glass. On the other hand, a mold that is too cool will produce a wrinkled surface on the glass, and surface checks may sometimes develop.

Drawing

Tubing

Nearly all tubing is made by one of three: Danner, Vello or downdraw.

Danner Process. In this process a continuous stream of glass flows over the surface of a rotating refractory mandrel, the axis of which is inclined slightly to the horizontal. The tubing is drawn from the free end of this mandrel, while air blown through the center of the mandrel maintains bore and diameter dimensions. A conveyer, consisting of asbestos-covered rollers, carries the tubing to the cutting machine, where it is cut into lengths.

Vello Process. Molten glass flows downward through the annular space between a vertical mandrel and a refractory ring set in the bottom of a special forehearth, called a bowl. Air blown through the mandrel maintains dimensions of both bore and diameter. The soft tubing assumes the shape of a catenary as it is drawn onto a horizontal conveyer that carries the tubing to the cutting machine.

This process has gained favor over the Danner process with several manufacturers because of its flexibility. It can accommodate a wide range of glass compositions as well as production rates varying from a few kilograms per hour to over 45 kg/min (100 lb/min). Dimensional control is good over diameters ranging from nearly o to 64 mm (2. 5 in). Under carefully controlled conditions, the standard deviation of diameter variation can be held to 0. 3 to 0. 5 percent of the nominal dimension. Thermometer tubing, in which the fine bore must be controlled precisely, is drawn on the Vello.

Downdraw Process. This process is similar to the Vello process. However, instead of bending the tubing from vertical to horizontal, the downdraw, as its name implies, draws the tubing straight down from the bowl in the forehearth. This permits larger diameters to be drawn than the Vello process is capable of, with good dimensional control. Diameters up to 280 mm (11 in) have been drawn. Production rates and glass compositions are both flexible, as with the Vello process.

Rod

Rod can be drawn by any of the tube-drawing process. When the air pressure through the mandrel is turned off, the glass collapses and forms rod instead of tubing.

Selected from "Glass Engineering Handbook, Third Edition, George W. McLellan and Errol B. Shand, R. R. Donnelley & Sons Company, 1976"

Words and Expressions

1. ring [riŋ] *n*. 垫环，密封环
2. punt [pʌnt] *n*. 钢棒
3. forehearth [ˈfɔːhɑːθ] *n*. 料道
4. danner process 丹尼法
5. vello process 维罗垂直拉管法
6. downdraw process 下拉法
7. mandrel [ˈmændrəl] *n*. 心轴，主轴
8. catenary [kəˈtiːnəri] *n*. 链，吊线
9. asbestos-covered 石棉被覆的

总 词 汇 表

A

abatement　*n*．减少，降低，抑制；废料
abrasion resistance　耐磨性
abrasive　*n*．废料；*a*．磨蚀（损）的
absorption　*n*．吸收
accessary　*n*．辅助设备；*a*．附加的
account for　是……原因
acrylamide　*n*．丙烯酰胺
acrylic　*a*．丙烯酸的；*n*．丙烯酸类树脂
activation energy　活化能
active-matrix　活化构造
adamantine　*a*．金刚石似的；*n*．金刚合金
additive　*n*．添加剂；*a*．添加的，加成的
additivity　*n*．加和性
adjunct　*n*．附属品
adularescence　*n*．泛蓝光，冰长石晕影
aerosol　*n*．气溶胶
aesthetic　*a*．美学的
agglomerate　*v*．（使）聚结，结块；*n*．，*a*．烧结块，团聚的
aggravate　*v*．使恶化，加重，变本加厉
aggregate　*n*．骨料；*v*．集结，使聚集
agitation　*n*．搅动
air-setting　气硬的
akin　*a*．同类的，同性质的
albumin　*n*．白蛋白
align　*v*．排齐
alite　*n*．阿利特，硅酸三钙石
alkali　*n*．碱性，强碱
alleviate　*v*．减轻，缓和
allochromatic　*a*．他色的，他色性的
allotropic　*a*．同系异型的
alumina　*n*．氧化铝
aluminosulphate　*n*．铝硫酸盐，硫酸盐
alumium nitride　氮化铝
alveolar　*a*．牙槽的，小泡的
amber　*n*．琥珀
ambient　*a*．周围的，外界的
amethyst　*n*．紫晶，紫罗兰色
amorphograghy　*n*．无定形网络
amphibole　*n*．闪石
anatomically　*a*．解剖（学）的
ancillary　*a*．辅助的，附属的
andalusite　*n*．红柱石
angle of repose　休止角
anhydrous　*a*．无水的
anion　*n*．阴离子
anisometric　*a*．（结晶等）不等轴的
anisotropic　*a*．各向异性的
annealing　*n*．*a*．退火（的）
annealing lehr　退火炉
annihilation　*n*．湮灭
annular　*a*．环形的
antioxidant　*n*．抗氧化剂，抗老化剂
antiparalle　*a*．反向平行；逆平行的
anti-solar glass　热反射玻璃
apatite　*n*．磷灰石
ape　*v*．模仿；*n*．类人猿，学样的人
appellation　*n*．称呼（号），名称
appliance　*n*．应用，器具，装置
applicant（s）　*n*．专利申请人
application number　*n*．申请号
approximately　*ad*．大约地
aquamarine　*n*．海蓝宝石，蓝绿色
aragonite　*n*．文石，霰石
argillaceous　*a*．粘土（质）的
argon　*n*．氩（Ar）
Argyle　*n*．阿盖尔，澳大利亚钻石产区
aristocracy　*n*．贵族统治，最优等的人
armour　*n*．盔甲，装甲
arrester　*n*．制动器，避雷针
arsenic　*n*．砷（As）
arsenide　*n*．砷化物
arterial　*a*．动脉的，主干的
arteriosclerosis　*n*．动脉硬化
asbestos　*n*．石棉
assemblage　*n*．组合，汇集
assignment of assignor's interest　*n*．专利转让人权益委托
asterism　*n*．星光效应，星座

asymmetry n. 不对称性
atomistic a. 原子（论）的
attainment n. 获得
attenuation n. 磨细（薄），冲淡，减少，衰减
attrition n. 摩擦，消（损）耗
Auger ES 俄歇电子能谱
augmentation n. 扩大，增加（长），增加物

B

back-scattered electron imaging 背散射电子影像
basalt n. 玄武岩
basaltic a. 玄武岩的
basic building block 基本组成部分
basic oxygen furnace (BOF) 碱性氧气转炉
basicity n. 碱性度
batch material 配合料
bauxite n. 铝土矿，（铁）矾土，铝矾土
bayerite n. 三水铝石（β-$Al_2O_3 \cdot 3H_2O$）
be attributed to 归因（结）于
be surrounded by 被……包围
belite n. 比利特，二钙硅酸盐
bentonite n. 膨润土
beryl n. 绿柱石
beryllia n. 氧化铍
bessemer n. 酸性转炉钢
bessemer converter 酸性转炉
bin n. 料仓
binder n. 粘结剂
binocular a. 双目（筒）的；n. 双目镜
bioactivity n. 生物活性
biocompatibility n. 生物相容性
bioglass n. 生物玻璃
bipyramidal a. 双锥的
birefringence n. 双折射，二次光折射
bisque firing 素烧（初次焙烧）
blank n. 料坯，半成品
blank mold 初模
blister n. 气泡
bloat v. a. 发胀（的）
blockage n. 堵塞，封锁
blow mold 成型模
bombardment n. 轰击，碰撞
bond strength 键强
borate glass 硼酸盐玻璃
borax n. 硼砂
boride n. 硼化物
braze v. n. 钎接，铜（钎，硬）焊
breakout n. 烧穿炉衬，金属冲击，突围
breunnerite n. 铁菱镁矿
bricklaying n. 砌砖
bridging oxygen 桥氧
buckle v. 弯折，压曲，挤弯作用
bulky a. 庞大的
buoyancy n. 浮力
bypass v. 越过，避开

C

cabochon a. 弧面的，凸面的
calcareous a. 碳质的
calcination n. 煅（焙）烧
calcine v. 煅烧，烧成
calcium sulfate 硫酸钙
calcium-aluminate glass 钙铝酸盐玻璃
cam n. 凸轮
campaign n. 炉龄（期）
canister n. 罐，容器
capacitor n. 电容器
capillary a. n. 毛细管（的），毛细作用（的）
capillary pore 毛细孔
carbide n. 碳化物
carboxylate n. 羧酸盐
carcinogenic a. 致癌的
carryover n. 飞料
casing n. 壳体，外壳
castable n. 浇注料
catalysis n. 催化
catalyst n. 催化剂
catastrophic a. 灾难的，不幸的，大变动的
catenary n. 链，吊线
cathode ray tube 阴极射线管
cathodoluminescence n. 阴极激发光
cation n. 阳离子
cavity n. 孔穴；a. 有空腔的
cell membrane 细胞膜
cellophane n. 赛珞玢，玻璃纸
cellular a. 细胞的，由细胞组成的，多孔的
cellulose n. 纤维素；a. 含纤维素的
cementitious a. 水泥质的，有粘性的
ceramisation n. 陶瓷化
cerium-rich a. 富铈的
certificate of correction n. 更正证书
chalcogenide n. 硫属化合物

characterization *n*. 表征
chatoyancy *n*. 猫眼效应
checker *n*. 格子砖
checkerwork *n*. 格子砖结构
chemical durability 化学稳定性
chemical vapour deposit 化学气气相沉积
chimney *a*. 烟囱状的
chip *n*. 薄片，集成电路片
chrome-magnesite 铬镁矿
chromite *n*. 铬铁矿，亚铬酸盐
chrysoberyl *n*. 金绿宝石
chunky *a*. 矮矮胖胖的
circuitry *n*. 电路（图），线路（图），电路学
circumference *n*. 圆周
class：current *n*. 类别：当前
cleavage *n*. 解理，劈开处
clinical *a*. 临床的
clinker *n*. 熟料（水泥），熔块
close-packed structure 紧密堆积结构
clumping *n*. 凝聚，团集
cluster *n*. 群，集，簇；（原子）团；集聚
coagulant *n*. 凝结（血）剂
cobalt *n*. 钴
cohesive *a*. 内聚力的，聚在一起的
cold-top electric furnace 冷炉顶电炉
collagen *n*. 骨胶原
collar *n*. 套管（环），卡圈
collision *n*. 碰撞
colloidal *a*. 胶体（态）的
combustion gas 燃烧（产生）的气体
commonplace *a*.，*n*. 平凡的（事），平常话
compile *v*. 编辑
comply *v*. 遵照，根据
composite *a*.，*n*. 混合的，复合的，复合物，合成物
compressive strength 抗压强度
conchoidal *a*. 贝壳状的
concrete *n*. 混凝土
confer *v*. 授（赠）予，协商
configuration *n*. 构形；（电子）排布
congruently melting compound 一致融化合物
consecutive *a*. 连续的
consistometer *n*. 稠度计
constrain *v*. 限制，约束
construction ceramics 结构陶瓷
contaminant *n*. 杂质
contamination *n*. 污染，杂质
contour *n*. 轮廓，外形
convective *a*. 迁移的，传送性的
coordination number 配位数
coordination polyhedron 配位多面体
coral *n*.，*a*. 珊瑚（的）
cordierite *n*. 堇青石
corrosion-resistant *a*. 抗腐蚀的
corundum *n*. 刚玉
counter blow 反吹气
crack initiation resistance 抗裂缝发生性
crack-propagation-resistant 抗裂缝发生性的
crawling *n*. 缩釉
crazing *n*. 细裂，龟裂
creep *n*. 蠕变
creme de la creme （法语）精华，最优秀的分子
cristobalite *n*. 方石英
critical value 临界值
cross-section 横截面
crown *n*. 炉顶
crucible *n*. 坩埚
cruciform *a*.，*n*. 十字型（的）
crystal growth 晶体生长
crystallinity *n*. 结晶度，（结）晶性
crystallisation *n*. 结晶（作用），晶化
cubic *a*. 立方晶系的
cullet *n*. 碎玻璃

D

damper *n*. 烟道，隔板
danner process 丹尼法
darkertoned *a*. 色调暗淡的，色淡的
day tank 日池窑
dead-burned 死烧，烧僵
decarbonate *v*. 去除二氧化碳，除去碳酸
decompose *v*. 分解
decomposition *n*. 分解
defect crystal chemistry 缺陷晶体化学
defernite *n*. 碱式碳酸钙
deflocculant *n*. 抗絮凝剂
deflocculate *v*. 反絮凝，解胶
deform *v*. 使变形
degastification *n*. 脱（除）气，去气作用
degrade *v*. 降（裂，分）解，降低，衰变
deleterious *a*. 有（毒）害的，有害杂质的
deliberately *ad*. 故意地，审慎地

dendrite *n*. 树枝状晶体
densification *n*. 密实化
dentistry *n*. 牙科（学）
dephosphorization *n*. 除（去）磷
depletion *n*. 耗尽
deposit *v*. （使）沉积
derivative *a*. 衍生的，被诱导的
destruction *n*. 破坏，毁灭
destructive expansion 破坏性膨胀
deteriorate *v*. 劣（退）化，变坏
devitrification *n*. 失透，析晶
devitrite *n*. 失透石
diagnostic *a*. 诊断的，特征的
diaphaneity *n*. 透明性（度）
diaphanity *a*. 透明的
dice *v*. 切割，切成小片
dichroism *n*. 二色性
dichroscope *n*. 二色镜
dielectric constant 介电常数
diffraction *n*. 衍射
diffusion *n*. 扩散
digestion *n*. 消化，吸收，（加热）溶解
dilational *a*. 膨胀的
dilatometer *n*. 膨胀仪
dinas *n*. 硅石
diode *n*. 二极管
diopside *n*. 透辉石
discrepancy *n*. 不符
disintegrate *v*. （使）崩溃，（使）分裂，（使）分解
disintegration *n*. 瓦解
dislodge *v*. 移动，除去
dispersion *n*. 色散，分散
displacement *n*. 移动，取代，位移
displacive *a*. 位移性的
disrupt *v*. 破坏，使分裂
dissipation *n*. 消耗，散失
dissociate *v*. （使）分离，离解，游离
distortion *n*. 扭曲，变形
divalent *a*. 二价的
diverge *v*. 分离，逸出，偏离
dodecahedron *n*. (pl. -dra) 菱形十二面体
doghouse *n*. 投料口，加料室
doloma *n*. 煅烧白云石
doloma-zirconia 煅烧白云石锆质，锆白云石质
doping *n*. 掺杂
doublet *n*. 二层拼合石，双合透镜，双重线
dough *n*. 面团
downdraw process 下拉法
draft *n*. 抽力，通风
draught *n*. 通（抽）风
drilling mud 钻井注浆
ductile *a*. 可延展的，易变形的
dull *a*. 麻木的，（色彩，光线）不鲜艳的
duplex film 双层膜

E

eclogite *n*. 榴辉石（岩）
eddy *n*. 涡流，旋涡
effringite *n*. 钙矾石
elaboration *n*. 精制，精品
electrical resistivity 电阻
electron hole 电子空穴
electron multiplier 电子放大器
electronegativity *n*. 电负性
electrophretic *a*. 电泳的
eletrolyte *n*. 电解质
elevator *n*. 提升机
elucidate *n*. 阐明，说明
emanate *v*. 发出，放射
emerald *n*. 祖母绿，绿宝石；*a*. 翠绿色的
emission *n*. 发射
empirical *a*. 经验的
emulsification of nutrient 营养乳化作用
emulsifier *n*. 乳化剂
emulsion *n*. 乳浊液，乳液
encapsulate *v*. 密封，封装
enhancement *n*. 优化，提高，增强
enstatite *n*. 顽火辉石
entail *v*. 使……承担
entity *n*. 实体，统一体
entrap *v*. 诱捕
entropy *n*. 熵
enumerate *v*. 数，计，列举
enzyme *n*. 酶
epitaxy *n*. 外延，（晶体）取向生长
epithelial *a*. 上皮的，皮膜的
equalise *v*. 使相等
equilateral triangle 等边三角形
erode *v*. 腐蚀，侵蚀
eruption *n*. 爆发，喷发物
ESCA 化学分析电子能谱

ethylene *n*. 乙烯
evacuate *v*. 撤离，排空，转移
EXAFS 扩散 X 射线吸收谱
exothermic *a*. 放热的
exotic *a*. 奇异的，外国产的；*n*. 舶来品
expanded flow 扩展流
expanditure *n*. 消费，支出
expectancy *n*. 期望（待）
exsolution *n*. 脱溶（作用）
extractor *n*. 分离器
extrude *v*. 挤压
extrusion *n*. 挤出，挤压
exude *v*.（使）渗出，发散

F

face-sharing *a*. 共面的
facet *n*.（多面体的）面，刻面；*v*. 在……上刻面
facilitate *v*. 使容易，使便利
fancy *a*. 花式的，奇特的
feldspar *n*. 长石
femoral *a*. 大腿骨的
ferrite *n*. 铁氧体，（水泥中）铁铝酸四钙
ferroelectric *a*.，*n*. 铁电体（的）
ferroeletricity *n*. 铁电（现象）
ferromagnetism *n*. 电磁性
field of search *n*. 搜索领域
filament *n*. 细丝，长纤维
file *n*. 锉刀，文件
fine agent 澄清剂
fireclay *n*. 耐火粘土（泥）
flactuation *n*. 波动，起伏
flash set 瞬凝
flaw *n*. 裂纹（痕）
flexural strength 抗弯强度
flowability *n*. 流动性
flue gas 烟道气
forehearth *n*. 料道
forklift *n*. 铲车，叉式升降机
formula weight 分子量
formwork *n*. 模板，（膜具用）材料
forsterite *n*. 镁橄榄石
fracture toughness 断裂韧性
frictional forces 摩擦力
frit *n*. 熔块，玻璃料
frontier *n*. 新领域，前沿
fumigation *n*. 消毒
fusion-cast 熔铸

G

gallium *n*. 镓（Ga）
galvanic cell 电流表，原电池
garnet *n*. 石榴石；石榴红色
gelatine *n*. 明胶
gelatinous *a*. 胶状的
gem *n*. 宝石
gemmology *n*. 宝石学
gemstone *n*. 宝石
geothermal *a*. 地热的
germanite *n*. 赭石；亚锗酸盐
germanium *n*. 锗（Ge）
GIA Gemmological Institute American 美国宝石学院
gibbsite *n*. 三水铝石（α- $Al_2O_3 \cdot 3H_2O$）
glacier *n*. 冰川（河）
glaze *n*. 釉料，上釉；*v*. 施釉
glazing *n*. 釉，上釉，玻璃窗
global *a*. 综合的，全面的
globules *n*. 液滴，水珠
glost-firing *n*. 釉烧
glycerin *n*. 甘油基，丙三基
gob *n*. 料滴
goggles *n*. 护目镜
grain boundary 颗粒界面，晶界
grain size 粒度
granite *n*. 花岗岩
granulate *v*. 使粒化
granulometry *n*. 粒度分析
graphite *n*. 石墨
green body 生坯
grit *n*. 磨料
grog *n*. 熟料
grouping *n*. 集团
gunning mixes 喷补料
gypsum *n*. 石膏
gyrolite *n*. 白钙沸石

H

hackly *a*. 粗糙的，参差不齐的
halide *a*.，*n*. 卤化物（的）
handicap *n*. 不利条件，缺陷
haphazard *n*. 偶然性

haze n. 薄雾
heat n. 次（包龄），熔炼
heat sink 散热片
heat-setting a. 热硬性的
hematite n. 赤铁矿
herbicide n. 除草剂
heterogeneous a. 异种的，非均质的，多相的
heterogeneity n. 异质，不同成分，多相
hexagonal a. 六方晶系的
hierarchical a. 体系的
homeopolar a. 相似极化的
homogeneity n. 均化，均（质，相）
homogeneous a. 均匀的，均（质，相）的
honeycomb n.，a. 蜂窝状物（的）
hopper n.（料，仓）斗
hose a. 软管
hue n. 色相（调），色的浓淡
humidity n. 湿气，湿度
hybrid n. 杂化物；a. 杂化的，混合的
hybridization n. 杂化
hydrophobic a. 憎水的
hydrostatic load 液体静压力
hydroxy apatite 羟基磷灰石
hydroxyl group 氢氧基团，羟基（OH^-）
hyperthermia n. 高热疗法
hypothesis n. 假设
hysteresis n. 磁滞现象，滞后，迟滞（性）

I

idiochromtic a. 自色的，自色性的
igneous a. 岩浆的，火的
igneous magma 岩浆
igniter n. 发火装置，点火器
iliac a. 肠骨的
imitate v. 仿制（造），模仿
impact erosion 冲击腐蚀
impair v. 削弱，损害
impart v. 给与，分给
impede v. 阻碍（止）
impediment n. 阻碍，妨碍（物）
impenetrable a. 难以渗透的
impermeable a. 不可渗透的，不透水的
impinge v. 撞击
implant n. 植入物，移植物
implementation n. 实现
impregnate v. 注入，浸渍（透，润）
improve on 提高，改善
impurity n. 杂质
in contrast to 与……相反，与……对比
in sita 原地，现场（操作）（拉丁文）
incandescent a. 白炽的，炽热的，灿烂的
incitation n. 激励
inclusion n. 夹杂（物），掺杂
incompatibility n. 不相容性
indentor n. 压痕计
in-depth a. 深入的
index of refraction 折射率
indispensable a. 必不可少的，责无旁贷的
indistinguishability n. 难辨性
inertness n. 惰性
infrared a. 红外的
ingenious a. 有创造性的，巧妙的
inherent a. 固有的
inhomogeneity n. 不（均）匀性，不同质，多相（性）
initial approximation 初步估算
injection molding 喷射模制成型
inteferometer n. 干涉仪
integrity n. 整体，实体
intercalate v. 添加，插入
interconversion n. 互变现象
interfacial transition zone 界面过渡带
interlocking a. 互联的
intermediate oxide 中间体氧化物
internodal a. 节间的
interparticle a. 粒子间的
interstitial a. 间隙的
interstitial mechanism 填隙机理
intervertebral disc 脊椎骨间盘
iolite n. 堇青石
ion exchange 离子交换
ion-thinned 离子减薄的
IPC class n. 国际专利分类
iridescence n. 晕（虹）彩
isostatic pressing 等静压成型
isostructural a. 同种结构的
isotherm n. 等温线
isotropic a. 均质的；各向同性的
issued/filed dates 公布/建档日期
ivory n.，a. 象牙（似的），象牙制成的

J

jack arch 平拱

jadeite *n*. 硬玉
jamb wall 侧墙
jekyll and hyde 双重人格的人

K

kaliophilite *n*. 钾霞石
kiln *n*. 窑，炉
kinetics *n*. 动力学
krogh-Moe complex 螯合物
kyanite *n*. 蓝晶石

L

labradorescence *n*. 拉长石晕彩
lacquer *n*. 漆，漆黑
ladle *n*. 勺，长柄勺，厨钢桶，钢（铁）水包
ladpis lazuli 青金石（岩）
lamellae *n*. 薄片（板，层）
laminate *v*. 分层，成薄片，层叠
landmark *n*. 里程碑
landmass *n*. 陆地，大片陆地
lanthanide *n*. 镧系元素；镧（系卤）化物
laser envelope 激光罩
latch *n*. 阀钮，插销
lath *n*. 板条状
lead *n*. 铅（Pb），铅制品
ledge *n*. 壁架，架状突出，矿层
legal status：gazette data code 法定状态：公布日期号码
legislation *n*. 立法，法律（规）
leucite *n*. 白榴石
levitation *n*. 漂（悬）浮
lighter-toned *a*. 淡色调的
lignite *n*. 褐煤
lignosulfonate *n*. 本质素磺酸盐
lime *n*. 石灰，氧化钙
limpid *a*. 明显的，清晰（澈）的，平静的
linkage *n*. 键合，联结
liquidus *n*.，*a*. 液相线，液相的
lithia-alumina-silica system 锂铝硅系统
lithium ferrite 铁酸锂
lithrarge *n*. 方铅矿
logistical *a*. 逻辑的，计算，后勤的
long range order 长程有序
look-a-like *a*. 与……相似的
loupe *n*. 放大镜
lubrication *n*. 润滑（作用）

M

macle *n*. 钻石的三角薄片双晶
macro-defect-free 宏观无缺陷的
magic angle spinning nuclear magnetic resonance （MAS-NMK） 幻角角旋，核磁共振
magnesia-chromium 镁铬质
magnesia-dolomite 镁质白云石
magnesia-spinnel 镁尖晶石
magnesia-zirconia 镁锆质
magnesite *n*. 菱镁矿
magnesium *n*. 镁（Mg）
magnetoplumbite *n*. 磁铁铅矿
malleable *a*. 有延展性的，可锻的
mandrel *n*. 心轴，主轴
manganese *n*. 锰（Mn）
mantle *n*. 地幔
marl *n*. 灰泥，泥灰岩
martensitic *a*. 马氏体的
masonry *n*. 砌筑，炉墙
matrix *n*. 基体（质）
mature *v*. 老（陈）化，成熟
mauve *a*.，*n*. 淡紫色（的）
membrane *n*. 薄膜，膜片
memory switch 记忆开关
metabolic *a*. 变化(形)的，同化作用的，代谢的
metallurgical *a*. 冶金学的
metamict *n*. 混胶状
metamorphic *a*. 变质（形）的，改变结构的
metamorphic rock 变质岩
metamorphism *n*. 变质作用
metasilicate *n*. 偏硅酸盐
metastable *a*. 亚稳的
methane *n*. 甲烷
methylcellulose *n*. 甲基纤维素
methylene iodide 二碘甲烷
micell *n*. 胶末，胶态原子团
microanalysis *n*. 微量分析
microchannel plate 微通道板
microcrack *n*. 微裂纹
microstructure *n*. 显微结构
mineralizer *n*. 矿化剂
miscible *a*. 可溶混的
modification *n*. 改变，修改，变体
modulate *v*. 调整，调制，转调
modulus of rupture 断裂模量

MOHS hardness scale　莫氏硬度表
moist curing　湿养护
moldable　*a*. 可塑的，可模制的
molecular dynamics simulation　分子动力学模拟
molybdenum　*n*. 钼（Mo）
momentum　*n*. 动量
monoclinic　*a*. 单斜的
monolithic　*n*.，*a*. 单片（块），整体（的）
monorail　*n*. 单轨道
monosulphate　*n*. 单硫酸盐
morphology　*n*. 形貌
muller-type　碾盘型
mullite　*n*. 莫来石
mullitzation　*n*. 莫来石化
multicomponent　*a*. 多成分的，多元的
mutual orientation　相互取向

N

naat　*n*. 钻石中的结节，晶节，扁平的钻石双晶
near-eutectic　接近共晶（共熔）的
nepheline　*n*. 霞石
nephrite　*n*. 软玉，闪石
nested crucible　套坩埚
network former　网络形成体
network modifier 网络调整体
neutralisation　*n*. 中和（作用，法）
nitridation　*n*. 氮化
nitride　*n*. 氮化物
nomenclature　*n*. 术语，命名法
non-bridging oxygen 非桥氧
notation　*n*. 表示法
notch　*n*. 槽口
notoriously　*ad*. 声名狼藉地
nucleant　*n*. 核化剂
nucleation　*n*. 核化

O

obviate　*v*. 消除，排除
occlude　*v*. 夹杂，挡住
occupancy　*n*. 占据
octahedral　*a*. 八面体的
olivine　*n*. 橄榄石
opacity　*n*. 不透光（性），浑浊度，不透明（体）
open hearth furnace　平炉
optical crown　冕牌光学玻璃
optical flint　火石光学玻璃
orbital hybridation　轨道杂化
orentational　*a*. 定位的，取向的
orifice　*n*. 孔，小洞
orthorhombic　*a*. 斜方晶系的，正交晶系的
orthosilicate　*n*. 正（原）硅酸盐
oscillate　*v*. 振荡，振动
oscillation　*n*. 振荡，振动
osmium　*n*. 锇
osseous　*a*. 骨（状）的
overlap　*v*. 与……重叠，与……部分一致
oxalate　*n*. 草酸盐
oxide gel　氧化物胶体
oxyacetylene　*a*. 氧乙炔的
oxy-fuel　含氧燃料

P

pad　*n*. 底座
palladium　*n*. 钯
palletization　*n*. 造球，球粒化
pan-type　盘型
paraelectric　*a*. 顺电的
paraformaldehyde　*n*. 仲（多聚）甲醛
Paraiba　*n*. 帕拉伊巴（巴西东北的州名）
parison　*n*. 型坯
particle size distribution　粒径分布
particulate　*n*.，*a*. 粒子（的），细粒（的）
parting　*n*. 裂理（开），分裂（离）
paste molds　石膏模
Pauling crystal radii　鲍林晶体半径
pellet　*n*. 丸，球（柱），片；*v*. 压片
per se　本质上（拉丁文）
percolation　*n*. 渗滤，渗透
periclase　*n*. 方镁石
peridotite　*n*. 橄榄岩（石）
periodicity　*n*. 周期律
periodontal　*a*. 牙周的
perlite　*n*. 火山岩玻璃
permeability　*n*. 渗透性
permeation　*n*. 渗入，透过
perpendicular　*a*. 垂直的
pesticide　*n*. 杀虫剂，农药
petrochemical　*a*.，*n*. 石油化工（的），石油化工产品（的）
pharmaceutical　*a*. 制药的，医药的；*n*. 药品
phase diagram　相图
phase transition　相变

phenolic *a*. 酚的，酚醛树脂的
phonon *n*. 声子
photoconductive *a*. 光电导的
photonics *n*. 光子学
photosynthetic *a*. 光合的
pigment *n*. 色素，颜料
pinacoidal *a*. 底面的，轴面的
pitch *n*. 沥青
pitch-impregnated 沥青浸渍的
plasma *n*. 等离子体（区）
platinum *n*. 铂
pleochroism *n*. 多色性
plunger *n*. 活塞，插棒
pneumatic *a*. 风力的，气动的
point of emergence 出露点
poise *n*. 泊（粘度单位）
polariscope *n*. 偏光镜
polarization *n*. 极化，偏振
polarize *v*. （使）极化，（使）偏振化
polyaluminate *n*. 多聚铝酸盐
polycrystalline *a*. 多晶的
polyethyllene *n*. 聚乙烯
polyhedron *n*. 多面体
polymorph *n*. 同质多形体
polymorphic *a*. 多晶的
polyphasic *a*. 多相的
polypropylene *n*. 聚丙烯
polyvinyl *n*.，*a*. 聚乙烯
porosity *n*. 气孔率，多孔性
Portland Cement 波特兰水泥，普通硅酸盐水泥
positron *n*. 正电子
postulate *v*. 假定
pot furnace 坩埚窑
pozzolanic *n*. 火山灰的
precursor *n*. 前驱物
predominate *v*. 掌握，支配
premature *a*. 早熟的，过早的
premium *n*. 奖赏（金），（喻）非常珍贵
prerequisite *n*.，*a*. 前提（的），先决条件（的）
priority number 优先号
prismatic *a*. 棱柱（镜）的，斜方晶的
probe *v*.，*n*. 探针，探测器，（以探针）探察（测）
producer gas 发生炉煤气
projection *n*. 喷射
propagate *v*. 传播（导），扩散（展）
propagation *n*. 传播，扩展
prophylactic *a*.，*n*. 防病的，预防药
prosthesis *n*. 修复术，假体
protein *n*. 蛋白质
pseudophase *n*. 伪相
punt *n*. 钢棒
puttylike *a*. 油灰似的
pyrolize *v*. 热解，高温分解
pyrosilicate *n*. 焦硅酸盐
pyroxene *n*. 辉石

Q

quenching *n*. 淬火，骤冷
quicklime *n*. 生石灰
quote *v*. 引用，举证

R

radiotherapy *n*. 放射疗法
radius ratio criterion 原子半径比准则
radome *n*. 雷达无线罩，整流罩
ram *v*. 捣打
reaction sintering 反应烧结
rearrangement *n*. 重排
rebound *n*.，*v*. 回弹，脱落
reciprocate *v*. 往复运动，上下移动
reconstructive *a*. 重建的
recuperate *v*. 回复，再生
redox *n*. 氧化还原
reducer *n*. 还原剂
refining *n*. 澄清，提纯，精炼
refractometer *n*. 反射仪
refractoriness *n*. 耐火度
refratory *n*. 耐火材料；*a*. 耐（难）熔的
regenerator chamber 蓄热室
regression *n*. 回归
repercussion *n*. 影响
replenishment *n*. 补充
requisite *n*. 必不可少的；*n*. 要素
residual stone 结石
resonator *n*. 谐（共）振器
resorbable *a*. 可重新吸收的
respiration *n*. 呼吸
retarder *n*. 阻滞剂，缓凝剂
retrogression *n*. 逆反应
revive *v*. 复活，苏醒
rheological *a*. 流变学的

rheology *n*. 流变学
rhombohedral *a*. 菱形的，三角晶系的
ridge *n*. 脊，螺纹
rigid body 刚性体
rigorous *a*. 严厉（酷）的
ring *n*. 垫环，密封环
ring mechanism 环形机理
rotational *a*. 旋转的
rubellite *n*. 红色碧玺，红电气石
ruby *n*. 红宝石

S

sag *v*. 下落（重）
sagger *n*. 匣体
sanitary ware 卫生洁具
sapphire *n*.，*a*. 蓝宝石（色），淡蓝色的
scatter *n*. 散射（布），分散
schist *n*. 片岩
Schottky defect 肖脱基缺陷
scorch *v*. 烧（烤）焦，使枯萎
scourge *n*.，*v*. 侵（磨，烧）蚀
screw dislocation 螺旋位错
scrub *v*. 洗涤
sealing glass 封接玻璃
sear *v*. 烙，烧灼
second nearest neighbour 次近邻
sedimentary *a*. 沉积的
sedimentary rock 沉积岩
seed *n*. 小气泡，灰泡
segregation *n*. 分层
selanium *n*. 硒（Se）
self-consitent *a*. 首尾一致的，一贯的
self-leveling 自水平的
sensor *n*. 传感器
setting point 固化点
setting time 凝结时间
settle blow 扑气
sewage *n*. 污水，污物
shaft kiln 竖窑
shale *n*. 页岩
shearing *n*. 切变，剪切
short range order 近程有序
shotcreting *n*. 喷射混凝土
shred *v*.，*n*. 撕碎，碎片
shringage *n*. 收缩（量，率）
shroud *n*.，*v*. 覆盖，罩
sidewall *n*. 侧墙
siliceous *a*. 硅酸的，硅土的
sillimanite *n*. 硅线石
silo *n*. 料仓
singlet *n*. 零自旋能级
sinterability *n*. 烧结性
sintering *n*. 烧结
sisal *n*. 剑麻
sizing *n*. 胶料；量尺寸，分级
skeletal *a*. 骨架状的
skull *n*. 结渣，渣壳
slab *n*. 厚平板，扁锭
slag line 渣线
slip casting 注浆成型，泥浆浇注
slosh *v*.，*n*. 溅，泼；泥浆
socket *n*. 穴，孔
sodium *n*. 钠（Na）
solidify *v*. 固化
solid-solution *n*. 固溶体
sonar *n*. 声纳
sooty *a*. 乌黑的
spall *v*.，*n*. 弄碎，剥落，散裂，碎片
spalling resistance 抗剥落性
spark plug 火花塞
spatial orientation 空间取向
special surface area 比表面积
specific volume 比容
spectroscopic method 光谱学方法
spherically *ad*. 球地，球形地
spherule *n*. 小球体
spine *n*. 脊柱
spinel *n*. 尖晶石
splintery *a*. 裂开的，易破裂的，锯齿状的
spondumene *n*. 锂辉石
spray-drying *n*. 喷雾干燥
sputter deposition 溅射沉积
square pyramid 四方锥
stabilizer *n*. 稳定剂
stack *n*. 烟囱
standard deviation 标准偏差
standard specification 标准规范（格）
stave *n*.，*v*. 狭板，蕊盒；*v*. 击穿，凿孔
stochastic *a*. 随机的，推测的
stockpile *n*. 储备，蕴藏量
stoichiometrical *a*. 化学计量的
strain point 应变点

stress concentrator 应力集中
stringent *a*. 最高的，高过，优于（to）
subatomic *a*. 亚原子的
sub-lattice *n*. 亚晶格
submicrometer *n*. 亚微米
subscript *n*. 下标
substitutional *a*. 取代的
substructure *n*. 亚结构
subtle *a*. 微妙的，微细的
superalloy *n*. 超耐热不锈钢
superconductor *n*. 超导体
supercooled *a*. 过冷的
superduty *a*. 超耐用的，超耐高温的
superficial *a*. 表面的
superfine *a*. 超细的
superimposition *n*. 重叠，添加，附加物
superplasticizer *n*. 超塑化剂
supersaturetion *n*. 过饱和
supersede *n*. 代替，取代
superstructural unit 超结构
superstructure *n*. 上部结构，超结构
surface-catalycal-chemistry-based technology 表面催化化学技术
surface-space-charge-based copying 表面空间电荷复印
surfactant *n*. 表面活化剂
suspension *n*. 悬浮液
syenite *n*. 正长岩

T

tactile *a*. 触角的，能触动的
take up the slack 抓紧松弛环节
tank furnace 池窑（炉）
tantalum *n*. 钽
tap hole 出钢口
tape casting 带式浇注（成型）
tape extrusion 带式挤压（成型）
tar *n*. 焦油
tell-tale *a*. 搬弄是非的，泄露秘密的
tendon *n*. 腱
ternary *a*. 三元的
tetragonal *a*. 正（四）方晶的，四方的
tetrahedron *n*. 四面体
tetravalent *a*. 四价的
texture feature 结构特征
texture perception 构造感觉
thermal conductivity 热传导率
thermal expansion coefficient 热膨胀系数
thermal shock resistance 抗热震性
thermistor *n*. 热敏电阻
thermochemistry *n*. 热化学
thermocouple sheath 热电偶套
thermoluminescence *n*. 热致发光
thick film ink 厚膜料浆
thickening time 稠化时间
thixotropic *a*. 触变性的
three-dimensional fluctuation 三维波动
threshold *n*. 限度，界限，阀
tibial *a*. 胫骨的
titanate *n*. 钛酸盐
tobermorite *n*. 水化硅酸盐
topaz *a*. 黄玉，托帕石
topological *a*. 拓扑学的
torsional *a*. 扭转的
tough *a*. 韧性的
tourmaline *n*. 碧玺，电气石（色）
toxicity *n*. 毒性
transformation *n*. 转变
transition temperature 转变温度
transmission *n*. 透射
tremolite *n*. 透闪石
triaxial test 三度实验法
tribology *n*. 摩擦学
tricalcium silicate 硅酸三钙
trichroism *n*. 三色性
triclinic *a*. 三斜的
tridymite *n*. 鳞石英
trigonal *a*. 三方的
trigonal bipyramid 三方双锥
trim away 修剪，去掉，刨平
trimming *n*. 修整，微调；边角料
triplet *n*. 三层拼合石，三个一组
trundle *n*. （使）滚动，推动
tumor *n*. 肿块，肿瘤
tungstun bronze 钨青铜
turbocharger *n*. 涡轮增压器
turguoise *n*. 绿松石（色）；*a*. 青绿色的
twilight *n*. 微光，曙光；*a*. 微明的

U

ubiquitous *a*. 普通的，无处不在的
ultramarine *n*. 佛青，群青；*a*. 深蓝色的

unattenable *a*. 不能获得的，难以得到的
uncertainty *n*. 不确定性
undercooled *a*. 过冷的
underfired *a*. 欠火（烧）的
underline *v*. 在……之下
underscore *v*.，*n*. 划线于……之下，强调，底线
unshaped refractory 不定形耐火材料
uprate *v*. 改进
UPS 紫外光电子能谱（学）
urchin *n*. 海胆
utensil *n*. 器皿（具），用具
utilization *n*. 利用
UV-VIS spectral region 紫外到可见光谱范围

V

vacancy mechnism 空位机理
vacancy *n*. 晶格空位
vacuum envelope 真空罩
valency *n*. 价，原子价
valorization *n*.
van der waals forces 范德华力
vanadium pentoxide 五氧化二铅
varistor *n*. 压敏电阻，可变电阻
vello process 维罗垂直拉管法
velvety *a*. 天鹅绒般的，软滑的，温和的，可口的
vertebra *n*. 椎骨，脊椎
vibratable *a*. 可推动的
vice verse 反之亦然
vinylalcohol *n*. 乙烯醇
vitrification *n*. 玻璃化
vitrify *v*. （使）玻璃化
vitrography *n*. 玻璃网络
void *n*. 空位，空隙；*a*. 空的
volatile *a*. 可挥发的
vulnerability *n*. 弱点，要害
vulnerable *a*. 易受攻击的

W

walnut *n*. 胡桃树
wave function 波函数
wear *v*. 磨损
weblike *a*. 网状的
wetting *n*. （变，润，浸）湿
whisker *n*. 晶须
wisp *n*. 一缕
wollastonite *n*. 硅灰石
workability *n*. 成型性
WPS

X

XAS X-射线吸收谱
xerograph *n*. 静电印刷术，干印术，静电复印术
xonotlite *n*. 硬硅钙石

Y

yttria *n*. 氧化钇
yttrium *n*. 钇

Z

zeolite *n*. 沸石
zinc *n*. 锌
zircon *n*. 锆石
zirconate *n*. 锆酸盐
zirconia *n*. 氧化锆